LAND REFORMS AND TRIBAL DEVELOPMENT

LAND REFORMS AND TRIBAL DEVELOPMENT

Dr. S. Thirunavukkarasu

Publications

KALPAZ PUBLICATIONS

DELHI-110052

Land Reforms and Tribal Development

ISBN: 81-7835-499-3

Published in 2006 in India by
Kalpaz Publications,
C-30, Satyawati Nagar, Delhi-110052
E-mail : kalpaz@hotmail.com

Laser Typesetting at : Master Computers, Delhi
Printed at : Salasar Imaging System, Delhi

Contents

Preface 9

List of Abbreviations 13

Glossary of Terms 15

List of Tables 17

1. **Introduction** 23
Problem of the Study • Period of the Study • Objectives • Hypotheses • Methodology • Selection of Taluk and Sample Villages • Identification of Tribes and Target Families • Plan of the Study.

2. **Review of Literature** 39
Food Gathering and Hunting • Shifting Cultivation • Settled Cultivation • Land Alienation • Shifts in Occupation • Indebtedness • Forest • Land Reform in Selected Countries.

3. **Various Land Reforms** 69
First Five Year Plan • Second Five Year Plan • Third Five Year Plan • Abolition of Intermediary Tenures • Reduction of Rents • Security of Tenure • Resumption of Tenancies • Ceiling on Agricultural Holdings • Consolidation of Holdings • Fourth Five Year Plan • Abolition of Intermediaries • Tenancy

Reforms • Ceiling on Land Holdings • Consolidation of Holdings • Fifth Five Year Plan • Abolition of Intermediary Tenure • Tenancy Reform • Ceiling on Agricultural Holdings • Consolidation of Holdings • New Strategy of Land Reforms • Programmes for Institutional Changes • Operational Programmes • Implementation Machinery • People's Involvement • Financing of Land Reforms • Mass Campaign of Land Reform • Tribal Sub-Plan and the Kalrayan Hills • Sixth Five Year Plan • Seventh Five Year Plan • Eighth Five Year Plan • Ninth Five Year Plan • Tenth Five Year Plan.

4. **Background of the Study Area** 109

Geographical Location • Rainfall and Irrigation • Origin of Malayali Tribe in the Hills • Kalrayan Hills Under the Jagirdars Administration • Kalrayan Hills in the Government's Direct Administration • Revenue Administration • Amenities Provided to the Tribals • Demographic Characteristics of Karayan Hills Tribes • Distribution of Tribal Population in the Sample Villages • Literacy Level of Tribals • Occupational Characteristics • Distribution of Land and Cropping Pattern.

5. **Progress of Land Reforms in the Kalrayan Hills** 159

Land Reform Measures • Modus Operandi of the Act • Survey and Settlement of Land • Progress of Land Reforms in the Sample Villages • Abolition of Bondage • Package Measures • Large Size Multipurpose Societies • The Tribal Co-operative Marketing Federation of India Limited • Cooperative Farming.

6. Analysis of the Tribal Economy of Kalrayan Hill **181**

Analysis of Socio-economic Conditions • Age Structure of Sample Tribals • Caste • Occupation of Tribals • Educational Status of Tribals • Analysis of Economic Characteristics of Tribals • Wealth Composition • Land Use Pattern • Cropping Pattern • Employment Details of Sample Tribals • Income Level of the Tribals • Expenditure Pattern of the Tribals • Indebtedness Among the Tribals • Analysis of Agricultural Production • Paddy Crop • Results of Multiple Regression Analysis for Varagu and Samai Crops • Ragi • Tapioca • Test of Hypothesis.

7. Summary and Suggestions **229**

Appendix 1 243

Appendix 2 245

Bibliography 247

Index 261

Preface

Land is the fundamental productive asset of the tribal people. They have an emotional attachment towards land. Tribals and land are inseparable. Adding to this, Indian tribals predominantly dwell in the forest area. Presently in the tribal area the lands are under the control of the Revenue Department while the forest is governed by the Forest Department. This dual administration with varied approach has altered the tribal people and their area. The Land reform measures have failed to address this burning issue in the tribal areas of our country. It is because the land reform measures meant for the non-tribals are extended to the tribal area. Therefore, unique land reforms are imperative to the tribal areas.

The entry of Forest Department permits the tribals to use the forest and forest land subject to their rules and regulations. The minor forest produce which is an important source of income to the tribals is under the mercy of Forest Department. Further, the entry of non-tribals has brought monetization, market and all sorts of other culture to the tribal areas. In the event of poor safeguard measures; the legal system is not effective to protect them from exploitation and the growing land alienation. Altogether, the tribals moving area is shrunk in size, given their illiteracy and ignorance exploitation is high and they face variety of problems. With these, I tried to study the efficacy of land reforms in Kalrayan Hills, where land reforms were implemented in large scale in 1976 and it is still incomplete here. I tried to evaluate the problem as simple as possible with simple statistical and econometric analysis.

I am indebted to my research supervisor Dr. A.R.Veeramani, M.A., (Econ.), M.A., (Pol. Sc.), M.Phil., Ph.D., Professor of Economics, Thiruvalluvar University, Vellore, Tamil Nadu, for his valuable guidance, suggestions and help in the preparation of the thesis.

I am grateful to my teachers: Dr. T.C. Mohan, M.A., M.Lit., Ph.D., formerly Vice Chancellor of Annamalai University, Annamalai Nagar, and Dr. K. Ganesan, M.A., Ph.D (USA), formerly Principal and Head of the Department of Economics, RKM. Vivekananda College, Chennai-4, for guiding me initially and their help to pursue the research work. I am obliged to Dr. R. Elango, M.A., M.Phil., Ph.D., Professor and Head of the Department of Economics, Annamalai University, Annamalai Nagar, for his useful suggestions to improve this work.

I am grateful to Dr. P. Govindarajan, M.A., Ph.D., formerly Head of the Department of Economics, Presidency College, Chennai-5; Dr.M.Muralidhran, M.A., Ph.D., Professor of English, Prof. N. Balasubramanian, M.Sc., M.A., M.Phil, Professor of Economics, and Dr. R.V. Srinivasan, Head of the Department Economics, RKM. Vivekananda College, Chennai-4. My thanks are due to Prof. T. Nandakumar for his appreciation and encouragement. I also thank Prof. N.G. Shanker, M.A., M.Phil., Dr. S. N. Sugumar, M.A., M.Phil., Ph.D and other colleagues in the Department of Economics.

I take this opportunity to thank the Revenue Department, Forest Department, Directorate of Statistics, Survey and Settlement, Land Reforms Department, Directorate of Adi-dravida and Tribal Welfare, Co-operative Department, State Planning Commission, Block Development Office, LAMP Society, Surveyor's Office at Thanjavur,

Thiruvannamalai and Kallakurichi, and other Departments of Government of Tamil Nadu. I am grateful to the University of Madras for permitting me to publish this research study.

Above all my thanks are due to the Tribals of Kalrayan Hills for providing the necessary information during my primary data collection.

I am indebted to my mother, wife, children and brothers for having spared me time and the atmosphere during my two decades of the research work.

S. Thirunavukkarasu

List of Abbreviations

HYVP	:	High Yielding Varieties Programme.
IRDP	:	Integrated Rural Development Programme.
ITDP	:	Integrated Tribal Development Programme.
LAMPS	:	Large-Size Multipurpose Societies.
MADA	:	Modified Area Development Approach.
MLA	:	Member of Legislative Assembly.
MP	:	Member of Parliament.
NEFA	:	North Eastern Frontier Agency.
SADT	:	South Arcot District.
SC	:	Scheduled Caste
ST	:	Scheduled Tribe
TRIFED	:	The Tribal Co-operative Marketing Federation of India Limited.
TSP	:	Tribal Sub-Plan.

List of Abbreviations

TRIFED	The Tribal Co-operative Marketing Federation of India Limited
TSP	Tribal Sub-Plan

Glossary of Terms

Adivasi	:	Synonymous with Scheduled Tribe.
Bhudan	:	Movement aimed to persuade land-owners to donate excess on unused land to the landless.
Cumbu	:	Bulrush or spiked millet or pearl millet, pennisetum typhoidum.
Cholam	:	Sorghum vulgare-a variety of crop raised in dry lands.
Firkha	:	A sub-division of a taluk.
Inam	:	Village, or part of a village's land, held revenue-free or at a reduced rate of revenue for village service, or for charitable or religious purposes.
Jagirdari	:	System of land tenure under the control of Jagirdars.
Khariff	:	Main growing seasons which begins in June or July and ends with the fall of harvest.
Kadu	:	Land for cultivation.
Patta	:	A deed or lease given by the district collector to the cultivator, specifying the particulars of his holding, including the tax payable for it.

Poromboke	:	Land in a village reserved for purposes other than cultivation, and held free from taxation.
Punal Kadu	:	Land under shifting cultivation.
Punal Kadu Nellu	:	A local paddy variety raised under rainfed conditions.
Ragi	:	A millet, elcusine coscorana.
Ryotwari	:	Division of all arable land into fields, with each assessed at a fixed rate payable to the Government.
Samai	:	A millet raised in hill areas.
Scheduled caste	:	Term used to refer a caste in India and also called Adi-Dravida.
Scheduled Tribe	:	Term used to refer a caste also synonymous with Adivasi.
Shifting cultivation	:	Slash-and-burn mode of cultivation practiced traditionally in the hill areas.
Taluk	:	A sub-division of a district.
Tapioca	:	The root of the cassava plant.
Thinai	:	A millet usually raised in rainfed areas.
Varagu	:	A millet raised in hill areas.
Vuzhavukadu	:	Land used for cultivation.
Zamindari	:	System of land tenure under the control of zamindars.

List of Tables

1.1. Details of sample villages, Hamlets, Total Population, Total Households and Sample Households of Vellimalai Taluk 34

4.1. Amenities Available in the Sample Villages as per 1981 Census 114

4.2. Comparative Tribal Population Statistics as per 1981 and 1991 Census 118

4.3. Distribution of Malayali Tribes in the Major Hills of Tamil Nadu. 119

4.4. Distribution of Total Population by Social Groups in the Sample Villages of Kalrayan Hill 120

4.5. Literacy level of Tribals in the Study Area 121

4.6. Distribution of Categories of Workers in the Study Area as per 1981 Census 123

4.7. Broad Industrial Categories of Main Workers in the Sample Villages as per 1991 Census 125

4.8. Land use Pattern in the Kalrayan Block from 1986 to 1996 (in Hectares) 127

4.9. Cropping Pattern in the Kalrayan Block from 1986 to 1999 (in Hectares) 129

4.10. Cropping Pattern in Nochimedu from 1989-1996 (in Hectares) 131

4.11. Land use Pattern in Mavadipattu from 1989-1996 (in Hectares) 133

4.12. Cropping Pattern in Mavadipattu from 1989-1996 (in Hectares) 134

4.13. Land use Pattern in Karialur from 1989-1996 (in Hectares) 136

4.14. Cropping Pattern in Karialur from 1989-1996 (in Hectares) 137

4.15. Land use Pattern in Vellimalai from 1989-1996 (in Hectares) 138

4.16. Cropping Pattern in Vellimalai from 1989-1996 (in Hectares) 139

4.17. Land use Pattern in Vazhapady from 1989-1996 (in Hectares) 140

4.18. Cropping Pattern in Vazhapady from 1989-1996 (in Hectares) 141

4.19. Land use Pattern in Kundiyanatham from 1989-1996 (in Hectares) 142

4.20. Cropping Pattern in Kundiyanatham from 1989-1996 (in Hectares) 143

4.21. Land use Pattern in Kendikkal from 1989-1996 (in Hectares) 144

4.22. Cropping Pattern in Kendikkal from 1989-1996 (in Hectares) 145

4.23. Land use Pattern in Pottiyam from 1989-1996 (in Hectares) 146

4.24. Cropping Pattern in Pottiyam from 1989-1996 (in Hectares) 147

4.25. Land use Pattern in Malliampady from 1989-1996 (in Hectares) 149

4.26. Cropping Pattern in Malliampady from 1989-1996 (in Hectares) 151

5.1. Progress of Land Reforms in the Kalrayan Hill-1979-80 (in hectares) 163

5.2. Progress of Land Reforms in the Kalrayan Hills as per Forest Department Records (in Hectares) 164

5.3. Progress of Land Reforms in the Sample Villages from 1979 to 1996 (in Hectares) 165

5.4. Development Programmes for Agriculture in the Kalrayan Hills from 1976-1996 170

5.5. Cooperative Farming in Kalrayan Hills from 1994-1995 (in Rs) 176

6.1. Size of Family of the Tribals in the sample villages of Kalrayan Hills 183

6.2. Distribution of Sample Population in different Age Groups (Age in years) 185

6.3. Occupation-wise Distribution of Sample Tribes in the Kalrayan Hills 186

6.4. Literacy Level of Sample Tribals in the Kalrayan Hills 187

6.5. The Total Value of Wealth Composition of Sample Tribals in the Study Area (in Rs.) 189

6.6. Distribution of Land among Sample Tribals in the selected villages of Vellimalai Taluk (in acres) 191

6.7. Cropping Pattern of the Sample Tribals in the Vellimalai Taluk (in acres) 193

6.8. Average Number of Days Employed by Sample Tribals in the Study Area 196

6.9. Total Income of the Sample Households in the Study Area (in Rs.) 197

6.10. Annual Total Household Expenditure Pattern of the Sample Tribals in the Study Area (in Rs.) 198

6.11. Total Loans Outstanding of Sample Tribals in the Sample Villages (in Rs.) 200

6.12. Average Cost of Cultivation of Paddy Crop by the Tribal Farmers in the Selected Villages (per acre) 202

6.13. Results of multiple-Regression Analysis for Paddy Crop by Sample Farmers in the Study Area. 204

6.14. Results of multiple–Regression Analysis for Varagu and Samai Crops in the Study Area. 209

6.15. Results of Simple Regression Analysis of Ragi Crop in the Study Area 215

6.16. Results of Simple Karl Pearson's Correlation Coefficient for Tapioca crop 216

6.17. Spearman's Rank Correlation Coefficient for the Vellimalai Block 221

6.18. Results of Spearman's Rank Correlation Coefficient for Kendikkal Village 222

6.19. Results of Spearman's Rank Correlation Coefficient for Karialur Village 222

6.20. Results of Spearman's Rank Correlation Coefficient for Vellimalai Village 223

6.21. Results of Spearman's Rank Correlation Coefficient for Nochimedu Village 224

6.22. Results of Spearman's Rank Correlation Coefficient for Mavadipattu Village 224

6.23. Results of Spearman's Rank Correlation Coefficient for Kundiyanatham Village 225

6.24. Results of Spearman's Rank Correlation Coefficient for Pottiyam Village 226

6.25. Results of Spearman's Rank Correlation Coefficient for Malliampady Village 226

1

Introduction

Land reforms for rural development have suffered a setback worldwide in recent years. Perhaps, it is the consequence of the change in the acumen and policy of the International Monetary Fund and the World Bank. Moreover, these banks have focused in favour of market reforms as against land reforms.[1] Such a change at the global level and the conditionalities imposed by these banks for sanctioning loans appears to have influenced the New Economic Policy of the Government of India. That is, the New Economic Policy, which commenced its operation on 1st July 1991, "does not explicitly say anything on the role of land reforms".[2]

However, in the persisting agrarian structure, land continues to have its crucial importance in the absence of alternative production resources in rural India. Further, even after forty seven years of planning with a number of organisational and administrative reforms, we still have vast inequalities in the distribution of land, an acute scarcity of capital, especially among small and marginal farmers and an overcrowding of landless agricultural labour. Therefore, land reforms are inevitable requirement for the socio-economic development of all the sections of peasantry, at least for the following two reasons:

First, even for a successful functioning of market mechanism, land reforms with their comprehensive connotations are essential, as this would transform the unproductive character of agrarian structure. Thereby this would release such forces of growth leading to rapid development of agriculture and industry. Secondly, given the unequal agrarian structure and the factor market, it is necessary that land reform should precede market reform for rural development. Further, more emphasis is required for the tribal economies where the land reform measures are indispensable for protecting them from exploitation.

The concept of land reform is, "to denote any integrated programme that aims at reorganising the institutional framework of agriculture in order to facilitate social and economic progress in accordance with the philosophy, values and creed of the community concerned".[3] Since there are large-scale inter-regional variations in the implementation of land reforms and their impact on agriculture and rural development, the need for continued and yet suitably modified land reform measures on the basis of economic structure of various regions, does exist. Further, when land reforms are considered relevant even for relatively open economies of rural areas, they are all the more necessary for the comparatively closed system of tribal economy.

In India, land reform is a State subject and hence, sharp variation in the implementation of land reform measures has been observed. These reform measures of distributist type are uniformly applied both in tribal as well as non-tribal area but, land reform measures should differ in tribal areas from non-tribal areas, because, of the subtle distinction observed in both the areas. Further, it is simple and complex while introducing land reform measures in the tribal areas. It is simple, because, the allotment of land is only to the tribals of a particular locality. While it is complex due to: insufficient land records owing to heritage ownership, socially, culturally, economically diverse tribal groups and the tribal areas are generally inaccessible. This situation is indeed tragic, for all the tribal people, since they were land owners in the beginning and their right on land was not recognised and there was total absence of official agencies or legal authorities in the tribal areas.

The early effect of the extension of the formal system from the non-tribal areas had troubled their right over forest as well as land. Moreover, the tribal people are presently depending on officials and non-tribals for their livelihood. Further, they have to depend on these people to recognise their traditional rights and access to the land and forest which that they had enjoyed over a period. The entry of non-tribals as contractors, moneylenders and businesspersons had brought indebtedness and land alienation. Consequently, "alienation of tribal land has continued unabated notwithstanding enactment of a bevy of laws and promulgation of regulations for protecting the same".[4]

The distinguishing feature of the tribal people is their peculiar association with the area in which they dwell. If it is happened to be land and invaluable forest, others always have an eye on these natural assets of the tribals. Therefore, "the first blow to this ingrained belief came to an end with the reservation of forests in the name of Scientific Management done by the colonial rulers for the purpose of revenue".[5] In course of time, even the right of the tribals to collect the Minor Forest Produce has not been allowed by the authorities. It is because, such lands are declared as 'forest land", exclusively under the control of the Government in order to arrest the deleterious deforestrating effect of shifting cultivation, land slide and soil erosion.

The tribals of India are not a solid monolithic mass but as an assorted collection of socially, economically, politically, technologically and culturally diverse groups living under different and ecological conditions. Tribals like the Irular, the Kadar and the Malayalis, are still in a very low technological level, compared to the tribes of khasi and Garo Hills of Meghalaya and the Apatanis of Arunachal Pradesh. They are in a comparatively better standard of living with the help of their highly developed mode of agriculture and horticulture.[6]

In fact, considering the multiplicity of factors and complexity of problems the Indian tribes are classified into: (1) Territorial distribution (2) Linguistic affiliation (3) Physical and racial characteristics (4) Occupational economy (5) Cultural contact and (6) Religious belief. Considering these any measure or reform should be linked with the tribal way of life, physical conditions of land, social customs, traditions and belief of each of the tribal areas. For that matter, even among the tribals a clear distinction is warranted between tribals living outside the Scheduled Areas termed as "Dispersed Tribals" and tribals living with in the Scheduled Areas described as "Predominantly Tribal areas".[7]

In these circumstances, any conventional land reform measure or developmental programme will not provide the solution to the complex problems and intricate issues of tribals. As, "these people have a holistic view of life which cannot be neatly dissected into personal, social, religious and economic slices which may be separately handled. Accordingly, it is not possible to make a distinction between the so called developmental and non-developmental facets of administration. They are so indistinguishably interwoven that one without the other may have no meaning, nay, may even become dysfunctional".[8]

Therefore, any economic measure of the type of land reforms will have to be suitably designed taking care of the special situation prevailing in each of these tribal areas. This factor appears to have very much influenced the latest tribal development programme viz., Tribal Sub-Plan (TSP) approach evolved by the Planning Commission during the Fifth Five Year Plan. However, the Report of the commissioner for Scheduled Caste and Scheduled Tribes has observed that the outlays and expenditure relating to the Tribal Sub-Plan during the Sixth Five Year Plan had clubbed together almost all sorts of programmes under one demand and have not helped to realise the objective of a Tribal Sub-Plan.[9]

Economic reforms of right type with concern for the tribal people should be undertaken in the tribal areas. This is mainly due to the fact that the importance of studying the basic economic structure or the attendant economic condition of any given tribal areas has not been recognised, and both the Centre's and the State's efforts in this direction are lacking. Even though the central government has shown its recognition of the distinctive features of Tribal Development Programmes as seen in the Special Central Assistance Programme, but the government agencies and officials in charge of implementing these programmes both at the central and State level do not appear to have had any scientific approach in the form of a perspective plan evolved for the sustained development of agriculture in the tribal areas. Even in their routine application of conventional reform measures, they have been considering the whole sub-plan activities as an agglomeration of all the general schemes usually taken-up in non-tribal areas. They simply apply them blindly to the tribal areas without any admiration of the fact that the situation in tribal areas is different.

Land reform measures undertaken in the tribal areas expose that the officials are more influenced by the overly desire for assimilating the tribals with their non-tribal culture. The officials, being persons from the non-tribal areas, are more inclined to think that the tribal culture is traditional and it needs to be changed, to reap the benefits of the measures. Perhaps they may be well-meaning officials with interest in developing the tribal areas, but they have only the background of information supplied by Sociological and Anthropological studies. And this has resulted in the overenthusiastic implementation of Land Reforms in the tribal areas. Further, the framework laid down in the land reform measures is not in consonance with the genuine need for Tribal Development i.e., without changing drastically either their culture or their way of living. Although, their problems have been very clearly visualised by the First Prime Minister of India, Late Pandit Jawaharlal Nehru, his warning about the neighbouring non-tribal's influence on the tribal's living appears not to have been taken notice of.[10]

Hence, the danger of assimilation is very much lurking in a tribal economy which is in close proximity with non-tribal area. Therefore, while implementing land reform special care should be taken to ensure that any approach by way of reform should concede the preservation of co-existence of the numerous tribal groups living in different tribal areas. In this context, the study of land reforms for tribal areas not only assumes considerable importance but also proves to be academically challenging.

Some studies on land reforms reveals that India was successful in the abolition of intermediaries.[11] But slow or incomplete in the case of ceiling on land holdings and tenancy reforms. It is due to "landed aristocracy and embedded bureaucracy and administrative machineries totally aloof to the peasant beneficiaries, diluted the reform efforts".[12] However, even the much-claimed success in the abolition of intermediaries as part of land reform measures was implemented very late in the Kalrayan hills i.e, only in 1976.

Problem of the Study

Kalrayan hill of Tamil Nadu is chosen for case study in this research work. The inhabitants of the hill are called "Malayalis', who are the homogenous single tribal group without any racial or communal differences. During the King Krishna Devaraya's regime, three Jagirdars viz., The Ariya Goundan Jagir, The Kurumba goundan Jagir and The Jadaya Goundan Jagir were appointed by the King to collect the revenue from the tribals. But, they slowly took over the hill's administration and ruled their respective villages till 1976. In the Jagirdars' period, no individual land record was maintained. However, the tribals were using the land and the forest by paying taxes to the tribal's chieftains. A government report says that the tribals were made as slaves to the Jagirs. Therefore, in order to free the tribals from the clutches of Jagirdars, on 25.8.1976, the Government of Tamil Nadu took over the hill from the Jagirdars by applying the Inam Estate (Abolition and Conversion into Ryotwari) Act of 1963 and the Bonded Labour System (Abolition) Act of 1976.

As a part of the land reform measures, fresh survey and settlement operations were carried out and lands were assigned to the tribals. Similarly, to supplement the land reform measures, several package measures were implemented in the Kalrayan hill from the Fifth Five Year Plan onwards. But, the resultant condition of tribals due to these reform processes is too complex and intricate. That is, the tribals are passing through a unique phase from Jagirdar's administration to the direct Government's administration. Further, they are not able to comprehend the magnitude of the change and the response needed on their behalf to face the new challenge.

It is imperative to note that in Tamil Nadu, Land Reform Acts have been uniformly applied both in tribal and non-tribal areas. Therefore, the routine extension of land reforms within the conventional frame had put a question mark on the tribal's right over land and other resources. Further, when the Kalrayan hill was opened to the non-tribals they entered or settled in the tribal area as moneylenders, contractors, merchants and officials. As a consequence of this indebtedness, alienation of tribal lands and tribal's right over forest resources, continued inspite of several regulations implemented by the Government. Such, ominous development is fundamentally due to the unscientific approach of the government while implementing the land reform measures in the hill. Now the tribals are in transitional stage and the land problem remain unsolved.

Period of the Study

In the absence of government machinery in the Kalrayan hill, before 1976, no concrete statistics are available about the hill, except "The Manual of South Arcot, compiled by J.H.Garstin in 1878"-perhaps an important document available about the hill, when the researcher tried to collect historical evidence spanning over 200 years. The hill area was left blank in the census reports up to 1981 Census report. The taluk Surveyor's document and the records of Registrar Office at various levels are available only from 1980. In this research work, every efforts has been made to collect such records, reports and documents as are available and relevant to the study.

However, the present research work will cover a period from 1989 to 2000. The year 1989 is chosen because in that year the Government of Tamil Nadu, passed an Order (G.O. No. 1168 dated 25.7.1989) to stop any further land reform process in the hill area. Since, no fresh land assignment is possible after 1989, the tribals actual economic condition due to land reform measures will be analysed in this research work.

Objectives

The major objectives of the study are:

1. To study the origin and present conditions of the Kalrayan hill tribes.

2. To review the land reforms and tribal development measures implemented in the various five year plans.

3. To study the method and progress of land reform measures undertaken in the study area.

4. To study the socio-economic conditions of tribals in the post-reform period.

5. To study the inputs used and output of various crops cultivated by the beneficiary tribals, and

6. To suggest an alternative strategy for tribal development.

Hypotheses

The main hypotheses are:

1. Land reforms of the conventional type had resulted in the land disputes between the government and the tribals.

2. Land reform measures have not significantly changed the land use pattern in the post-land reform period.

3. There is no significant variation in the cropping pattern inspite of land reform measures undertaken in the study area.

4. The production possibilities with inputs use and output of various crops favour cultivating traditional crops rather than the newly introduced agricultural package schemes under the Tribal Sub-Plan.

Methodology

The Kalrayan hill of Tamil Nadu is purposively chosen for the present research work, because:

1. Land reform measures have been undertaken in large scale from 1976 and the reform process is not yet completed till date.

2. It is an area with majority of tribal population, which is the largest tribal population of the State.

3. The study area adjoins agriculturally and industrially advanced urban and semi-urban non-tribal agglomerations.

4. The tribals are in a state of transition from non-ryotwari to ryotwari system and they have been freed from heritage bondage and assigned with some lands supplemented with government development programmes.

5. Non-tribals have entered into the hill area as moneylenders, contractors, or officials and many of them have settled in the tribal area. This is a sensitive issue in the tribal areas and more so, in the Kalrayan hills, and

6. The Kalrayan hill is known for its rich forest resources.

These facts provide enough scope for a study on, "Land reforms and Tribal Development; A case study of Kalrayan hills, Tamil Nadu".

Selection of Taluk and Sample Villages

The Kalrayan hill contains three taluks viz., Vellimalai Taluk, Mottampatti Taluk and Seerapattu Taluk. Of which the Vellimalai Taluk is chosen for our case study because;

It represents majority of the villages and more number of tribals, than the other two taluks; and

Vellimalai is the head quarters of the Block Development Office and LAMP society.

In the Vellimalai Taluk, of the 25 villages, 9 villages have been chosen for the study, representing lower hill villages (3 villages) and upper hill villages (6 villages). The sample villages have been chosen in such a way that the result drawn from the study will be representative of the other villages. The sample villages located at 30 to 60 Kilometers away from Kallakuruchi (nearest urban centre). Further, most of the villages are inaccessible and located in the interior forest without road facilities.

Identification of Tribes and Target Families

The tribes are identified by their culture, common name, common dialect, common territory, customary laws and by considering all other economic and social factors.[13] These differences can be narrowed down by evolving an acceptable definition suitable to the tribes of the study area. That is, "Adivasi or tribe mostly small in size to the total population of a country, settled in hill and plain areas, known for their own unique social, cultural and economic systems, ruled by their own people, ownership of land should be hereditary, speaks common language and absence of literacy". Thus, sufficient care was accorded in the identification of tribes, who are the target groups of the land reform measures in the Kalrayan hills.

The target groups in the land reform measures are the land allottees. The allottees were identified by their land holdings allotted by the government. Since, all the tribals are the beneficiaries of land reform measures; the question of the impact of land reform on non-beneficiaries does not arise. The following table exhibits the names of sample villages and sample households, chosen for study in this research work.

Table 1.1 portrays that the nine sample villages chosen for study included 24 hamlets and its distribution is more in Kendikkal (5 hamlets) and Vazhapady (4 hamlets) and less than 3 hamlets in other revenue villages. The nine villages included 1537 households to the total of 3693 households of the Taluk. Finally, 10 per cent of the households were contacted with a specially prepared pre tested questionnaire. Map 1.3 shows the sample villages chosen for study in this research work.

Table 1.1 : Details of Sample Villages, Hamlets, Total Population, Total Households and Sample Households of Vellimalai Taluk

S. No.	*Name of Revenue Village*	*No. of Hamlets*	*Names of Hamlets*	*Total Population*	*Total House holds*	*Sample House holds*
1.	Pottiyam	2	Kattukottai and Mayampadi	1001	302	31
2.	Malliampady	1	Paranginatham	1061	134	14
3.	Kundiyanatham	2	Melparigam and Kalpady	337	81	9
4.	Nochimedu	1	Kodunthurai	269	56	6
5.	Vazhapady	4	Melvazhapady, Kannumathivaluvu Meldevanur and Thaldevanur	727	172	18
6.	Mavadipattu	3	Kurathikundru, Sundapadi and Alathi	615	109	11
7.	Kendikkal	5	Melkendikkal, Kottaputhur, Thalmadur, Nadumadur and Melmadur	1465	318	32
8.	Karialur	3	Pulavapadi, Thalvellar and melvellar	975	202	21
9.	Vellimalai	3	Thalvellimalai, Thalsathanur and Melsathanur	458	163	17
	Total	24	—	6908	1537	159

Source: Government of Tamil Nadu: Block Development Office, Vellimalai.

In addition to primary data collected from the tribals, all necessary secondary data had been collected from Adi-Dravida and Tribal Welfare Department, Government of Tamil Nadu, Office of the Survey and Settlement and Department of land Reforms, Government of Tamil Nadu, office of the State Co-operatives, Madras, Land Record offices at Thanjavur, Kallakuruchi and Thriuvannamalai, Taluk offices at Kallakuruchi and Sankarapuram and Block Development office at Vellimalai, Divisional Statistical Office at Sankarapuram and Kallakuruchi and Forest Department at Madras and Vellimalai. The primary and secondary data collected were pooled and put into computer analysis in order to check the validity of the hypothesis. In the research work, Karl Pearson's correlation coefficient, multiple regression, and Spearman's rank correlation coefficient were used in the thesis. Finally, to test the hypotheses 'F' test, 'χ^2' test, test of concordance and test for Spearman's' correlation co-efficient were adopted and discussed in the chapters.

Plan of the Study

The present research work is presented in seven chapters. The First chapter deals with the introduction to the study, statement of the research problem, the period of the study, main objectives, hypotheses and research methods.

In the second chapter, the researcher has tried to dwell upon all the salient aspects of available literature probing into land reform measures undertaken in various tribal economies. It is observed from the literature on land reforms in the tribal areas, that no single author had covered all the aspects of land reform measures. The lacuna in these studies leaves enough scope for a micro level study conducted afresh in the kalrayan hills of Tamil Nadu.

The Third chapter portrays the general as well as specific land reforms and the accompanying tribal development package measures recommended in the Five Year Plans. In this chapter, the importance is given to the Fifth Plan because, such programmes as implemented in the study area commenced only from 1976. The chapter also highlights fact that many such schemes are not need-based and are drawn from the conventional frame meant for the non-tribals.

The Fourth chapter delineates the background of the kalrayan hill tribes and their condition before and after 1976. General information like geographic location, topography and soil condition, rainfall and irrigation facilities, general and specific information about the tribals in the country and the State are also discussed in the chapter.

The Fifth chapter deals with the progress of land reform measures undertaken in the Kalrayan hills. The chapter exhibits some of the legal aspects of land reforms implemented in the hill and all details about the assignment of land to the tribals.

In the Sixth chapter, an analysis of the Kalrayan hill's tribal economy during the post reform period is given. The chapter is divided into two parts viz., first the socio-economic characteristics of the tribals like, education, age group and family size, wealth, income, employment, cropping pattern indebtedness and alienation of lands are discussed in detail. Secondly, an empirical analysis of inputs' used and output of different crops cultivated by the tribals are examined with correlation and regression analysis. Finally test of hypotheses with statistical techniques is presented.

The Chapter Seven deals with summary and suggestions. The suggestions given would provide a concrete need-based strategy for land reforms and package measures required for a compact tribal development strategy.

References

1. Haque, T. "Land Reforms and Rural Development" in SINGH, Tarlok. et. al, Impact of Land Reforms on Agriculture and Rural Development (National Institute of Rural Development,

Hyderabad, and Indian Association of Social Science Institutions, New Delhi, 1992), p. 13.

2. Hanumantha Rao, C.H. "New Economic Policy, Land Reforms and Rural Development-Tasks Ahead", *Ibid.*, p. 209.

3. Jacoby, E.H. and Jacoby, C.F. Man and Land: The Fundamental issues in Development, [Andrew Deutsch, Ltd., London, 1971], p. 24.

4. Government of India: Report of the Commissioner for Scheduled Castes and Scheduled Tribes, (Manager of Publications, New Delhi, 28th Report, 1986-87), p. 14.

5. *Ibid.*, pp. 14-21.

6. Kottakayam, Jacob John. Social Structure and Change among the Tribals (D.K. Publishing House, New Delhi, 1983), p. 53.

7. Government of India: Report of the commissioner, *op. cit.*, p. 387 "since there were special provisions under the Fifth and Sixth schedules to the constitution in regard to the administration of the Scheduled Areas and the Tribal Areas, the areas of tribal concentration had to be treated as distinct areas for which special provisions special laws and regulations and special pattern of administration were to be adopted. In other words, a clear distinction had been drawn between tribals who lived within these concentrations known as the Scheduled Areas and tribals who were outside the schedule areas. The former were recognised to be more backward and requiring special attention from government".

8. *Ibid.*, p. 57.

9. *Ibid.*, p. 384.

10. "The goals of tribal development in India, were best summarised in Nehru's forward to Verrier Elwin's book on NEFA as: (1) People should develop along the lines of their own genius and we should avoid imposing anything on them. We should try to encourage in every way their own traditional arts and culture. (2) Tribal rights in land and forest should be respected. (3) We should try to train and build up a team of their own people to do the work of administration and development. Some technical people from outside unit no doubt be needed, especially in the beginning but we should avoid introducing too many outsiders into tribal territory. (4) We

should not over-administer these areas or over-whelm them with multiplicity of schemes. We should rather work through and not in rivalry to their own social and cultural institutions. (5) We should guide results not by statistics or the amount of money spent, but by the quality of human character that is involved". Adapted from Ashok R. Basu, Tribal Development Programmes and Administration in India, (National Book Organisation, New Delhi, 1985), pp. 38-40.

11. Joshi, P. C. Land Reforms-A Trend Report in a Survey of Research in Economics, Vol. 4, ICSSR Study, 1975, and SIDHU B.S. Land Reform : Welfare and Economic Growth [Vora and Co. Pub. Pvt. Ltd., Bombay, 1976] pp.240-244.

12. Bandyopadhyay, Rekha, "Global Review of Land Reform-A critical Perspective", Economic and Political Weekly, March 16, 1996, p. 686.

13. Imperial Gazettier of India, Oxford Dictionary, Ralph Linton, Lucy Mair, G.W.B. Huntingford, D.N. Majumdar, I.M.Lewis and T.B. Naik, as quoted in Jacob John Kottakayam, *op. cit.*, pp. 13-15.

2

Review of Literature

In India, agriculture remains the major economic activity, despite the attempts for diversification of the economy. Agriculture contributes to the process of transformation and lot of interactions and interdependencies are found between industry and agriculture. The distribution of land in the country is highly skewed, i.e., of the total number of cultivators about 80 per cent are marginal and small farmers and their share in the total cultivable land is only 20 per cent. About 35 per cent of people engaged in agricultural operations are landless agricultural labourers. The money and efforts spent on the transfer of population from agriculture to industry have not yielded the expected results. Therefore, a suggested remedy is to redistribute the available land among all those who are dependent upon it so that every one will have an equal opportunity to employ himself on his own land.[1]

In this chapter, an attempt is made to review the available studies on the major problems of the tribals. The present review is limited to certain special activities of the tribals like food gathering and hunting, shifting cultivation and terraced cultivation, and their major problems like land alienation, occupation, and indebtedness. Further, a brief review of land reforms undertaken by various countries is also presented in the chapter.

Food Gathering and Hunting

Food gathering and hunting is very high among nomadic and semi-nomadic tribes, where, "as one should expect concerning food-gatherers, among whom the connection of man with land is the loosest and its existence abundant, there is little of what may be called land ownership... often the place in which they hunt or glean is said to belong to the community, village, or clan, because they would resent any interference from outsiders or prevent any other persons or group from using the space reserved to themselves for making a living".[2] Such lands will be perpetual and tribals use it individually or collectively according to their own system. These types of tribals are found in Kerala, Tamil Nadu, Andhra Pradesh, Maharasthra and Andaman in India[3] and the Kalamath food gatherers of North America, Vedar of Ceylon Maidu of California, Negritos of Malay and Australian aborigines.[4]

Where the tribes practice such food-gathering and hunting activities, they lack sufficient resources, agricultural implements, use in appropriate technology and mostly a subsistence economy. In these areas, economic development will be slow, because, they have to devote much of their time in such activities. Therefore, development programmes in these territories should begin with accepting their fundamental right of hunting in the forest. For example, in Bihar and Maharashtra no special freedom is given to tribals for hunting in the forest, while in Manipur, the tribals are given the freedom of hunting wherever they like.[5] With regard to the tribals of the Kalrayan Hill, hunting is not a predominant occupation. When the officials regulate the tribal's entry into the forest the hunting by tribals automatically ceases.

Shifting Cultivation

Indian tribes as cultivators, practice either shifting cultivation or settled cultivation. Shifting cultivation[6] is an age-old institution adopted by the tribals of Assam, Orissa, Madhya Pradesh, Bihar and to certain extent in the other tribal areas. It is used not because of any deep-rooted superstition but because of absence of an alternative to it.[7] Contrary to this, Baigas of Madhya Pradesh and Orissa, practice shifting cultivation by considering it as an order from Bhagwan. According to them "the legend grew out of the concept of mother earth and the mother earth should not be tortured through the dagger of plough. Since the shifting cultivation does not require any ploughing, the mother earth blesses the Baiga for the respect shown to her. They also believe that adoption of plough cultivation shall bring misery".[8] On the other hand shifting cultivation is done with simple implements by the Korku, Baiga, Korwa and Maria tribals of Madhya Pradesh and Naga tribes of Assam, because, they cannot afford to buy costly agricultural implements.[9]

A study conducted in the Himalayan region reported that, in the North-East-region, of the total cropped area of 4.2 million hectares, about 2.7 million hectares i.e., 64 per cent of land under shifting cultivation. The gross return per hectare in paddy cultivation was Rs. 2404 and Rs. 2374 in Jhuming.[10] The difference of Rs. 70 does not assign much weight for settled cultivation. However, due to population explosion, more and more areas are brought under shifting cultivation. Thus, reduction in the duration of shifting cultivation cycle, lead to the loss of valuable forest, loss of soil fertility and biodiversity, soil erosion, reduction in rainfall, landslide and depletion of forest based products.

To efface shifting cultivation various measures have been taken by State and Central Governments. These measures are legal measures and welfares measures implemented through package of schemes. Shifting cultivation is banned in most of the states except in a few pockets of Madhya Pradesh and Northeastern region. The tribals who violate the rule are fined or prosecuted, otherwise collective fines are imposed on all the inhabitants of the area. Welfare measures with package of schemes to control shifting cultivation in Northeastern States include soil and water conservation, construction of bench type terraces and creation of irrigation facilities. In Assam, an attempt is made to resettle the Jhumia tribes in rubber and coffee plantations. On the other hand in Meghalaya a two hectare terraced land with a subsidy of Rs. 2000 per family for construction of dwelling houses are provided. Further, "a top sequencing of crops is recommended with forestry on hill tops, horticulture on moderate slopes and crop production on low lands". The existing techniques of extension education by conducting demonstrations, training and visit system have failed under the hill conditions. Therefore, farming system apparels is suggested for providing package of measures suitable to the tribal area.[11] In states like Andhra Pradesh, West Bengal and Madhya Pradesh establishment of agricultural colonies are attempted to wean way the tribals from shifting cultivation to settled cultivation. In such colonies, each tribe was given some cultivable wasteland along with other amenities for cultivation. The scheme was not successful due to mismanagement and non-acceptance of tribals in the lower plan areas.[12]

Tribals adopt shifting cultivation, even though the yield is less, due to scarcity of fertile land: relatively costless method of cultivation and farm operation needs only simple agricultural implements. Further, "the notion widely held that shifting cultivation is responsible in the main for large scale soil erosion needs to be effectively dispelled. The correct approach to the problem of shifting cultivation lies in accepting it not as a necessary evil, but recognising it as a way of life; not condemning it as an evil practice but regarding it as an agricultural practice evolved as a reflex to the physiographical character of land. For quite some time, jhuming has been condemned out of hand as a curse to be ashamed of, a vandalism to be decried. This attitude engenders an inferiority complex and unhealthy atmosphere for the launching of any development scheme seeking to improve the current practices.[13] Even now, it is followed in countries like India, Africa, Central and South America and account for 10 per cent of world population.[14] In the Kalrayan hill, shifting cultivation was practiced in the name of Punal Kadu by paying a tax to the erstwhile Jagirs. However, it ended when Jagirs were taken over in 1976 and totally vanished when specific lands were allotted through land reforms.[15]

Settled Cultivation

The transition from shifting cultivation to settled cultivation is possible only if the cultivation is confined to permanent plough land. The transformation should be gradual; otherwise, a hasty decision may ruin the tribals' fundamental right to land. Without shifting cultivation, "the Mizos of Mizoram and the Apatanis of Apatani Valley in Arunachal Pradesh are the two such examples of shifting cultivators emerging as expert permanent cultivators".[16] Similarly, Santhal Oraon and Ho of Bihar and Bengal, Tharu and Korwa of Uttar Pradesh, Saora of Orissa, Badaga of Nilgiri Hills of Tamil Nadu, Gond, Bhill and Bhilala of Madhya Pradesh are the tribals who turned out to be better settled cultivators.[17] The acceptance of settled cultivation shows their cultural and ecological adaptability and its impact on tribal economy.

A study on cropping pattern was conducted in Nilgiri district of Tamil Nadu for a period from 1966-67 to 1976-77. It reveals that the cropping pattern is affected by the topography, rainfall, soil and irrigation facilities. Further, "while the cropping pattern in the plains is more elastic, it is considered to be inelastic in the hill areas due to certain limitations".[18] The finding also emphasized that the cropping pattern changes according to the demand for crops and soil condition. According to the study, the cropping pattern in the district over 10 years did not change, except for a small increase in the cultivation of vegetables. On the other hand, one more study on cropping pattern argues that land allocation for different crops is influenced by physical, economic, biological and social factors and if it is adopted wisely it would bring more output and income to the tribals.[19]

The impact of new technology adopted by the tribals of Chotanagpur regions of Southern Bihar was studied in 1988-89 with specific objectives: to identify the level and determinants of the adoption of new technology; and to assess the impact of technology on labour absorption and income distribution.[20] The level of technology adoption was computed by regressing the adoption index, literacy index, area under high yielding varieties, quantity of fertilizers used, scores on irrigation applied and recommended. The adoption function is derived in the form of multiple regression and the results shows that "The level of adoption was positively associated with size of farms; cropping intensity and per hectare crop income tended to increase with the increase of farm size".[21] With regard to labour absorption and income, distribution the study found that human labour absorption was relatively higher on farms with low adoption than on those with higher adoption, by causing disparity in the income distribution. These conclusions presents an overall view, hence the findings may not represent all the tribal areas due to the fact that agriculture in tribal area is generally labour intensive and widespread low level of technology adoption in the tracts.

A study in Meghalaya revealed that the expected yield from terraced farming was the lowest of 15 quintals per hectare as against 6 to 7 quintals per hectare in shifting cultivation.[22]

However, the gross return per hectare in Darengini village in the Garo Hills of Maghalaya as shown by another study[23] was Rs. 1617 per hectare from terraced land. Further, except paddy crop yields from podu fields as compared to settled cultivation were reportedly less by 1.25 and 2.85 times in the hill tract of Korapur in Orissa.[24]

The land and its distribution in hill tribal areas are classified into forestland, land unfit for cultivation, grazing land, trees, poramboke land, cultivable land etc. The cultivable land is minimum and the pressure arising out of ever-growing population is apparent which decreases in the land availability. For example in Gujarat in 1959, out of 459 tribal families surveyed, only 12 were landless and the rest had on an average 5.32 acres of land. In Madhya Pradesh, it was 15.95 acres 4.40 and 5.95 acres in Dungarpur and Banswara district of Rajasthan, and 2.80 acres in Manipur.[25] It was 1.74 hectares in 1981 and 1.6 hectares in 1991 in the Kalrayan hills.[26]

Land Alienation

The pressure on land, chronic indebtedness and loopholes in the existing acts causes land alienation in the tribal areas. Land alienation is a complex problem, because, very often, tribals lose control on their land by the tricks of moneylenders, tribal chieftains and others.

In the tribal areas, indebtedness and land alienation are inter-related because, moneylenders insist on land as a surety for lending money. Further, land alienation is also an outcome of development programmes implemented and extension of infrastructural facilities from the nearby non-tribal areas. Land alienation is a fundamental problem in the tribal areas caused mostly by the moneylenders. Accordingly, various States have enacted laws.

The recommendation of the Commissioner for Scheduled Castes and Scheduled Tribes in this regard are "the law concerning alienation of land belonging to Scheduled Castes and Scheduled Tribes and restoration of illegally or irregularly transferred lands should be made stringent. The Central Government should prepare a model Regulation/Law in this regard which may be forwarded to the States for adoption within a stipulated period of not more than one year. The Act should prohibit all future transfers of land by members of Scheduled Castes and Scheduled Tribes in favour of members of other communities as also to such Scheduled Tribes women who may be married or may be living with a non-tribal; prohibit transfer of land by a member of one tribal community to members of other tribal community; prohibit sale of land of a Scheduled Castes/Scheduled Tribes person in realisation of dues including loans advanced by individuals, cooperatives or institutions notwithstanding the provisions in the law of the decree or court; prohibition of consent of passing of decrees by courts which may involve transfer of land by a Scheduled Castes/Scheduled Tribes person; prohibition of appearance of pleaders in cases involving restoration of lands to Scheduled Castes/Scheduled Tribes persons; provisions for summary proceedings in cases involving alienation of land belonging to SC/ST persons; provision for only one appeal in cases where transfer of land by a SC/ST person is held by the court as illegal or malafide; provision for compulsory restoration of land after the decision in favour of a SC/ST person and within a stipulated period but not later than the harvesting of crop, if any, already in the field and prohibition of stay orders by the appellate authorities in case an appeal is preferred; and occupation of land within three years of the date of restoration of land to a Schedule Castes and Scheduled Tribes person by any person whoever should be made a cognizable offence".[27] These recommendations cover a variety of disciplines through which land alienation erupts into tribal areas and escalate their problems. Therefore, to safeguard the tribals such measures should be made mandatory on the part of the State Governments by the Central Government. Otherwise, the exploitation of the people will continue in spite of the protective laws in the tribal areas.[28]

In Himachal Pradesh, land alienation is one of the complex problems in the tribal areas of Bharmour and Pangi sub-divisions. In order to protect the tribals from the fundamental problem arising out of land alienation number of protective land laws has been passed.[29] These laws restrict on : transfer of land by sale or mortgage from tribals to non-tribals; transfer of land to any person with flexible approach in respect of persons belonging to the same tribe; transfer of land to any person, non-tribal or tribal; sale of land to other non-scheduled tribe, scheduled caste or other backward classes; and reserved areas for tribals.[30]

Land reform laws in Himachal Pradesh include: Punjab Tenancy Act, The Punjab Tenants Security of Tenure Act, 1950; The Punjab Tenancy (H.P. Amendment) Act, 1952; The Himachal Pradesh Tenants (Rights and Restoration) Act; 1952; The Punjab Tenants (Security of Tenure) Act, 1950; The Abolition of the Big Landed Estates and Land Reforms Act, 1953; The Himachal Pradesh Consolidation of Holdings Act, 1953; The Himachal Pradesh Land Regulation Act, 1968. With these, the state government provided safety measures to the tribals, either by amending the acts or extending the general acts to the tribals, of which, The Himachal Pradesh Land Regulation Act, 1968,[31] states that, "no person belonging to any Scheduled Tribes shall transfer his interest in his land by way of sale, mortgage, lease, gift or otherwise to any person not belonging to such tribe except with the previous permission of the Deputy Commissioner of the District. Every transfer of land, in contravention of the previously mentioned section shall be void. Thus, in Himachal Pradesh many such provisions in the Acts are in the line with the overall national policy as recommended by the Commissioner of Scheduled Castes and Scheduled Tribes.

In Gujarat, land alienation is caused due to soil condition, poor technology, social and other obligations.[32] In this State, the Tenancy act's Section (165) prevents land transfer and on the other hand, section (168) provides for lease of land on yearly contract. If the lease exceeds certain time limit, the land is considered to have passed on to the person who cultivates it. Further, landlords manipulated the records in such a way that the tribal lands were taken away before passing the Tenancy Act. The binami transfer of land due to ignorance and widespread illiteracy is very common in the State. In Gujarat, for the unpaid loan the Cooperatives Societies auctioned the tribals' lands. Further, the tribals are forced to part with their land for charitable, religious, educational, industrial, irrigation, mining and other purposes. To prevent land alienation number of legislations have been passed viz; The Bombay Tenancy and Agriculture Land Act, 1948, The Land to the Tiller Act, 1957 and the general orders of the Government relating to the disposal of waste land. The Bombay Land Revenue Code prohibits land transfer in areas where survey and settlement is pending and without the permission of the officer concerned.

Land alienation in West Bengal is by manipulating the settlement records, by force, or by taking advantage of the poverty of the people. Land alienation and indebtedness are directly related. Therefore, to prevent this number of protective measures have been implemented in the state. The West Bengal Land Reforms (Amendment) Act, 1965, Section 14(c) of Chapter II(A) exempt land transfer to public and charitable purposes, simple mortgage to the government or to a registered cooperative society, simple mortgage or mortgage by deposit of title deeds in favour of a scheduled bank, cooperative land mortgage bank or a corporation owned and controlled by the Central or State Government or by both for the development of land or improvement of agricultural production and a gift or will to a person belonging to a Scheduled Tribes.[33] Further, a team consisting of officials and tribal MLA's recommended for modification in the existing Land Reform Act in order to prevent land alienation. In West Bengal, land transfer to non-tribal is illegal but the same by the government agencies is not considered as an alienation of tribal land in the State.

Non-tribals from Andhra Pradesh caused land alienation in Orissa who actually charges exorbitant interest ranging from 100 to 300 per cent, with ultimate intention of grabbing the tribal land. To solve this problem, the government provided a fairly effective network of staff and officers to enforce the protective Acts and Regulations viz., Orissa Debt Bondage Abolition (Regulations), 1948; Orissa (Scheduled Areas) Money lending (Regulation), 1967; Orissa (Scheduled Areas) Debt Relief Regulation, 1967; Orissa (Scheduled Areas) Debt Relief Regulation 1967; Orissa (Scheduled Areas) Transfer of Immovable Property (Amendment) Act, 1975; Land Improvements Loans Act, 1983; The Agriculturalist Loans Act, 1984; The Minimum Wages Act, 1948; The Orissa Land Reforms Act of 1960; The Orissa Cooperative Societies Act, 1962.[34] In addition to the legislative measures, the revenue field staff, tribal welfare officers and non-official agencies like Panchayat Samities and Gram Panchayats individual MLA's and MP's are involved in the detection of illegal land transfers. About 6000 cases of illegal transfers were detected in 1975 and so for 5018 cases, orders were passed for the restoration of land to the extent of 4032 acres of land. In the first quarter of 1976, 2588 cases have been detected and most of the cases were ordered for restoration of tribal land. However, the illegal and binami transfer of land makes the legislative measures an ineffective one. Further, several punishment to the moneylenders, an alternative credit avenues and awareness among the tribals have been advocated for better results. The detection of illegal transfer of land and settling the same by the "Team" is a milestone in finding the solution to the land problem, and a revelation to the other states on this line to tackle land alienation problems in the tribal areas.

The State governments seriously view land alienation and hence a number of protective laws have been passed. However, in Tamil Nadu, there is no legislation or law to provide protection to Scheduled Caste and Scheduled Tribe against alienation of land. However, according to Revenue, standing order once if land is assigned to these groups subject to the condition that it should not be alienated for 10 years from the date of allotment and beyond 10 years, it should be transferred only to their own people if necessitated. Any transfer is null and void and would cause resumption of land without compensation.[35] However, during the primary data collection, it was noticed that about 44 acres of land was sold to non-tribals and about 17 acres of land to their own tribals. Hence, separate law pertaining to land alienation like the one The Himachal Pradesh Transfer of Land (Regulation) Act, 1968, must be passed to safeguard the tribals from land alienation in Tamil Nadu.

Shifts in Occupation

According to V. Saravanan[36] the work force did not shift largely from the primary to secondary and tertiary sectors. Therefore, some economic changes in the occupations of the tribals cannot be ignored. He observed an occupational transformation within the primary sector in the hills of Salem District. The proportion of cultivators to the total working force in the primary sector continued to decrease in all the hills till 1981. Similarly, the trends of occupational transformation of the tribal females within the primary sector deteriorated.

Harshed R. Trivedi[37] has analysed the occupation and leisure time activities in the tribal area of Valsad District. Migration and occupational change is due to monsoon, lack of employment opportunities, draught, scarcity, inadequate rainfall etc. The occupations of tribals were job in mines, forests, collection of minor forest produce, bamboo work and some times bonded labour.

C. Gangaiah[38] found that small and marginal farmers were shifting their primary occupation from agriculture to secondary occupations like dairy, poultry, fish farming, sericulture, floriculture etc., During drought conditions these occupations provides livelihood to the people.

G.C. Pande[39] has observed that in Tharu tribal community nearly 96 per cent were involved in agricultural activities. However, presently in this community during the third generation shift in occupation was found towards industry. In some other tribal community, the author found that the shift was from primitive type of employment to agriculture.

Indebtedness

Tribal areas are opened to the outsiders and non-tribals. They entered into the tribal regions as moneylenders, businessmen, contractors etc. Most of the tribal economies are in transition; hence, the need for money exists to fulfill their social, cultural and economic needs. Monetization, market penetration and abject poverty necessitate borrowing money from different sources, in the absence of their own source of money. The sources of finance are from organised sectors viz. Commercial Banks, Cooperative Bank and LAMPS, while the unorganized sector consists of private moneylenders and contractors. The financial institutions under the organised sector sanction loan and performs banking as well as non-banking business like purchase of minor forest produce etc. These institutions cannot sanction fresh loan to a defaulter tribe, hence, the only alternative source for them are the moneylenders and contractors.

Tribals normally borrow money from the moneylenders for different purposes, but the moneylenders give credit with single goal that is to grab the land from the tribals.[40] Land alienation accentuates indebtedness in tribal areas; hence, remedial measures are essential to break the vicious circle of indebtedness. The foremost, is the Fifth Schedule of the Indian Constitution, which empowers the Governor of the States to regulate the activities of the moneylenders in the tribal areas. Following this, there are a number of legislative measures implemented / enacted in each state. Some of the laws in different states to control money lending, debt-redemption and debt bondage are ; the Andhra Pradesh Scheduled Areas Moneylenders, Regulation, 1963; The Agency Debt Bondage Abolition Regulation, 1964; The Assam Moneylender's Regulation 1968; The Bihar Moneylenders (Regulations of Transaction) Act, 1939; The Bombay Agricultural Debtor's Relief Act, 1947; The Kerala Money lending Act, 1958; The M.P. Anusuchit Jan Jati Rini Sahayata Act, 1966; The Madras Indebtedness Agriculturists (Repayment of Debts) Act, 1955; The Mysore Pawn Brokers Act, 1961; The Orissa Money Lenders (Application of Certain Provisions) Regulation, 1950; and The Rajasthan Sagri System Abolition Act, 1961.[41] Therefore, it is recommended that, "No programme of economic development is likely to have any impact on the tribal economy unless vigorous measures are taken to rescue the tribes from the clutches of the moneylenders".[42]

Forest

Tribals depended on forest and forestland not only for its natural vegetation but also as a source of livelihood and, "the ties with the forests go back to times immemorial. Further, they have enjoyed freedom to use the forests, in whatever manner they like, to such an extent that they have developed a conviction that they belong to the forests and the forest belongs to them".[43] The forest policy in India began from 1894, since then many forest policies were evolved for regulating the use of forest. The Report of Committee on Forest and Tribals[44] recommended that:

(i) "Forest policy and forest system should be directed towards managing a renewable endowment of vast potential for sub serving national, regional as well as local development goals. In facts, the individual tribal, the local tribal community and national interest should be regarded as three corners of a triangular forest policy. Forest policy must fulfill three sets of needs

(a) ecological security,

(b) food, fruit, fuel, fodder, fibre, timer and other domestic needs of particularly the rural and domestic needs of particularly the rural and tribal population; and

(c) cottage, small, medium and large industries including the requirements of defense and communications;

(ii) "Wherever community rights exist on forest land, they should be recognised and adapted to serve the urgent needs of the soil and water management and re-afforestation of denuded tracts by suitable species; Conjoint efforts of government, cooperative, community and private sectors are necessary to increase production of fuel-wood, fodder, fruit and industrial wood;"

(iii) "Social forestry, farm forestry, community agro forestry, should be encouraged as multi-use land resources pattern in the context of national land use policy and for increased production of fodder, fuel wood, fertilizer, generating employment, improving environment, and relieving rural women from drudgery and hardship of finding fuel wood;"

(iv) "A programme of large-scale plantation should be taken up with the help of tribals giving them rights on the trees planted by them in assigned areas and usufruct. Possibilities of short-term subsidy programmes for implementing forestry programmes may be concretised;"

Considering that, forestry is being recognised as more important in the economy for energy, ecology, employment, poverty, alleviation etc. In India, the forest policy is not uniformly adopted in all the states. For example in Gujarat, forest lands are given to forest settlers and will not be disturbed as long as the users abide by the conditions laid down during the grant. In Maharashtra, forestlands are given on yearly lease for agri-sylvi cultural purposes. In States like Manipur, hunting is allowed in the forest while it is denied in Bihar and Maharasthra. Contrary to this in other states including Kalrayan hill area the tribals are fined or prosecuted when the tribals violate the forest-law. No doubt, forest must be safeguarded, not by delinking tribals from forest but by integrating them with forest.

Therefore, Commissioner for Scheduled Castes and Scheduled Tribes recommended that, "The Government of India may consider formally adopting a resolution accepting and development of forestry resources so that desired changes can be effected in the perceptions of the administration and of the people about the forestry and suitable modalities for future action may be worked out".[45] In majority, of the tribal areas land problem remain unsettled and the forest department people are overambitious in safeguarding the forest from deforestation.

Land Reform in Selected Countries

The global experience of land reform measures initiated with different ideologies and processes have had universal aims:[46] to interrupt the vicious cycle poverty, ignorance and stagnation, to alter the existing unequal distribution of land by ensuring agricultural and economic development. Studies probing into the post-reform efforts delineate conflicting results about the reform measures. The depressing picture of reform achievements worldwide was due to overenthusiastic implementation of land reform measures; delay and loopholes in the laws; poor administrative setup; landed aristocracy; and unrealistic and unachievable ideologies.[47] A brief summary of land reforms implemented in selected countries are presented in this section.

In Africa, the transition in the tribal economy from isolation to open economic system was out of commercial market penetration due to colonial conquest. The introduction of cash crops and western line of administration also changed their native identity. This has encouraged land manipulation not only by foreign commercial interest but also by tribal chieftains, tempted by the prospect of becoming feudal lords or capitalist farmers.[48]

Further, farmers in Africa suffered due to undefined land policies, mostly influenced by western concept of individualization that aims at settlement and resettlement of tribal people. Few of the land tenure models undertaken in Africa[49] provide a concrete measure for consideration or adoption in tribal areas.

The Nucleus Plantation schemes funded and run by foreign firms in Nigeria is managed as a cooperative organization or like a company in partnership with the government. In Tanzania, the post-settlement policy aimed at changing the land tenure and land use pattern by reorganizing and mobilizing the peasant population. Multi-tribal 'collective socialist villages' called "Ujamma Vijjini" are formed and the return in shared among the tribal members. The societies are formed in their own communal traditions and the tribals who are not willing to become members can receive land elsewhere in the area.[50]

In Uganda, land settlement is based on individual ownership pattern. The important effort was the establishment of "group settlement", where the tribals were allotted land. The tribals are provided with tractor and technical services with government subsidy.[51]

In Cameroon, land tenure policy has a positive approach because, as per the Law passed in 1959, the legitimate right of tribal communities on land will be protected and it prevents even the government in utilizing the excess tribal land and water resources. However, Government amended the Law and provided for establishing National Collective Patrimony to be established from the surplus land acquired from the tribals. Therefore, allotment of such lands is provisional and will be revoked if it is not used within a specified time.[52]

In Tunisia, legislation pertaining to land provided for an organised rural settlement. In such settlement areas, modern farm techniques extension services and institutional arrangements have been provided for the inhabitants of the area. The subdivision of land holdings is prohibited. Any change in the ownership is subject to approval of the Government. The size of individual holding has a fixed ceiling and excess land is be expropriated by the government by paying compensation to the owners of land. The consolidation of land holding is implemented in case of excessive fragmentation. Land policies of both the countries aimed for better utilization of natural resources attached with improved institutional arrangements.[53]

Jan Breman[54] at the outset discussed the economies of scale, fixing floors for landholdings and the way in which small and marginal farmers were converted into landless agricultural labourers in India. He is for a forced agrarian proletarianization, which has to be carried out in India on an abstract level similar to Indonesia. Further, he recommended organising the unemployed and the underemployed in groups, brigades of tens, hundreds and thousands, like military, and basic military training is to be given to them for 3 to 9 months. The trained people should be sent for public works projects of the different parts of the country for one year, after that they should come for receiving more skills or military training. The group was called 'Development Bridges', the ratio of the group should 70:20 to the total population and 10 per cent of them should be given tasks other than public works. According to him, India lags behind in fixing floor on land holding.

Keith Sutton[55] reviewed the functioning of land redistribution programme in Algeria. In Algeria, the basic land redistribution proceeded in three phases. The first-phase, in 1972-73 concerned about state and communal land and land belonging to religious endowments. The second phase was from 1973-75. The third phase commenced in 1975 and concerned communal and private land and livestock in the pastoral sector. A suggested fourth phase could affect the forested and alfalfa zones. Further, after independence, Algerian government took possession of 2.8 million hectares of land and converted into state farms.

Number of agencies in Algeria monitors land redistribution. A 'land bank' the Fonds National de la Revolution Agraire (FNRA) was established for expropriation and redistribution of land. The land allottees were given a 'setting-in-subsidy' of 290 dinars per month. They also should be member of Co-operative Agricole de Production de da Revolution Agraire (CAPRA). They collectively carry out purchases, sales, and farming operations. The total income is divided among the members based on number of hours worked. In CAEC (Cooperative Agricole d' exploitation commune) the members have right of ownership, but, they should adopt the collective cultivation plan of the society. The Groupment de mise en valeur (CAPCS) provides inputs and market farm output and to support the establishment of peasant's (UNPA) with landless peasants and small holders, including the reform beneficiaries of pre-existing small holders. These agencies and its formulation is a good model for an ideal rural development programme.

The importance of land reform is felt in capitalist countries like U.S.A. also. Geisler and Popper[56] analysed the problems of land reforms in America. The Americans have historically looked upon land reform as an "issue" in developing nations and an irrelevancy at home. However, now Americans are becoming more concerned about the fairness and efficiency of domestic pattern of land distribution. The concern of people over the land reform is noticeable both in rural and urban areas. The land ownership and its distribution in various states, made them to think 'land reform' both as a phase and as a concrete policy and have increasingly claimed the attention of planners, politicians, lawyers, conservationists, community activitists and property owners. The land reform movement illustrates the political nature of American land allocation and it emphasises redistribution of land ownership rather than regulation of land use pattern.

In most of the Latin American[57] countries like Argentina, Brazil, Chile, Colombia, Ecuador, Guatemala and Peru, the agrarian condition was not conducive for economic, social and political development. It is because of the outdated land distribution pattern, wasteful use of agricultural resources and labour extensive farming practices. The concentration of land ownership was in the hands of large landowners who decided about production and employment pattern. Further, "The typical land distribution pattern in Latin America, however, is equally detrimental from the point of view of land use. Almost everywhere, the separation of ownership from management of land, common in many other parts of the world, is aggravated by further separation of management from labour. The fact that cultivation practices, such as use of fertilizers, weed-killers, pesticides etc. which determine the quality of investment, are not decided by the owner or manager of land but left entirely to the agricultural labourer whose miserable wage does not increase with higher yields, is an additional reason for the very low productivity of agricultural land".[58]

In Latin America, the constitutional action for land redistribution is far from encouraging. The "Declaration of the American President in 1967 which gives top priority to regional integration... was far more than a diplomatic postponement of agrarian reforms; it was an important political decision which has shifted the problem of structural changes in Latin America from the evolutionary to the revolutionary level". This is an important factor as it ignites public opinion and the social consciousness of the masses.

Land reform and Peasant Association is the special nature of agrarian situation in Ethiopia. The problems of land concentration in different social classes resulted in land reform by force due to peasant uprising. Accordingly, a committee of military officers (DERGUE) introduced the reforms programme. To this effect, it abolished all private title to land, retaining ownership as the collective property of the people. The ceiling limit is 10 hectares.[59]

In Cuba, "agrarian reform was at the top of the revolutions' priorities because inequality in land holding was seen as the central factor underlying Cuba's economic, social and political ills. The great majority of land was held in large estates, 70 per cent of land being owned by less than 10 per cent of farms. Control of the most important agricultural activities, sugar and cattle was even more concentrated. At the time of revolution, for example, the 28 largest sugar companies owned 1437 thousand hectares and controlled another 617 thousand hectares through rental agreements. They thus controlled 20 per cent of the total farmland. Similarly, the 40 largest cattle launch covered 992 thousand hectare or almost 10 per cent of the farm land".[60] That is, about 57 per cent of the operational area was in the hands of foreigners and local landlords.

However, the whole picture changed after the revolution. After the revolution, the actual land redistribution of land was relatively simple. "The revolutionary government expropriated the large plantation units and limited landownership in the remaining part of agricultural area to 30 caballerias (402 hectares) but soon lowered the ceiling to 5 caballerias (67 hectares) giving the tenants full ownership rights." The Cuban revolution benefited the agricultural workers the most in terms of security and appropriate real wages. The Cuban government also contributed enormously to the success of land reforms. The formation of socialist agriculture to consolidate the land is an attempt to utilize land and labour. Thus, Cuba is able to break the traditions of decades and redistribute the land only after the revolution.

In Yugoslavia, the land redistribution is revolutionary one. German minorities controlled more than 1,600,000 hectares of land. During and after the Second World War the government redistributed the land. After that, many enactments were passed for consolidation of holdings and new agricultural policy[61] was evolved.

Land reform in China was a revolutionary type and, "The revolution that ended after thirty years of civil war and 200 years of foreign intervention in China is fundamentally an agrarian revolution with gigantic dimensions. In contrast to Tzarist Russia where the revolutionary movement spread from the urban centres into countryside, the Chinese movement began by winning the support of the peasants and established its principal basis in rural areas" The Chinese land reform started with redistribution of land, drought animals, implements and houses confiscated from large landlords. About 40 to 50 per cent of the arable land was redistributed to poor peasant and landless labourers benefiting 60 to 70 per cent of the rural population. The reform carried out within a short span of one generation with a minimum of bloodshed. However, mere redistribution did not fetch much to the beneficiaries. Therefore, in 1956, more than 95 per cent of households collectively organised as 'higher' cooperatives. In 1958, the agricultural cooperatives were amalgamated into the large units of people's communes, to establish multi-purpose units.

Further, "The composition of commune is undoubtedly a most suitable institutional framework for the gradual introduction of technical innovations and for creating an administrative 'infrastructure' for the transfer of responsibilities which encouraged the substitution of labour for capital wherever needed and provided an essential incentive for additional efforts. It has been observed quite rightly that remuneration on the work team level may easily be associated with individual performances and thus puts pressure to bear on those members of the team who work slowly or do not show any initial interest".[62] However, in late 1980's a new system is introduced for more private initiative to the collectivised organisation.

It is generally felt that all over the world irrespective of their environment and system, land reforms is accepted for speedy economic development. The need for land reform to serve as a means to interrupt the vicious cycle of poverty, ignorance and stagnation to pave the way for agricultural and economic development in the tribal areas. If it is properly implemented to the needs of the people, it is capable of increasing the income, employment production and consumption of the beneficiaries. The studies of land reform in tribal areas in India and other countries leave enough scope for a fresh study of land reform in the Kalrayan hills of Tamil Nadu.

References

1. Dandekar, V.M. and Rath N., "Poverty in India", *Economic and Political Weekly*, January 2, 1971, pp. 70-73 and Singh, Hoshiar."Oh, to have a Piece of Own Land", *Kurukshetra,* Vol. XXXI, No. 18, June 16-30, 1983, pp. 6-8, Joshi, P. C. "Problems of Land Reforms in the Second Stage" in Mahajan, V.S. (Ed.,) Studies in Indian Economy (Deep and Deep Publications, New Delhi, 1983) pp.152-176, Aziz, Abdul. The Rural Poor: Problems and Prospects (Ashish Publishing House, New Delhi, 1983), Arora, R.C. *Development of Agriculture and Allied Sectors: Command Area Development Approach* (Sultan Chand and Company Limited, New Delhi, 1982) pp. 39-46.

2. Gisbert P. Tribal India: A Synthetic View of Primitive man (Rawat Publications, Jaipur, 1983), p. 168, *op. cit.*, p. 168.

3. *Ibid.*, pp. 166-175 and according to Jacob John Kottakayam, "most of such tribes are found in Southern India and prominent among them are the Kadar inhabiting the forests of Cochin, Malapatram, Paliyam, Pamiyan, Irula and Kurumba of Tamil Nadu and Chenchu dwelling in the Annamalai mountain range of Andhra Pradesh. Besides, the Birhor and the Kharia of Bihar, Kamar, Baiga and Abhujmaria of Madhya Pradesh, Yenadi of Andhra Pradesh, Koya and Kontareddi of Tamil Nadu and Katkar of Maharashtra may also be included in this category. The Onge, Jarwa etc. of Andaman Islands also fall in this category". *Ibid.*, p. 45.

4. Gisbert, P. *Ibid.*, p. 169.

5. Kottakayam, Jacob John, *Ibid.*, p. 93.

6. Shifting Cultivation is called Jhum in Assam, Maghalaya, Tripura, Mizoram and Arunachal Pradesh, Bewar or Dahya in Madhya Pradesh, Podu in Andhra Pradesh, Koman or Bringa in North Orissa and Punal Kadu in Kalrayan Hills.

7. Sain, K. "Economic analysis of shifting cultivation", Indian Journal of Agricultural Economics, Conference Number, Vol. XXXIII, October-December 1978, p. 9.

8. Kottakayam, Jacob John, *op. cit.*, p. 87.

9. Shah, S.L. "Tribal Economy in India with Special Reference to the Himalayan Region-Important Development Issues", *Indian Journal of Agricultural Economics*, Conference Number, Vol. 47, No. 3, July-September. 1992, p. 381-390.

10. Saika, J.N. "Potentiality of Pineapple Cultivation as an Alternative to Shifting Cultivation. A Study in East Khasi Hill District of Maghalaya" as quoted in SHAH, S.L. *op. cit.* pp.381-390.

11. Shah, S.L. *op. cit.* pp.381-390.

12. Government of India : *Report of the Scheduled Areas and Scheduled Tribes Commission,* 1961 and *Report of the Study Team on Tribal Development Programmes,* (Planning Commission, New Delhi, 1969).

13. Chaturvedy, M.D. as quoted in Jacob John Kottakayam, *op. cit.*, p. 88.

14. Sain, K. *op. cit.* pp.8-11.

15. The details are discussed in Chapter V.

16. Kottakayam, Jacob John., *op. cit.*, p. 47.

17. *Ibid.*, p. 47

18. Sridharan, B. and Radhakrishnan, S.A. "A study on the Factors Affecting Changes in the Cropping Pattern in Nilgiri District, Tamil Nadu", *Indian Journal of Agricultural Economics*, Vol. XXXIII, Oct-Dec.1978, No. 8, pp. 14-20.

19. Singh, Katar and Rahim K.M.B. "Identification and Evaluation of Optimal Cropping System for a Typical Water land in Uttar Pradesh Hill", *Ibid.*, pp. 29-32.

20. Chandra, Naresh, and Singh, R.P. "Determinants and Impact of New Technology Adoption of Tribal Agriculture in Bihar", *Indian Journal of Agricultural Economics*, Vol. 47, No. 3, July-Sep.1992, pp. 397-399.

21. *Ibid.*, pp. 397-399.

22. Gupta, Tirath. and Sambrani, Shreekant. "Control of Shifting Cultivation: The Need for an Integrative Approach and Systematic Appraisal", *Indian Journal of Agricultural Economics, op. cit.*, pp. 1-7.

23. Borah, Durgeswar. "A Comparative Study of Crop Production Under Shifting Cultivation and Terrace Cultivation: A case studies of Garo Hills, Meghalaya", Agro-Economic Research Centre for North-Eastern India, Assam Agricultural University, Jorhat, 1977.

24. Hasan, Mohammed. "Shifting to Settled Cultivation-A Transition in Farming in Hilly Tract of Koraput, Orissa", *Indian Journal of Agricultural Economics, op. cit.*, p. 426.

25. Kottakayam, Jacob John. *op. cit.* pp.82-82.

26. Census Repot of 1981 and 1991.

27. Government of India : *Report of the Commissioner for Scheduled Casts and Schedule Tribes,* (Manager of Publications, New Delhi, 28th Report, 1986-87) pp.15-16.

28. *Ibid.*, pp. 15-16.

29. Basu, Ashok R. *Tribal Development Programmes and Administration in India* (National Book Organisation, New Delhi, 1985) p. 92.

30. Burman, Roy B.K. "Perspective for Administration and Development of the Scheduled Tribes" as quoted in Ashok R. Basu, *Ibid*, p. 38.

31. Basu, Ashok.R *op. cit.*, p. 95.

32. Dubey, S.L. "Gujarat" in Dubey, S.N. and Murdia, Ratna. (Ed.) *Land Alienation and Restoration in Tribal Communities in India.* (Himalaya Publishing House, Bombay, 1977). pp.76-84.

33. Roy, U.K. "West Bengal" in Dubey, S.N. and Murdia, Ratna. *Ibid.* pp.112-125.

34. Jha, Vinod. "Orissa", *Ibid.* pp.126-137.

35. Murdia, Ratna. "Land Allotment and Land Alienation Policies and Programme for Scheduled Caste and Scheduled Tribes", *Economic and Political Weekly*, Vol. X, No. 32, Aug.1975, pp. 1204 to 1214 and Government of Tamil Nadu, *Annual Tribal Sub-Plan*, 1992.

36. Velayutham Saravanan, Economic Transformation of Tribals in Tamil Nadu since the Colonial Rule 1972-1991, unpublished Ph.D., Thesis, University of Hyderabad,1994, pp. 155-160.

37. Trivedi, Harshed R., Tribal Land Systems, Land Reform Measures and Development of Tribes, (Concept Publishing Company, New Delhi, 1993), pp. 255-271.

38. Gangaiah, C., "Floriculture Earn Higher Farm Returns", Southern Economist, May, 15, 2001, pp. 16-19.

39. Pande, G.C., (1991), Indian Tribes, Anmol Publications, New Delhi, pp. 216-231.

40. Borrowing cash loan is common in all the tribal areas. In Maharashtra, tribes borrow seed and pay packs 3 to 4 times more than the quantity they had borrowed. In Tripura, moneylenders purchase the crop in advance of harvest at a very low price and in Maharashtra and West Bengal the borrowing is also for buying agricultural implements-Jacob John Kottakayam, *op. cit.* pp.76-87.

41. Kottakayam, Jacob John. *Ibid.*, p. 81.

42. Government of India: *Report of the Study Group on Tribal Development Programme* (Planning Commission, New Delhi, 1969).

43. Kottakayam, Jacob John. *Ibid.* p. 90.

44. Government of India: *Report of Committee on Forest and Tribals in India, Government of India,* (Ministry of Home Affairs, Tribal Development Division, New Delhi, 1982) pp. 101-117.

45. Government of India: *Report on the Commissioner op. cit.* pp. 60-62.

46. Bandyopadhyay, Rekha. "Global Review of Land Reforms : A Critical Perspective", Economic and Political Weekly, March

16, 1996, pp. 680-685 and Sidhu, B.S., Land Reforms, Welfare and Economic Growth (Vora and Co. Publishers Pvt. Ltd, Bombay, 1976), pp. 20-25.

47. *Ibid.*, p. 686.

48. Jacoby, E.H. and Jacoby, C.F. *Man and Land: The Fundamental Issue in Development* (Andre Deutsch Limited, London 1971), pp. 275-281.

49. Griffin, Keith, *Land Concentration and Rural Poverty* (The Macmillan Press Ltd, Madras 1976) pp. 15-70.

50. Jacoby, E.H. and Jacoby, C.F. *op. cit.*

51. *Ibid.*

52. *Ibid.*

53. Dooren, P. J. "State-Controlled Changes in Juniria's Agrarian Structure" from Tropical Man (Royal Tropical Institute of Amsterdam, Leiden, 1968) as quoted in Jacoby, C.H. and Jacoby, C.F.*op. cit.*

54. Breman, Jan. *Control of Land Labour in Colonial Java : A Case Study of Agrarian Crisis and Reform in the Region of Cirebon during the First Decades of the 20th Century* : Foris Publications, (Holland 1983) as reviewed by Arvind N. Das. "Process of Agrarian Transitions in Indonesia", *Economic and Political Weekly,* Vol. XX, No. 10, March 9, 1985, pp. 398-404.

55. Sutton, Keith." Agrarian Reform in Algeria-Progress in the Face of Disappointment, Dilution and Diversion", Jones, Steve. *et. al.*, (Ed.,) Rural Poverty and Agrarian Reform (Allied Publishers Pvt. Ltd., New Delhi, 1982) pp.356-373 and Griffin, Keith. *Land Concentration* and Rural Poverty, *Op.cit,* pp. 16-42.

56. Geisher, Charles C. and Popper, Frank J. *Land Reform American Style,* (Rowman and Allanheld Publishers, 1984).

57. Sethi, Narendra K. "Land Reform in Economic Development: A case study from Latin America", *Southern Economist,* Vol. XII, No. 17 and 18, January 1, 1969, pp. 37 and 38.

58. *Ibid.,* pp. 37-38.

59. Abata, Alula. and Teklu, Tasfaye. "Land Reform Peasant Associations in Ethiopia : A Case Study of two Widely Different Regions", in Amit Bhaduri and M.D. Anisur Rahman's *Studies in Rural Participation* (Oxford and IBH Pub. Co., Bombay, 1982), pp. 58-59 and Bandyopadhyay, Rekha. "Global Review of and Reform: A Critical Perspective," *op. cit.*, p. 683.

60. Macewan, Arthur, "Agrarian Reform and Economic Transformation in Cuba" in Steve Jones, *et al.*, *op. cit.* p. 229 and Bandyopadhyay, Rekha. "Global Review of Land Reform: A Critical Perspective, *Ibid.*, p. 683.

61. Dorner, Peter. *Land Reform and Economic Development, op. cit.*, p. 124.

62. Jacoby, E.H. and Jacoby, C.F. *op. cit.*

3

Various Land Reforms

In India, there are 573 tribal communities accounting which for 7.9 per cent of the total population. They vary vastly in Socio-economic,, cultural and linguistic features and are also widely dispersed all over the country in hilly, forest and plain areas. The persisting poor economic condition of the tribals made the Government to implement a number of development measures, through Five Years Plans to achieve social justice and economic development.

The tribal development measures of the plans included; distribution of land to the tribals, development of lands under cultivation, protection to the tribals from moneylenders, development of cottage or village industries and establishment of various developmental projects.[1] These development measures are prepared on a broad basis and given to the State Governments, for implementation. In Tamil Nadu, such land reforms and other tribal development measures have been put into operation as early as in any other State in India. In this chapter, a brief review of the progress of reforms and tribal development measures implemented during plan periods is attempted.

First Five Year Plan (1951-56)

The Draft of the First Plan was prepared in July 1951. After a careful analysis of the main projects of the plan, the final report was submitted to the Government on December 7, 1952, and ratified by the Parliament in 1953.[2] However, the plan was to be effective from April 1951 to March 1956.

In the plan, agriculture gave the top most priority, with the objective of changing agriculture from subsistence farming to economic farming. Further, land reform was part and parcel of the objectives of the plan. By considering the weakness of Indian agriculture, land policy was evolved for, "The reconciliation of the interests in land between the contending economic classes, such as intermediaries, large owners, small and middle owners, tenants and landless workers; and the reorganization of the agrarian structure (the system of land holding) so that it can continuously be adapted to an increasing efficiency basis".[3]

The Plan suggested uniform land reform measures for the whole country. These measures include the abolition of intermediaries, ceiling on land holdings, tenancy reform and consolidation of holdings. Similarly, the plan recommended "Co-operative Village Management" to sole the inherent weaknesses of Indian agriculture. Perhaps, this was initiated to pool the uneconomic land holdings, in order to make them more viable, manageable and to increase agricultural output and employment. In fact, many State Governments had enacted legislations to abolish the intermediaries. As a result, about 20 million cultivators were brought under ryotwari system and 57.7 lakhs hectares of land was distributed to the landless agriculturists. The drastic statutory compulsions on the subject had cost Rs. 670 crores to the Government, by way of compensation paid to the erstwhile zamindars.

Ceiling on land holdings was considered because of the unequal distribution of land, which persisted even after the abolition of zamindari system. This plan recommended that, "where land is managed directly by substantial owners and there are no tenants in occupation, public interest requires that there should be an absolute limit to the amount of land which any individual may hold".[4]

In the plan, the land ceiling was based on family holding. According to the land ceiling Acts of various states, such portion of land that is in excess to the ceiling or limit, should be declared as 'Surplus land', by following a procedure and would be taken over by the government. These lands will be distributed to the landless peasants. The States concerned provided the new owners with financial and technical assistance.

Tenancy reforms were initiated with regulation of rent, security of tenancy and land to the tiller. All the State Governments had enacted legislations to effect tenancy reforms as suggested by the Planning Commission. Like the ceiling on land holdings, there were exemptions to the tenancy viz., people serving in the defense forces, unmarried women, widows and mentally and physically retarded persons. The rent was fixed at one-fifth of the total produce and in case of higher rent proper explanation was demanded from the owners.

Yet another land policy of the plan was the consolidation of land holdings. The plan proposed that all the States should have legislation to prohibit further sub-division and fragmentation of lands, below a minimum of land, as fixed by the States. The consolidation of land holdings was accepted by most of the states by passing legislation except States like Tamil Nadu.[5]

The first plan considered co-operative farming as an indispensable instrument of democracy. To quote from the plan, "In a farm of substantial size it is possible to eliminate several wasteful operations and to ensure better planning of the use of land, including selection of crops, crop rotation, soil conservation, development of irrigation and introduction of improved techniques. Economies which cannot be availed of by small farms are available to large ones".[6]

The plan felt that the cooperative farming is capable of increasing agricultural production, by applying new agricultural techniques and it will create a demand for labour to be employed on large-sized co-operative lands. Further, it will also increase the income of the peasants.[7] However, the success of co-operative farming depends upon the acceptance of peasants. Similarly, the functioning of such farming should be regulated by specific land management legislation.

The plan identified 245 tribal communities constituting 5 per cent of the total population. The concentration of tribes was maximum in Assam (33.0 per cent), followed by 29.8 per cent in Manipur and it was only 1.1 per cent in Tamil Nadu. According to the Plan, "The tribal population in India is accepted to be the oldest-population of the land. The communities have lived for centuries in the forest and hilly regions, and at present they are found in a wide central belt beginning with the Aravalli Hills in the west and extending into parts of Bombay, Madhya Pradesh, Bihar, Orissa, West-Bengal and Assam. There are tribes in the north, in the southern ranges of Himalayas, and also in the South in the Western Ghats and Eastern Gnats in the Vindhya and Satpura mountains".[8] These tribals have suffered from various social and economic disabilities. Therefore, various schemes were taken up during the Five Year Plans under the general development programme. "But due to their comparative social, economic and educational backwardness, they could not possibly catch up with the other advanced communities of India hence special provisions had been made in the plan to secure their advancement in such a way as to bring them to the level of the rest of the community".[9]

The tribal development programmes of this plan included schemes for development of communication, water supply, forest economy, agriculture, community development, arts and crafts, health and hygiene, education and leadership. The communication programme of the plan emphasized for laying roads and communication facilities in the tribal areas. The outlay earmarked for the scheme was separated from the usual road grants allocated by the Union and State Governments. Since, the tribal people live in hilly, rocky and forest-areas, there was shortage of water, i.e., both for drinking and cultivation. Therefore, efforts were initiated in the plan to construct new wells and to improve irrigation facilities.

The plan felt that the quality of land in tribal area was generally poor and no land record was maintained. Further, the tribals have become landless due to famine and other economic conditions. Therefore, the plan proposed that, "The problem of land restoration and distribution is linked up with the larger problem of land reform affecting all agriculturists, but the tribal population could be induced and assisted to move to large uncultivated areas which are suited to their modes of living".[10]

The Plan observed that the tribals practiced widespread shifting cultivation, settled cultivation and terraced cultivation in various tribal areas. The First Plan recommended the introduction of new methods of agriculture, which is suited to the local condition of the tribal areas. At the same time, in order to accelerate agricultural development, community development projects were started in Assam, Bihar, Orissa, Madhya Pradesh and Tripura. Similarly, Co-operative activities were initiated in several tribal areas with the help of social workers. During the plan, Multi Purpose Cooperative Societies and 653 Forest-Labour Co-operatives were established.

The first plan realised that, the growth of "Criminal Tribes" in certain tribal pockets, "are made up of a few pastoral communities, which could not adjust themselves to the economy of settled life; small sections of forest tribes which broke away from larger tribes because they could not adjust themselves to economies resulting from the forest and land policies of successive governments; and certain groups which were temperamentally and psychologically unable to adjust themselves to a law-and-order society and found it profitable to take advantage of concentrated properties in settled economies rather than to earn their livelihood by productive labour".[11] To solve this problem a series of programmes were worked out by the Government. The initial step was that the criminal tribes should be dealt with seriously only if they are proved guilty by the Court of Law. In this connection the Criminal Tribal Act has been repealed with effect from 30th August 1952.

The first plan document clearly indicates the keen intention of the Government on tribal development. However, many programmes and recommendations were drawn from the conventional frame meant for the non-tribals. Further, according to the plan document "it is not easily practicable when tribal life has been influenced by social forces from without, and tribal communities have reached a certain degree of acculturisation accompanied by the penetration of communication into the tribal areas and of social services for the betterment of their lives".[12] It is rueful to note that in the First Plan itself the concept of preserving the tribal identity was not given serious consideration by the Government.

Second Five Year Plan (1956-61)

In the Second Plan, the emphasis shifted from agriculture to industry. However, with the progress of land reforms in the First Plan, even in the Second Plan, the programme on land reforms were to continue with abolition of intermediaries, tenancy reform, ceiling on land holdings and agrarian reorganisation.

The abolition of intermediaries like zamindars, Jagirdars, Inamdars etc., which was more than 40 per cent of the total area of the country, had almost been completed during this plan. The intermediaries were given compensation for the loss of their rights. During the Second Plan, the total compensation paid to the intermediaries was Rs. 2250 million. In the second plan, the tenancy reform began with defining the term "personal cultivation". According to the plan document, the personal cultivation should contain three elements viz., risk of cultivation, personal supervision and labour.[13] The Plan recommended that all the State Governments should consider the three points while evolving tenancy legislation. All the measures on tenancy reform aimed at restoring the right on land, if they are evicted from land by the landlords. Because of such reforms, the extent of tenancy was reduced to 12 per cent from 20 per cent during 1953-54.[14]

During the Second Plan, the planners experienced certain problems in tenancy with respect to small tenants, large tenants and the voluntary surrender of rights. A study observed that the eviction of small tenants was easier than large tenants and the purchase of lands was made by large tenants rather than by the small tenants.[15] Therefore, measures were taken to protective the small tenants and recommended only the voluntary surrender of rights of land.[16] However, the laws on tenancy were not without loopholes. Hence, the tenants continued to face problems in spite of the legislative provisions made by the States.

With regard to ceiling on land holdings, the plan suggested that, "Steps should be taken in each state to impose ceilings on existing agricultural holdings. The ceiling would apply to owned land held under personal cultivation".[17] The ceiling limit was to be fixed on unit basis i.e., husband, wife and dependent children. Further, the commission suggested that the level of ceiling may be lower or higher on the basis of population and availability of cultivable waste land.[18] Unlike the First Plan, the Second Plan recommended five types of exemptions to the ceiling laws viz., tea, coffee and rubber plantation, orchards in compact areas, specilised farms in cattle, dairying etc., sugarcane farms of sugar industries and efficiently managed farms.

Finally, land reform measure in the Second plan included consolidation of land holdings and legislation to prevent fragmentation of land holding under the agrarian reorganisation programme. The plan recommended cooperative farms on lands allotted to the landless people. Such programmes were completed in some states of North India, whereas no concrete steps were taken to prevent sub-division and fragmentation of land holdings.

The Plan tried to reconstruct the tribal economy on the basis of their culture, traditions, social, psychological and economic problems. The plan felt that while implementing the welfare programmes the tribals traditional beliefs and practices may be disturbed. Hence, it was suggested to win the confidence of the elders of the community. The important annual in the plan was the initiative taken to involve and train the tribals in the administration. They were appointed as welfare extensions workers in this regard. Further, the plan suggested forming a "Team" consisting of anthropologists, administrators, specialists and social workers who will approach the tribal problems with utmost sympathy and understanding.

The Plan document related shifting cultivation with the customs and traditions of the tribal people. It was proposed to wean the away tribals from shifting cultivation and to encourage them to go for settled cultivation. As an alternative to shifting cultivation, agricultural colonies were formed in many States. Further, the plan suggested an alternative land utilisation pattern, i.e., permanent afforestation in the upper hill regions, shifting cultivation in the lower hill regions without damage to forest, and terraced cultivation in the lower as well as on gentle slopes of the hill areas.

Collection of minor forest produce is also a main source of income to the tribals. The Government, by considering the penetration of the outside contractors into the tribal areas to buy the minor forest produce at a low price, established Forest-Labour Co-operatives in the tribal areas. During the First Plan, 653 such societies were established in the tribal areas of the country. In addition, about 312 Multi-Purpose Co-operative Societies were established in the tribal areas of Orissa, Bihar and Madhya Pradesh.

Yet another problem in the tribal area is indebtedness. These problems always end in land alienation in most of the tribal areas. Therefore, laws have been enacted to safeguard the tribals from indebtedness and land alienation in many States.

On Community Development and National Extension, programmes were worked out to encourage the settled type of cultivation in place of shifting cultivation, improvement of agriculture, provision of medical and public health services, improvement of communications, development of arts and crafts, organisation of co-operatives and the establishment of community welfare centres.[19] In the total outlay of Rs. 4672 crores, only Rs. 42.92 crores (0.9 per cent) was earmarked for tribal development. In the Second Plan, no drastic measure was taken to solve the land and forest issues of the tribal areas.

During the plan, on May 1, 1958, a committee on Special Multi-Purpose Tribal Blocks and the Central Advisory Board for tribal welfare were appointed to review the various schemes and programmes of the tribals. At the end of the plan, considering the bottlenecks in the implementation of welfare programmes for tribals, the President of India, had appointed a commission under the Chairmanship of U.N. Dhebar in 1960. The major recommendations of the commission were.[20]

1. The protective machinery for safeguarding the interests of the tribal people and protecting them from exploitation has not functioned properly. Large-scale transfers of tribal land have taken place. There is the need for strengthening and in some cases reorganising the administrative set-up for scheduled areas.

2. The requirements of personnel to work in the tribal areas have not been assessed adequately. There is need for a special institution for imparting orientation training to personnel of various levels.

3. There are special problems in tribal areas, which call for a scientific study and evaluation.

4. The non-governmental agencies have a crucial role to play in the development of tribal areas. They should be adequately assisted on the basis of programmes.

These recommendations paved way for a newer tribal development measures in the subsequent plans.

Third Five Year Plan (1961-66)

In the beginning of the plan, the 1961 census was released. According to the census, tribal population was 22.5

million. The criminal tribals were estimated at 4 million. The plan felt that the tribal people still live in isolation and their development was below the development of other communities. Hence, the plan had directed its development policy, on "education and provision of training facilities, improvement of agriculture, building up of communication, improvement of health and medical facilities and supply of drinking water".[21] Moreover, in the plan the tribal area administration and development were carried out by the trained force from within the tribal group with little outside technical guidance in the beginning. Here it is appropriate to quote from the plan document: "Should be development along the lines of their own genius, with genuine respect and support for their own traditional arts and culture and without pressure or imposition from outside".[22] Before we take up the third plan's approach to tribal development, we give in brief the general and specific land reform measures undertaken in the plan.

Land reforms in this plan restated the same two objectives: "The first is to remove such impediments to increase agricultural production as arise from the agrarian structure inherited from the past. This should help to create conditions for evolving as speedily as possible an agricultural economy with high levels of efficiency and productivity. The second object, which is closely related to the first, is to eliminate all elements of exploitation and social in justice within the agrarian system, to provide security for the tiller of soil and assure a quality of status and opportunity to all sections of the rural population".[23]

In pursuance of the above two objectives, the proposals of land reforms in the plan included: abolition of intermediary tenures, reduction of rents, security of tenure, resumption of tenancies rights of ownership for tenants, ceiling on agricultural holdings schemes of resettlement and consolidation of holdings. Even though these measures were already undertaken in the previous two plans, an analytical evaluation of such schemes in this plan would provide material to find out the change in the perspectives of reform process in this plan.

Abolition of Intermediary Tenures

Intermediary tenures, which accounted for 40 per cent of the country, were removed, except the tenures under religions and charitable institutions and service inams.[24] According to the plan document, about 20 million of tenants were brought into direct relationship with the State. Further considerable extent of cultivable wasteland and private forestland was also taken over by the Government. However, "there has been a measure of delay in the assessment and payment of compensation to intermediaries. Out of a total amount of Rs. 670 crores (Rs. 520 crores as compensation and Rs. 150 crores for interest charges, so far Rs. 164 crores was paid as compensation and that too mainly in the form of bonds.[25] This clearly indicates only further scope for vehement implementation of Acts pertaining to abolition of intermediary tenure and the speedy disposal of compensation in the Fourth Plan.

Reduction of Rents

The need for the regulation of rent by way of legislation arose due to the persisting vast inequality of the rent in the country. To quote the plan document, "in some states, as in Gujarat, Maharashtra and Rajasthan, the maximum rent now stands at one sixth of the produce. In Assam, Kerala, Orissa and Union Territories, the rent payable is about one fourth of the produce or less. In several States, the normal level of rent is still about a third of the produce. It is to be hoped that in these States rents will be reduced to the level envisaged in the first two plans so as to facilitate more rapid improvement in the economic conditions of tenants".[26] The plan recommended rent payment in cash rather than in kind.

Security of Tenure

Legislative measures were taken in many States to protect the tenants from eviction. There are three aims of such legislation, i.e., "firstly, that ejectments do not take place except in accordance with the provisions of the law; secondly, that land may be resumed by an owner, if at all, for "personal cultivation" only; and thirdly, that in the event of resumption, the tenant is assured of a prescribed minimum area".[27] The plan suggested simplifying the legislation. Further, voluntary surrender of land should be accepted only with registration. Similarly, the personal cultivation is a hindrance in the legislation. Hence, States have been asked to modify the definition of personal cultivation.

Resumption of Tenancies

In the first and second plans, it was advocated not to allow resumption of land beyond 5 years. Further, "owners with less than a basic holding (that is, one third of a family holding) should be free to resume their entire area for personal cultivation and to lease out their lands. As regards owners whose holdings lie between a basic holding and a family holding, they may be permitted to resume for personal cultivation, within a specified period, one-half of the area held by the tenant but in no event less than basic holdings. Where a tenant is left without any land or with area smaller than a basic holding, the Government should endeavour to find land for him to cultivate".[28] As a part of tenancy reform, right of ownership for Tenants was initiated in the plan. However, in Tamil Nadu, the Government took no such measure.[29] On the other hand, in states like Utter Pradesh, Gujarat, Maharashtra, Madhya Pradesh, Rajasthan, and

Delhi more than 3 million tenants with a holding of 4.5 million acres were brought under the control of the Government.

Ceiling on Agricultural Holdings

Legislation pertaining to ceiling on land holding had been enacted in all the states. With regard to fixing of ceiling, on land holdings, some states had chosen ceiling based on individual holding while in other states they considered ceiling on the basis of family size. For instance, in Assam, Gujarat, Kerala, Rajasthan and also in Madras and Mysore, the ceiling applied to the aggregate area held by a family.[30] In many states the transfer of land was prohibited from the date of legislation of the bill and in several states a date prior to the enactment of the legislation had been indicated. In Tamil Nadu the transfer after the legislation were disregarded. Similar to the previous plan, 5 categories of land were exempted from the ceiling. The ceiling proposals in the second plan continued even in the Third Plan.

Consolidation of Holdings

By the end of the Second Plan, about 36 million acres were brought under consolidation of holdings. This achievement was recorded only in Punjab, Uttar Pradesh, Maharashtra, Gujarat and Madhya Pradesh. Therefore, efforts were made to popularise the benefits of consolidation of holdings and extension of such programmes in the Southern and Eastern parts of the country. The third plan aimed to bring about 30 million acres under consolidation of holdings.

The third plan felt that legislation pertaining to land management was fairly old in the States. The specific guidelines laid down in the first and second plan for land management were not seriously viewed by the states. For instance, such legislation were enacted only in two states and in one Union Territory. Even here, the legislation was not implemented. Therefore, in the third plan, "efforts would be of value to bring together the best experience in land management practices for the guidance of farmers, cooperatives and panchayats, the question of enforcing legislative sanctions. The role of panchayats and panchayat samithis had to be studied further in consultation with the states and in the light of the experience gained by them in working the existing enactments".[31]

Finally, in the third plan a Panel on Land Reform was appointed to study the problems arising in the implementation of land reform in the states. The panel recommended updating the land records of states. The Planning Commission committed to provide central assistance to carryout cadastral surveys and to update the land records.

The plan proposed to give priority to economic rehabilitation to persons engaged in shifting cultivation. The major schemes in the plan included land settlement, land reclamation and soil conservation, minor irrigation, supply of seeds, manures, training facilities, financial support to artisans, cottage industries, establishment of service cooperatives and forest labour cooperatives, provision for education, scholarship etc. and establishment of maternity and child welfare centres.[32]

Further, the failure of the Multi-Purpose Cooperative Societies had forced the Government to a launch an alternative programme by establishing Tribal Development Blocks during the plan. The tribal development blocks were set up on Community Development project pattern. The total outlay of the plan was Rs. 15902 crores in which about Rs. 75 crores was earmarked for tribal development programmes. In the second plan, 43 Tribal Development Blocks were established and each block got Rs. 27 lakhs co sponsored by both Community Development and Ministry of Home Affairs.

Since, the orientation was changed in the plan only Rs. 22 lakhs for each block was spent.[33]

The planning commission constituted a study team in 1966 under the headship of P. Shilu Ao, to recommend suitable schemes for the fourth plan. The study team recommended schemes for agriculture, forest policy, tribal indebtedness, education, communication, transport, administrative changes in Tribal Development Blocks.

Fourth Five Year Plan

The third plan ended in 1965-66 and with a plan holiday in 1966-69, the fourth plan actually began only in 1969-70. The plan document focused on the reform measures in the same pattern of the previous three plans. To quote from the plan, "There are many gaps between objectives and legislation and between the laws and their implementation. It is necessary to identify the deficiencies and take steps for their elimination. One of the important tasks of the Fourth Plan was to try and ensure that land reform became a reality in the village and the field".[34] Land reform measures of the plan included the abolition of intermediary tenures, tenancy reforms, ceiling on land holdings and consolidation of holdings. These principal measures received attention in the recommendations of the Land Reforms Implementation Committee of the National Development Council.

The Chief Ministers' conference held in November 1969 also considered the same points. In this plan, the major thrust was given to identify the gaps and weaknesses in the existing laws and their implementation. Further, the Co-operative farming and Co-operative village management schemes were dropped in the plan.[35] The Fourth Plan mentioned that, "in Co-operative farming, priority will be given to the revitalisation of the existing weak and dormant societies. New societies will be organised only in compact areas and if they have a potential for growth".[36] Land reform measures undertaken in the plan are presented below.

Abolition of Intermediaries

In the 20 years of planning, Zamindars, jagirs, inams and other intermediary tenures have been abolished in our country. However, according to the Plan Document, "certain non-ryotwari tenures still remained. Legislation was yet to be enacted for abolition of temporarily settled estates in Assam, certain inams and tenures in Kerala, Maharashtra and Tamil Nadu, Goa, Delhi and Dadra and Nagar Haveli. Legislation was yet to be completed in respect of muttadari and malguzari tenures in Agency tracts and inams in Telangana area of Andhra Pradesh and Devesthan inams in Gujarat. It has been divided to take action of abolition of these remnants of the intermediary tenures by 1970".[37] The payment of compensation to ex-intermediaries was observed to be slow in States like Bihar, Orissa, Rajasthan, Uttar Pradesh and West Bengal. The plan also recommended the scrutiny of cases pertaining to evasion and obstruction by the intermediaries while implementing the land reforms. It was suggested to the States for an effective implementation of laws pertaining to abolition of intermediaries was strongly suggested to the states.

Tenancy Reforms

To convert tenants and sub-tenants as owners of land, considerable progress has been made by way of legislators in Maharashtra, Gujarat, Madhya Pradesh and Rajasthan. About 3 million tenants acquired ownership to the extent of 7 million acres of land in about 11 States. Whereas, 82 per cent of the total number of tenants mainly in the States of Andhra Pradesh, Assam, Bihar, Haryana, Punjab, Tamil Nadu and West Bengal, were not protected from tenancy reform laws. The effect of the insecurity of tenancy has "not only impeded the widespread abolition of high-yielding varieties but in some cases led to social and agrarian tensions".[38] Hence, bringing security of tenure is essential by declaring the existing tenancies as non-resumable ones by the owners of land.

Ceiling on Land Holdings

Land ceiling legislation with different level of ceilings, transfers and exemption from the laws have been implemented in all the States. As a result, about 9, 64,800 hectares of land had been declared as surplus and 6, 40,000 hectares have been taken possession of by the State Governments for distribution. However, due to problems in the distribution, only 464,174 hectares were reported to have been distributed. Moreover, "It has been observed that this gap has been due to, in some cases, administrative difficulties in selecting the allottees in accordance with the provisions given in the ceiling Acts stay orders obtained from High Courts and inferior quality land surrendered by the landlords".[39] This matter was discussed in the Chief Ministers' Conference held in November 1969, where it was also decided to review the provisions in the legislation and to hasten the implementation of reform measures. Further resettlement programmes for the landless agricultural labourers, distribution of cultivable surplus Government lands, reduction of land from the ceiling level and removal of a few exemptions were also considered in the Fourth Plan.

Consolidation of Holdings

The plan tried to extend the benefits of consolidation of holdings to all other States by reviewing the progress made in this regard by Punjab, Haryana and Uttar Pradesh. To implement the schemes in the plan, about Rs. 28.4 crores was earmarked by the Government.

The land reform measures undertaken in the previous plan periods faced problems not only in the implementation itself but also in the supply of inputs to the beneficiaries. Therefore, the plan suggested, a, "Periodical evaluation of land reform programmes is proposed to be undertaken both by the states and at the centre through suitable organisations and institutions. It is also considered necessary to provide for the contingencies, study of the problems of land reforms as well as the techniques of implementation adopted in different states with a view to imparting training both in methodology and in execution. It has accordingly been decided to establish for this purpose a Land Reforms Centre at Poona in the Campus of the Gokhale Institute of Politics and Economics".[40]

The Fourth Plan also continued with the typical tribal development measures as found in the Third Plan. The Plan felt that to implement tribal development programmes more effectively in the tribal areas, they should be protected from exploitation with legislative and executive measures. The plan highlighted the need for giving protection to the tribals in problems like land alienation, scaling down of debts, regulating money lending and control of rate of interest charged by moneylenders and reforming the existing administrative machinery in the tribal areas. The plan also recommended that the government and the voluntary agencies should work together to make it clear to the tribals that the tribal development measures are intended only for their economic betterment. Further, the plan suggested that the tribal welfare department in States should be closely associated with the planning and implementation machinery of tribal development programmes in the tribal areas.

The welfare programmes for tribes in the plan also included schemes for land allotment, grant of subsidies for the purpose of plough bullocks and improved seeds, schemes for soil conservation, land consolidation, minor irrigation, education, health and housing. Government of Tamil Nadu allotted Rs. 32.05 lakhs for education, Rs. 36.50 lakhs for development purposes. Rs. 106.37 lakhs for housing, water supply and other schemes and Rs. 39 lakh for Tribal Development Block were earmarked in the Fourth Plan[41] of the total outlay of Rs. 1934.14 crores, about Rs. 174.92 lakh was allotted by the Government of Tamil Nadu for various tribal development programmes.

Fifth Five Year Plan

The fifth plan was for the period 1974 to 1979. The plan was important for two reasons; the introduction of Tribal Sub-Plan; and the Kalrayan hills were brought under the direct rule of the Government in 1976. Like the earlier plans, the Fifth Plan also gave emphasis to land reforms and the same procedure. According to the Plan, "The objectives of land policy have been to remove such motivational and other impediments to the increase in agricultural production as arose from the agrarian structure inherited from the past, and also to eliminate all elements of exploitation and social injustice within the agrarian system so as to ensure equality of tenurial status and opportunity to all sections of the rural population".[42]

The programmes of the plan dealt with the abolition of intermediary tenure, tenancy reform, ceiling on land holdings, consolidation of holding, and implementation machinery of the Government.

Abolition of Intermediary Tenure

In the Fourth plan itself necessary legislative steps were enacted by all the State Governments to abolish intermediary tenures. However a few intermediary tenures continued to remain in the fifth plan period. According to the Plan Document, only Rs. 275 crores were paid to the ex-intermediaries from the total outlay of Rs. 670 crores earmarked for paying compensation.

Tenancy Reform

Tenancy Reform Acts were passed in several States even before the Fourth plan. However, maximum rates of rent were observed in states like "Punjab, Haryana, Jammu and Kashmir, Tamil Nadu and Andhra pradesh. In Punjab and Haryana fair rent was $33\frac{1}{3}$ per cent of the gross produce; in Tamil Nadu 33½ per cent to 40 per cent of the gross produce. The Andhra Pradesh State Assembly passed a bill fixing fair rent at the level of 30 per cent of the produce for irrigated land and 25 per cent for dry land. In Jammu and Kashmir, for tenants of landowners holding above 12½ acres of land, fair rent was 25 per cent of gross produce for wet land and 33 1/3 per cent for dry land; however, for tenants of landowners who owned less than 12½ acres of land fair rent was 50 per cent of the gross produce."[43] Such difference in the rent portrays the fact that these states should have passed legislation on Tenancy Reform by disregarding the guidelines given in the Fourth Plan.

Ceiling on Agricultural Holdings

Laws pertaining to ceiling on land holdings had been enacted in all the states except Punjab areas of Haryana and Punjab. Since, fixing ceiling was a state subject, wide variations between different states were observed. In this connection, the Central Land Reform Committee made certain recommendation in August 1971 to bring uniformity in the ceiling law of the states. Accordingly in the Chief Minister's Conference held on 23.6.1972, "Certain conclusions were reached with regard to the level of ceiling, unit of application, exemptions, compensation, distribution of surplus land etc., and subsequently national guidelines were issued on the basis of those conclusions."[44]

Consolidation of Holdings

Consolidation of agricultural holdings was completed in Punjab and Haryana, while good progress was observed in

Uttar Pradesh, Maharashtra and Himachal Pradesh. However, "No law for effecting consolidation of holdings has yet been passed in Andhra Pradesh, Kerala and Tamil Nadu."[45]

New Strategy of Land Reforms

The new strategy included programme for institutional changes; operational programmes; new implementation machinery; people's involvement for the success of the programme; financing of land reform; mass campaign for land reform and training of field officers. The new strategy gave the momentum and directives to the States on land reforms in general and the implementation machinery in particular. However, most of the schemes in the land reforms have been repeated in the new strategy of land reforms.

Programmes for Institutional Changes

At the outset, priority was given to the removal of gaps between policy, legislation and implementation. The institutional changes dealt with tenancy reform, land-ceiling laws, laws of land alienation and debt redemption and protection to weaker sections of the society. Further, legislation on tenancy reform differently defined the term' personal cultivation'. According to the plan, "In the prevailing rural situation, supervision, either by the landowner himself or a member of his family should be insisted upon, the term family being defined as in the ceiling law.[46] Such supervision would be possible only if the landowner or a member of his family resides in the same village or in an adjacent village. It will also be necessary to restrict the future transfer of agricultural land to persons who reside in the same village or in an adjacent village. Such a provision, if strictly enforced would reduce the incidence of absentee ownership of land."[47]

Regulation of tenancies was a problem to the Government. Hence, the plan recommended leasing out of land only in some cases, like specified disability or persons serving in the Defense forces with written contracts for a specified period. With regard to security of tenure and right of purchase in respect of homestead lands with the members of Scheduled Castes and Scheduled Tribes and other backward classes, the Plan recommended to enact such laws in States where there was no such legislation.

Operational Programmes

The operational programmes included three programmes viz., comprehensive programme of preparation and maintenance of record of tenancy; distribution of surplus land and consolidation of agricultural holdings. The first operational programme demanded necessary statutes for the preparation of land records. While preparing and updating the records the rights of share-croppers, should be protected. Further, high priority was accorded to the cadastral survey of the tribal areas.

Secondly, the distribution of surplus land with adequate supply of inputs and investment support was recommended in the plan.

Thirdly, the Plan felt the need for the identification of tenants and sharecroppers before introducing consolidation of holdings. According to the Plan, "where land consolidation was undertaken, the land of small holders, the surplus land and the Government and the Government waste land available for distribution to new assignees should be consolidated in compact blocks".[48] This scheme would facilitate the Government to have future public investments in irrigation and land development programme for the weaker sections of the society. The three measures discussed above are not new because such measures were already there in the previous plans.

Implementation Machinery

Administrative set-up and Land Reform Tribunals formed the core of the implementation machinery in the new strategy of land reforms. The administrative machinery at the state level should be Land Reforms Commissioner with the rank of the First member of the Board of Revenue, functioning directly under the Ministry of Land Reform, a District Land Reforms Officer with sufficient status at the district level and Patwaris, Karnams, Karmcharis at the village level.[49] The staff needed for the administration may be drawn from the General Revenue Administration.

The plan recommended that the function of Land Reform Tribunals is to bring justice in all land reform matters. For instance, in Tamil Nadu, "Every Land Tribunal shall have the same powers as are vested in a civil court under the Code of Civil Procedure, 1908 (Central Act V of 1908).[50] Each Tribunal shall have only one judicial officer not below the rank of Subordinate Judge or an officer not below the rank of District Revenue Officer. Further, against the decision of the Tribunal, an appeal may be made to the High court within thirty days from the date of judgment. The strategy for the implementation machinery of the plan is a landmark in the land reform measures as compared to the previous five-year plans.

People's Involvement

The plan felt for people's involvement by forming village committees and block committees to the success of land reforms. As per the plan, "it is recommended that committees of beneficiaries be established at the village and block levels to advice on the implementation of all measures of land reforms and provision of supporting facilities to beneficiaries of land reform".[51] The suggested village committee may have 5 to 7 members representing landless labourers, sharecroppers and smallholders of the village owning less than 2 acres of land. Finally, one of the members of the village committee will be elected to represent matters to the block committees. It is clear that such committees would help the beneficiaries of the programme and the government, in implementing land reform measures effectively.

Financing of Land Reforms

Inadequate financial allotment for implementing land reforms in the earlier plan had actually hampered the implementation of land reform measures. Therefore, the financial outlay for the Plan was increased for streamlining the tenurial status, strengthening the implementation machinery of the programme to the new landowners and an integrated programme in the consideration of holding.[52]

Mass Campaign of Land Reform

Another programme launched in the Fifth Plan was a mass campaign at the village level to educate the beneficiaries to know various provisions of the land reform laws. To affect the land reform laws were translated into regional languages of the states and published through the communication media. Perhaps, such a move from the Central Government forced the States to translate the land reform laws in their regional languages and enabled the people to know the procedure and provisions in the laws concerned.

Finally, training of field officers and supervisory officers was recommended in the Plan in order to impart field experience for an effective implementation of land reform measures. Thus, the fifth plan occupied an important place in the programmes and better implementation of land reforms, than the earlier plans.

The Tribal Sub-plan approach was evolved during the later periods of the Fourth Plan and it was effectively implemented only in the Fifth Plan. It is an annals in the tribal development programmes and. "Proposed that sub-plans for the geographically and administratively viable areas with tribal concentration should be prepared with the objective of narrowing down the gap between tribal and other areas; improving the quality of life of the tribal communities, and achieving social and cultural integration of tribals with the rest of the society".[53]

The tribal sub-plan approach consists of three main components viz., (i) integrated Tribal Development Projects (ITDP's) comprising generally administrative units like sub-division/Tehshils/Taluks with 50 per cent or more Scheduled Tribes Population (ii) 284 pockets of tribal concentration (MADA Pockets) having a total population of 10,000 or more and a Scheduled Tribe population of 50 per cent or more and (iii) 73 Primitive Tribal Group Projects.[54] The TSP is implemented in 17 States and 2 Union Territories. Other tribal population wise dominated States will have regular Plans for tribal development.

The strategy for tribal development during the fifth plan includes programme for institutional changes, concrete operational programmes, implementation machinery, people's involvement and the allocation of adequate funds for financing land reforms. It is also necessary to launch a mass campaign to educate both the officials and the beneficiaries about the provision of the various land reform laws in the states.[55]

The fund for the plan is raised from State Plans, special central assistance, central and centrally sponsored programmes and institutional finance. The investments on Tribal Development Programme during the plan was Rs. 1102 crores (3.01 per cent) to the total outlay of Rs. 39322 crores.[56]

The Tribal Sub-Plan was adopted in the areas where there was concentration of more tribal population. Moreover, to handle the tribal problems in an integrated and co-coordinated manner, the Integrated Tribal Development Projects, the Modified Area Development Approach and special prospects for the primitive tribes, were implemented in the Plan. The State will be classified into different integrated tribal development projects. Each integrated tribal development project will be known as a unit, which contains a group of blocks. Then, each block should formulate a separate five year plan on annual plan basis schemed to suit the local conditions for tribal development. Accordingly, the demand for money by each block will be taken into account while framing Integrated Tribal Development Project for the State.

Tribal Sub-Plan and the Kalrayan Hills

The Kalrayan Hill was taken over by the Government only in 1976. Hence, for the first time, the study area was directly brought under the tribal sub-plan in 1976. That is, from 1976-79 and subsequently in the annual plan from 1979-80. The sub-plan benefited 8100 families. The total outlay was Rs. 75.83 lakhs and the expenditure was Rs. 61.15 lakhs. The outlay included state plan schemes and centrally sponsored schemes. The state plan schemes contained programmes on education, employment generation, health, housing and economic development of tribals.

Sixth Five Year Plan (1980-85)

Land reform measures of the Sixth Plan contained only similar schemes of the previous five year plans. Therefore, only schemes for Tribal Development are presented in this section. The Sixth Plan, (1980-85) had new schemes for land reforms. During the plan, the State Governments were advised that they should earmark an amount as outlay for the Tribal Sub-Plan keeping in view : (1) proportion of the Tribal Sub-Plan area in the total geographical area of the State, (2) relative level of development of tribal areas vis-à-vis other areas in the State and (3) percentage which the tribal population in the State bears to the total population.[57] The draft of the Plan outlays that, "Tribal area development is a rural development activity with a different facet. The tribal areas not only require special attention, but one attuned to the cultural ethos of each area. Programmes will be taken up to achieve the objective of narrowing the gap between the levels of development of tribal areas and other areas and also to bring qualitative change in the life of the tribal community more rapidly. To translate these objectives into action, a strategy for consolidating the gains of protective measures will be adopted and programmes to provide full employment and to extend educational and health services will receive emphasis. Further, areas of tribal concentration will also be taken up for development by identifying pockets of 10,000 population living continuously of whom at least 50 per cent are tribals.[58] This approach was called the modified area development approach under the tribal sub-plan schemes.

The plan aimed at achieving full employment within 10 years with an integrated approach. The total outlay of the plan was Rs. 1,10,821 crores of which Rs. 5,468.46 crores was invested in tribal development programmes. The percentage of allocation in this plan was a maximum of 4.93 per cent compared to the previous five year plans. On the other hand in Tamil Nadu total outlay was Rs. 2456.06 lakhs and the expenditure was Rs. 2024.80 lakhs in the plan.

In the introduction of Integrated Tribal Development Programme (Tribal Development Programme), according to local nature of tribal areas was considered in the plan. The major thrust of Tribal Sub-Plan during the plan was on shifting cultivation, horticulture, credit-cum-marketing, minor irrigation, forestry oriented programme, programme for landless tribals, animal husbandry and education. These have been identified after a review of State's efforts in the implementation of the Tribal Sub-Plan.

The Tribal Sub-Plan formulated in the plan had very little need-based programmes in an integrated manner and also it included only State Plan Schemes. Shifting cultivation and the interest of forest villagers were not seriously considered in the plan.[59] During the plan, about 12884 tribal families were benefited under the tribal sub-plan scheme.

Seventh Five Year Plan (1985-90)

Seventh plan continued with the same land reform measures undertake in the previous plans. Whereas for tribal development, the major thrust was given to raise the socio-economic conditions of the tribals and strengthening the infrastructure in the tribal areas. The plan felt that the tribal areas were still traditional and exploited by the non-tribals. Therefore, the major tasks in the plan were to create awareness among the tribals and to emphasise stringent anti-exploitative measures.

The main objective of this plan are: taking up family beneficiary oriented programmes to raise productivity levels of the beneficiary families in the fields of agriculture, horticulture, animal husbandry, small industries etc; elimination of exploitation of tribals in the sphere of alienation of land, money-lending, debt bondage, forest etc.; human resource development through education and training programmes; infrastructure development; development of vulnerable tribal areas and groups like forest villagers, shifting cultivators, displaced and migrant tribals including tribal women; and up gradation of environment of tribal areas.[60]

The Tribal Sub-Plan strategy of the plan aimed at the identification of development blocks with more tribal population in order to adopt the schemes of the plan in an integrated manner. Further, to implement the programmes, money was earmarked with financial participation by central and state governments. On the other hand, for a successful implementation of the programme the administrative structures in tribal areas were revamped with appropriate personnel policies.[61]

The total outlay of the plan was Rs. 1,80,000 crores, of which the approved size of Tribal Sub-Plan was Rs. 6,955.63 crores, that is Rs. 6,199.63 crores under State Plans and Rs. 756 crores under Special Central Assistance. The flow of fund for the plan was from State Plan, Central plan and centrally sponsored schemes, Special Central Assistance and institutional finances. In Tamil Nadu, the total plan outlay for Tribal Sub-Plan was Rs. 5832.27 lakhs and the expenditure was Rs. 5380.06 lakhs. This shows that government's outlay on Tribal Sub-Plan increasing from after plan but the expenditure is decreasing.

The plan was also to cover the tribal people living in urban areas with family oriented programmes. The plan was to build up the economic base for about 30 lakhs tribal families under beneficiary oriented programmes, human resource development and infrastructure development. During the plan, every year about 10000 to 12000 tribal families benefited in the Kalrayan Hills.[62]

Eighth Five Year Plan (1992-1997)

Just after the Seventh Plan in 1990, two annual plans were adopted in 1990-91 and 1991-92. The total outlay for tribal sub-plan in the 1990-91 annual plans was Rs. 1626.12 lakhs and in the subsequent annual plan, it was Rs. 1660.12

lakhs in Tamil Nadu. The two annual plans had no special programmes for tribal development.

The Eighth Plan document focused on the problems like landlessness, unirrigated and poorly developed lands, agricultural worker and bonded labour system. Therefore, major ameliorative activities undertaken in the plan have been oriented towards the welfare of the tribal population by providing education, employment and housing. These schemes are provided through the tribal sub-plan schemes. An important change in the plan is to benefit the tribals living outside the sub-plan areas through a special programme called the Dispersed Tribal Development Programme.

According to the Plan, "The resource base and the social and cultural heritage of our Scheduled Tribe population is getting eroded through a combination of development intervention, commercial exploitation and ineffective legal and administrative systems. The trend needs to be arrested as it can undermine the very survival of these communities. There is growing articulation and recognition of the fact that mega projects in irrigation, power and transport often disrupt the life and environment of a large number of Scheduled Tribes families, while the benefits of these projects mainly accrue to the population in the plains.

It is necessary that the planning and administrative machinery at different levels shows greater awareness and sensitivity to their dimensions of development and takes steps to ensure that the lives of scheduled tribes are not disrupted in the name of national progress. More positively, programmes need to be devised with the involvement of the Scheduled Tribe themselves in the light of their own order of priorities to remove economic, educational and social disparities to which they are subjected".[63] The approach of the plan includes programmes for providing minimum social services, conservation of their scientific resources and improvement of irrigation systems. The plan also aims to restore their traditional rights to forest produce. Finally, the plan document projected for a revival of their right to market their produce and for due recognition of their traditional community organisation.

The Eighth Plan document of the Tamil Nadu Government had listed laws on land reforms and others to remove such impediments on concentration of land in a few lands, absentee landlordism, existence of number of intermediaries and exploitation of tenants and tillers of the soil by the big landholders.[64] The acts are:

1. The Tamil Nadu Cultivations Tenants Protection Act, 1955.
2. The Tamil Nadu Cultivating Tenants (Payments of Fair Rents) Act, 1956.
3. The Tamil Nadu Land Reforms (Fixation of ceiling on Land) Act, 1961.
4. The Tamil Nadu Public Trusts (Regular Administration of Agricultural Lands), Act, 1961.
5. The Tamil Nadu Agricultural Lands Records of tenancy rights Act, 1969.
6. The Scheduled Castes and the Scheduled Tribal (Prevention of Atrocities) Act, 1989.

With regard to land reforms, no firm law has been passed after 1980. As on 31st July 1992, about 1,46,074 acres of lands were assigned to 1,21,152 persons, of which only 174 were from Scheduled Tribes.[65] Further, Rs. 1000 (per acre) was allotted for the improvement of land. For all these schemes, the State Government had contributed Rs. 1 crore as its share to the Eighth Plan.[66]

Ninth Five Year Plan

The Ninth Plan tried to bridge the gap between Scheduled Castes/ Scheduled Tribes and the rest of the population. Infrastructural facilities like drinking water, streetlights, roads connecting the tribal areas with the plains, opening of tribal schools, health sub centres and primary health centres were provided during the Ninth Plan period. In the Plan, a sum of Rs. 775 crore was provided and the anticipated expenditure during the period is Rs. 621.39 crores.

For the TSP, an outlay of Rs. 274.55 crores was earmarked in the Plan and the anticipated expenditure is Rs. 94.73 crores. In addition to this, an amount of Rs. 131.79 crore has been released as special central assistance for implementing programmes under Tribal Sub Plan. In the Plan, 37,876 families were assisted for their economic betterment under various programmes of TSP as against the Ninth Plan target of 51,382 families.

Tenth Five Year Plan

The important objectives of the Plan are improving standard of living of SC & ST; reducing the incidence of poverty among SC & ST; improving the socio-economic status through various developmental and income-generating activities; improving the employment opportunities for educated youth of poor families; improving the educational status, enhançe the entrepreneurial capacity, and improving the living conditions.[67]

The new Special Economic Development Programme in the Plan includes skill development or building training to below poverty, line families for the promotion of micro enterprises, venture capital funding, vocational training, Talent Search Training programme for job placements in private sector. In this Plan, a sum of Rs. 1200 crore is provided for the welfare of Scheduled Castes and Scheduled Tribes. Of which, Rs. 1044.16 crores is provided for SCs and Rs. 155.84 crores for STs both ongoing and new schemes.

The objective is to reduce the percentage of SC/ST families living below poverty line to less than 10 per cent and to raise their economic status. The main tribes in Tamil Nadu are Malayali, Toda, Kurumba, Paniya, Irular, Kattunayakan, Kanikar, Palaiyan, Sholagar, Kadar, Veddar etc., of which Toda, Kurumba, Kattunayakan, Paniya and Irular are primitive Tribes.

The ITDP areas cover two lakh tribals, which is one third of the total tribal population. Operational holdings of tribals are 47,955 covering an area of 77,907 hectares. Incidentally, majority of the tribal population in Tamil Nadu live in forests except the Irulars in Kancheepuram district.

Under TSP, the resources available under various sources are pooled together and schemes are drawn up and implemented by various sectoral departments. The size of the State Plan is fixed at Rs. 40, 000 crores and the flow of funds to the tribal sub plan is expected to be Rs. 412 crores, which constitutes 1.03 per cent of the Tenth Plan outlay. A sum of Rs. 27.50 crore is expected from the LAMP Co-operative Societies as Institutional Finance. In addition, an amount of more than Rs. 15 crore will also flow to the Tribal Sub Plan as Centre's share under Centrally Sponsored Schemes. During the Tenth Plan, family oriented schemes like distribution of animal and birds, beehives, opening of vocational guidance centres, construction of houses, setting up pre-schools for the children etc., will be implemented at a cost of Rs. 25 crores.

In addition, schemes like art and culture; construction of storage points; fixing of minimum purchase price for minor forest products; establishment of Data Centre; State level employment exchange; opening of show room at Chennai for selling the tribal art and artifacts; opening of flour mills for processing of paddy and other food grains in tribal areas; and EDP to 2000 Tribal women were implemented during this Plan. The outlay earmarked for this purpose is Rs. 45 crore.

Land reforms and tribal development measures undertaken from the First to the Ten Five Year Plans were certainly in pursuance of the national goal to achieve economic development by removing all disabilities of tribal development. "However, in retrospect, it is clear that these programmes were notional and continued to be so up to the end of the Fourth Plan. More fundamentally all these correctives, old and new, general and specific were limited in their scope in so far as these related only to the inadequacy of the percolation effect and were designed to supplement or stimulate the same".[68] The Tribal sub-plan strategy of the Fifth Plan and the dispersed tribal development programme of the Eighth Plan considered be modifying and designing for benefiting the tribals, actually differ from the traditional tribal development programmes.

References

1. Government of India: *Report of the Commissioner for Scheduled Castes and Scheduled Tribes,* (Manager of Publication, New Delhi, 28th Report 1986-87) p. 5.

2. Bansil, P. C. Agricultural Problems of India (Vikas Publishing House Pvt. Ltd., New Delhi, 1975) p. 584.

3. Sidhu, B.S. Land Reforms Welfare and Economic Growth (Vora and Co. Publishers Pvt. Ltd., Bombay, 1976), pp. 70-72.

4. *Ibid.,* p. 243.

5. Dhingra, I.C. The Indian Economy: Resource Planning Development and Problems (Sultan Chand and Sons, New Delhi, 1988) p. 401.

6. Government of India: *Progress of Land Reform*, (Planning Commission, New Delhi 1963), p. 225.

7. Government of India: *First Five Year Plan*, (Planning Commission, New Delhi, 1952) p. 194.

8. *Ibid.*, p. 636.

9. Government of India: *Report of the Commissioner for Scheduled Castes and Schedule Tribes*, 1960-61, Part-I, p. 62.

10. Government of India: *First Five Year Plan, op. cit.*, p. 638.

11. *Ibid.*, p. 640.

12. *Ibid.*, p. 636.

13. Government of India: *Second Five Year Plan*, (Planning Commission, New Delhi, 1956) p. 86.

14. Sidhu, N.S. *op. cit.*, p. 88.

15. Khusro, A.M. Economic and Social Effects of Jagirdari Abolition and Land Reforms in Hyderabad. (Osmania University, Hyderabad, 1958), p. 169.

16. Government of India: *Second Plan op. cit.*, p. 11 and United Nations, *Report on the Progress in Land Reforms;* Fourth Report, (New York, 1966), p. 29.

17. Government of India: *Second Five Year Plan op. cit.*, p. 178.

18. *Ibid.*, p. 197.

19. Government of India: *Second Five Year Plan, op. cit.*, p. 589.

20. Government of India: *Report of the Scheduled Areas and Scheduled Tribes Commission*, under the Chairmanship of U.N. Dhebar, (Ministry of Home Affairs, 1961), *op. cit*, p. 29.

21. Government of India: *Third Five Year Plan,* (Planning Commission, New Delhi, 1961) p. 702.
22. *Ibid.,* p. 703.
23. *Ibid.,* p. 200.
24. *Ibid.,* p. 221.
25. *Ibid.,* p. 222.
26. *Ibid.,* p. 222.
27. *Ibid.,* p. 223.
28. *Ibid.,* p. 226.
29. *Ibid.,* p. 228.
30. *Ibid.,* p. 229.
31. *Ibid.,* p. 234.
32. *Ibid.,* p. 705.
33. *Ibid.,* p. 706.
34. Government of India: *Fourth Five Year Plan,* (Planning Commission, New Delhi, 1969) p. 174.
35. Sidhu, B.S. *op. cit.,* p. 102.
36. Government of India: *Fourth Five Year Plan,* p. 226.
37. *Ibid.,* p. 175.
38. *Ibid.,* p. 177.
39. *Ibid.,* p. 180.
40. *Ibid.,* pp. 182-183.
41. *Ibid.,* p. 140.
42. Government of India: *Fifth Five Year Plan,* (Planning Commission, New Delhi, 1976) p. 42.
43. *Ibid.,* p. 42.
44. *Ibid.,* p. 43.

45. *Ibid.*, p. 43.

46. Government of Tamil Nadu: *The Tamil Nadu Land Reforms (Fixation of ceiling on land) Act 1961, as modified upto 31.08.1989*, define family as person, the wife or husband and his, her minor sons and unmarried daughter and minor grandson and unmarried grand-daughters in the male lines, whose father and mother are dead. p. 17.

47. Government of India: *Fifth Five Year Plan*, p. 44.

48. *Ibid.*, p. 44.

49. *Ibid.*, p. 44.

50. *Ibid.*, p. 44.

51. *Ibid.*, p. 45.

52. *Ibid.*, p. 45.

53. Government of India: *Fifth Five Year Plan*. (Planning Commission, New Delhi, Vol. II), p. 285.

54. Government of India: *Report of the Commissioner op. cit.*, p. 361.

55. Government of India: *Fifth Five Year Plan, op. cit.*, pp. 284-286.

56. Government of India: *Report of the Commissioner, op. cit.*, p. 362.

57. Government of India: *Sixth Five Year Plan*, (Planning Commission, New Delhi, 1981) pp.419-421.

58. *Ibid.*, pp. 1048-1050.

59. Government of India: *Report of the Commissioner, op. cit.*, p. 384.

60. *Ibid.*, p. 385.

61. Government of India: *Seventh Five Year Plan*, (Planning Commission, New Delhi, 1986).

62. Government of Tamil Nadu: *Annual Tribal Sub Plan*, 1995-96.

63. Government of India: *Eighth Five Year Plan*, (Planning Commission, New Delhi, 1991) pp. 30-32.

64. Government of Tamil Nadu: *Eight Five Year Plan,* (State Planning Commission, January 1993), p. 193.

65. *Ibid.*, p. 194.

66. *Ibid.*, p. 498.

67. Government of Tamil Nadu, Tenth Five Year Plan, pp. 267-284.

68. Government of India: *Report of the Commissioner, op. cit.*, p. 4.

4

Background of the Study Area

Kalrayan hills of Villupuram District, located within the parallels of 13° and 11° of the North latitude and 80° and 78° of the East longitude. The total area of the Kalrayan hills is 600 square kilometers, which covers 0.46 per cent of the total geographical area of the State. The elevation of the hills ranges from 1000 feet to 3800 feet from the Mean Sea Level. The hills area is known for its rich forest resources like, sandalwood, jackfruit, lemon tamarind, curryleaf, galenut and millets. In this chapter, background of the study area, origin of the Malayali tribes in the hills, efforts taken by the Government to take over the hills from the Jagirdars, amenities available to the tribes, distribution of land, and crop pattern have been presented in detail for the Kalrayan hills and the sample villages using the secondly data collected from the Government offices.

Geographical Location

Kalrayan hills is located on the South-West part of the district, and the boundaries of the hills are: on the South the Attur taluk of Salem District, which is known for sago industries, cotton textile, steel plant and high quality mangoes; in the west, the Harur taluk of Dharmapuri district is situated which is famous for cotton textiles, manufacturing of wood and wooden products; in the Northern side of the hills the Chengam taluk of the Vellore District is located, which is known for tobacco products, textile, silk weaving, leather and leather products; Finally, on the East the Kallakuruchi taluk of Cuddalore District is located. The taluk is known for paddy cultivation, cotton textile, tobacco, groundnut, cashewnut and small and large scale industries. Thus, the boundaries of the hills clearly portray that it is situated in the midst of urban and semi-urban areas with agriculturally and industrially advanced districts.

Rainfall and Irrigation

The average rainfall in a year ranges from 722 millimeters to 889 millimeters and the maximum rainfall is usually in the months of October and November.[1] But, this is much below the State's average or normal rainfall of 943 millimeters per annum.[2] Further, the hills area is irrigated by Melmalai River, Kottaputhur River, Pulavapady Ponnanganni River, Gomugi River, Sundapady River, Manimuktha River and Mayura River. These rivers drain the rain water into the Gomugi dam and connecting rivers in the plain areas. Therefore, check dams have been constructed across the rivers, to stop the quick drain of rainwater into the plain areas.

Having discussed the general features of the hills, it is appropriate to trace the history of Kalrayan hills tribes and its administration, in the period before and after the taking over of the hills by the Government.

Origin of Malayali Tribe in the Hills

The inhabitants of the Kalrayan hills are known as Malayali Tribe. According to a Government report, they had come from Kancheepuram as Warriors belonging to Karalar community, said to have settled in the hills and later overpowered the native vedars (Hunter).[3] Whereas, another report says that they had come from Gingee and settled in the hills during the Mohammedan invasion of Carnatic.[4] However, the census reports from 1981 onwards, classify the hillsmen as Malayali tribe. The Malayali tribes were under the control of three Jagirdars over many centuries. That is, during the King Krishna Devaraya of Vijayanagar Kingdom (1378 AD), said to have given rights to three Jagirdars, as a reward to the services rendered by them to the King in a military operation.[5] Further, by about 1890, the three Jagirdars had obtained a title deed from the British Government to enjoy possession of land in their respective Jagris, by paying a "guit-rent" to the Government.[6] Moreover, in the Jagir's regime the hills was termed as a non-ryotwari area and there was no Government machinery in the hills.[7] The three Jagirdars were The Ariya Goundan, The Kurumba Goundan and the Jadaya Goundan.

Kalrayan Hills Under the Jagirdars Administration

According to the Manual of the South Arcot District, "The 96 villages on the Kalrayan hills are divided into three Polliams. The Poligars names are Jadaya Goundan, Kurumba Goundan and Ariya Goundan. They pay a small annual peishcush to Government viz., Rs. 225, Rs. 154 and Rs. 70 respectively. The Polliam of Jadaya Goundan is the Southernmost of the three which comprises 40 villages. The chief village in it, where he resides is called Chinnathirupathy. Kurumba Goundan's polliam adjoins that of Jadaya Goundan on the north. It comprises 42 villages, of which the principal one is Thumbai. That of Ariya Goundan's and comprises 14 villages, of which the chief one is Kallanur... the compiler was unsuccessful in his efforts to get full information from all the Poligars regarding their estates, but the following facts regarding the Pollium of Jadaya Goundan may most probably, be accepted as applicable, mutatis mutandis, to the two others. No information at all was procured from Ariya Goundan".[8]

The revenue administration during the Jagirdars regime exhibited a typical example of exploitation on the tribals. The tribals were forced to pay quite a number of taxes to the Jagirdars viz., plough tax, tax for cutting trees, tax for grazing, fax for citizenship, house tax, tax for shifting cultivation, bachelor tax i.e., tax on all bachelors who attained the age of 10 years tax for owning animals, tax for marriage, tax on widows i.e., widow or widower should re-marry otherwise liable for heavy taxes, and finally tribals were fined if they were found wearing chapels, shirts or wrist watches. Moreover, Jagirdars visited their villages once in a year. During their visit, they were carried on a Palanquin by the tribals up to the boundaries of their villages and passed on to the adjoining village, till the completion of his inspection of all the villages. Further, when the Jagirdar visited their villages, the tribals should lay or level the foot-path for the smooth pass of the Jagirdar. He used to levy a heavy penalty of Rs. 1000 for those who got insured while carrying him in the Palanquin in order to ensure his safety.[9]

The Jagirs were divided into four Nadu. In each Nadu, there were four officials viz., the Natan, the Moopan, the Goundan and the Kangani. They were appointed by the Jagirdar to help him in the revenue administration. The Natan and Moopan were to collect the rent and pay them to the Jagirs. The kangani was the policeman and the Goundan was the Natan's peon.

The tribals were freely moving from one village to another. They were non-offensive type and also reluctant to move with any outsider. The Kalrayan hills tribes were Hindus by religion and they used to offer Puja to their village Deity in a closed manner once in a year i.e., April or May. During the Puja days, outsiders were not allowed into the villages for a week. Further, they closed roads or foot-paths of their villages by indicating the Puja with three white lines at regular intervals.

The hills tribes were cultivating lands by paying taxes to the Jagirs and also being "bonded labourers" to the Jagirs, generation after generation. The plight was that they were deprived of minimum basic amenities like school, medical facilities, communication, roads etc., Further, they were compelled to sell their products only to the Jagirdars or to the contractors appointed by them. These, inhuman approach of the Jagirdars, forced the Government of Tamil Nadu, after a long silence, to take over the administration of the hills from the Jagirdars.

Kalrayan Hills in the Government's Direct Administration

The State Government made two attempts i.e., one in 1961-62 and again in 1975-1976 to bring the hills under its control and to evict the Jagirdars. In its first attempt, a Block Development Office was formed for the Kalrayan hills. But, the Government was not successful in its first course of action, due to the opposition by the Jagirs. In the second attempt, the Government invoked the Inam Estate (Abolition and Conversion into Ryotwari) Act 1963. But, the Jagirdars successfully stalled the whole course of action by obtaining a stay order from the Court. To quote a Government's report[10] "a major portion of these hills is still under the control of the Jagirdars who have a virtual local regime over the areas. When the Government of Tamil Nadu proceeded to take over the areas under the Inam Estate Abolition Act, the Jagirdars went to the court. The whole matter is under dispute and a case is pending in the court. Against this background, it has not been possible for Government to undertake any development work in the area particularly because of the stay order of the court. But it is this particular area which has been found to be very backward with practically no basic

Table 4.1 : Amenities Available in the Sample Villages as per 1981 Census

Sl. No.	Name of the Village	Educational	Medical	Drinking Water	Post and Telegraph	Distance of Market	Nearest Bus Stop
1.	Kendikkal	P(2)	10 km	R	PO	10 km	5-10 km
2.	Karialur	P(1)	5 km	W	PO	10 km	5 km
3.	Kundiyanatham	5-10 km	5-10 km	S	5-10 km	10 km	5-10 km
4.	Vazhapady	P(1)	5-10 km	W	5 km	10 km	5 km
5.	Nochimedu	5 km	5 km	S	5 km	10 km	5 km
6.	Vellimalai	P(1)	5-10 km	W	5 km	10 km	5 km
7.	Mavadipattu	P(1)	5 km	S	5 km	10 km	5 km
8.	Pottiyam	P(1)	10 km	R	PO	5 km	5 km
9.	Malliampady	P(2)	10 km	R	PO	5 km	5-10 km

Source: Census of India, 1981, Part XIII-B, Village and Town Wise. Primary census Abstract, South Arcot District, P-Primary or Elementary School, W-Well without-electricity, R=River S=spring.

infrastructure, no facilities like the roads, hospitals, schools, electricity, water, supply etc. The people are also very poor, illiterate, ill-fed, ill-clad and indebted to the hilt. There are no land records as they are itself has not been surveyed. This is the general picture of the area and as things stand the court decision is to be awaited before undertaking any development work in the area on a large scale".

However, the state Government by taking advantage of "Emergency" and the President's Rule, in 1976, efforts were made to evict the Jagirdars from the hills. Accordingly, a large number of Government officials from the Revenue Department with a large number of "coolies" to carry their baggage and camping tents and with a sizeable armed police force had entered into Karayan Hills area near Vellimalai in Jadaya Goundan Jagir through "Attur Pass" in Attur taluk of Salem District in the last week of August-1976, gradually took possession of the entire Hills area.[11] Thus, in the second course of action the Jagirdars could not retaliate to the supremacy of the Government. In the circumstances following a constructive dialogue with the District Collector, the three Jagirdars have announced that in the interest of the overall development of the area they would hand over the estates to Government.[12]

According to the Hindu, "After the imposition of the President's rule, the State Government took keen interest in the uplift of these tribals and the District collector succeeded in persuading the Jagirdars to hand over the estates to the authorities for development".[13] Finally, the Jagirdars withdrew the case against the Government on 25.8.1976. Therefore, on 25.8.1976 the Kalrayan Hills was fully taken over by the Government of Tamil Nadu.

Revenue Administration

The Government of Tamil Nadu sanctioned a special Deputy Collector (Vide Government of Order, Number 1711, dated 17.08.1976) for the Hills. The headquarters of the Special Deputy Collector was Mosttampatti. Kalrayan hills was divided into three taluks viz., Vellimalai taluk, Mottampati taluk and Killakkadu taluk, each representing the three erstwhile Jagirs i.e., Jadaya Goundan, Kunumba Goundan and Ariya goundan, respectively. Further each taluk was administered by a special Tahsildas. The Special Tahnsildars took over the Kalrayan Hills's administration on 25.8.1976 from the three Jagirdars.

Presently, entire Kalrayan hill's revenue administration is controlled by one Special Tahsildar. Because, the other two taluks viz., Mottampatti taluk and Kilakkadu taluk are kept in abeyance, due to non-viability and less work. Similarly, the then six Firkhas has of the Hills are reduced to one only Firkha, for the same reason mentioned above. The entire Hills is divided into 18 Village Administrative Offices and each villages administered by a Village Administrative Officer. The functions of the taluk is to maintain records about, distribution of land under various classification i.e., forest-land, wet land dry land, grazing land, cultivated land, cultivable land, cropping pattern, collection of taxes, record of birth and death and reporting to the Government about various events that are taking place in the Hills.

Amenities Provided to the Tribals

The amenities available in the Hills area after the Jagirs were taken over have increased to a considerable level. For example, from 1976 to 1996 of the 163 habitation about 119 habitations were electrified. The State highways roads were formed after 1978, which connects Kallakuruchi and Attur via Vellimalai. Now, limited bus transport facilities are available from Kallakuruchi to Vellimalai, Attur to Vellimalai, Kallakuruchi to Seerapathu and Kallakuruchi to Mottampatti. However, even now must of the village in the Hills do not have transport facility.

Kalrayan hills were shown as "Unsurveyed area" in the census report,[14] till 1981 census. However for the first time the 1981 census brings out the amenities available to the tribals of the hills. Table 4.1 portrays the amenities available to the sample villages chosen for case study in this research work. All the sample villages except Kundiyanatham and Nochimedu, have either primary school or elementary school. Further, after 1976, about 23 Government Tribal Residential Schools have been opened in the Hills. With regard to drinking water, all the villages have either well (without electricity), river or spring. Since it is a Hills area, only four villages have post offices and the tribals of other five sample villages have to walk from five to ten kilometres to avail the benefit. The market facilities in the sample villages are located at a distance of 5 to 10 kilometres.

Further, the tribals have to walk from five to 30 kilometres to reach the weekly shandy conducted at Vellimalai. Similarly, LAMP societies located in three places of the hills viz, Vellimalai, Kilakkadu and Mottampatti are also located at a distance of 5 to 30 kilometres from the tribal habitations. Finally, the bus stop on Kallakurichi to Attur via Vallimalai, Kallakurchi to Mottampatti and Kallakuruchi to Seerapattu bus route villages are located at 5 to 30 kilometers distance from the tribal villages. Thus, these amenities are created only after taking over the hills from the Jagirs. The tribals, without any hesitation or revolt, have also accepted such, facilities.

Demographic Characteristics of Kalrayan Hills Tribes

Population

The tribal population[15] in the State has increased by 10.37 per cent over 10 years from 1981. This increase is much below the increase of Scheduled Castes (20.62 per cent) and non-Scheduled Castes and Scheduled Tribes (14.27 per cent), compared to the decade increase in the total population of all the castes (15.39 per cent).[16] Further, the growth of tribal population in the Kalrayan hills from 1981 to 1991 was only 4.8 per cent. Thus, table 4.2 clearly indicates that the growth rate of tribal population in the state as well as the Kalrayan hills was comparatively less than the other caste.

Table 4.2 : Comparative Tribal Population Statistics as per 1981 and 1991 Census

Sl. No.	*Census Period*	*Tribal Population* Kalrayan hills	South Arcot District	Tamil Nadu
1.	1981	28143	53775	520226
		(5.41)	(10.34)	(100.000
2.	1991	29494	58009	574194
		(5.14)	(10.1)	(100.00)

(Figures in parentheses are percentages to the total).
Source: Tamil Nadu census 1981, Part IX, Special Tables for Scheduled Tribes, and Census of 1991. Final Population Atlas, series 1.

The 1991 census identified 573 tribal communities in the whole of India. In Tamil Nadu there are 36 tribal communities, of which, the Malayali tribes are the predominant tribal community (40.18 per cent) and they inhabited mostly in hills and forest areas like, Kalrayan hills, Jawadhi hills, Kolli hills, Sitteri hills, Sherveroy hills, Palani hills and Pachamalai hills. These hills located in Salem, South Arcot, Dharmapuri, Trichy and North Arcot districts of the

State. The distribution of major tribal population is presented in table 4.3.

Table 4.3 : The Distribution of Malayali Tribes in the Major Hills of Tamil Nadu

Sl. No.	*Name of the District*	*Name of the Hill Area*	*Area of the Hills (sq.km.)*	*Tribal Population of Hills*	*Total Population of Hills*
1.	Salem	Kolli hills	224.85	30665	38449
				(79.76)	(100.00)
2.	Salem	Yercaud hills	147.50	21678	33353
				(65.00)	(100.00)
3.	Salem	Kalrayan hills	319.21	20665	21398
				(96.59)	(100.00)
4.	Salem	Aranuthumalai	29.02	6604	11879
				(55.59)	(100.00)
5.	Salem	Pachamalai	109.92	6583	24161
				(27.25)	(100.00)
6.	North Arcot	Jawadhi hills	310.35	49962	59488
				(83.99)	(100.00)
7.	South Arcot	Kalrayan	600	29991	32756
				(91.56)	(100.00)
8.	Dharmapuri	Sitheri	188	14353	29890
				(48.02)	(100.00)
9.	Trichy	Pachamalai	128.83	7894	13397
				(58.92)	(100.00)

(Values in parentheses are percentages).

Source: Government of Tamil Nadu: Annual Tribal Sub-Plan, (Director of Adi Dravidar and Tribal Welfare, Ezhilagam, Chennai. 1996-97), p. 3.

Table 4.3, depicts that in Salem district there are five tribal areas, in which the Salem Kalrayan hills spread over 319.21 square kilometers and has 96.59 per cent of the tribal

Table 4.4 : Distribution of Total Population by Social Groups in the Sample Villages of Kalrayan Hills

Sl. No.	Name of the Village	Scheduled Tribes			Non-Tribes			Total Population		
		1991	*1981*	*1971*	*1991*	*1981*	*1971*	*1991*	*1981*	*1971*
I.	Kalrayan hills	29494	28143	NS	6266	4617	NS	35760	32760	NS
1.	Kendikkal	730	1444	NS	-	20	NS	730	1464	NS
2.	Vellimalai	797	390	NS	133	68	NS	983	458	NS
3.	Vaxhapady	822	723	NS	-	4	NS	822	727	NS
4.	Karialur	903	921	NS	197	56	NS	1100	975	NS
5.	Mavadipattu	726	611	NS	35	4	NS	761	615	NS
6.	Nochimedu	431	268	NS	-	1	NS	431	269	NS
7.	Kundiynatham	246	316	NS	-	21	NS	246	337	NS
8.	Pottiyam	504	690	NS	78	371	NS	582	1061	NS
9.	Malliampady	538	524	NS	42	535	NS	580	1059	NS

NS- Not Surveyed.

Source: 1. Census of India-1971, South Arcot District-Part I.
2. Census of India-1981, South Arcot District-Part I.
3. Census of India-1991. South Arcor District-Part I.

Table 4.5 : Literacy Level of Tribals in the Study Area

Sl. No.	Name of the Village	Male	1991 Female	1981 Total Village Population	Male	Female	Total Village Population
I.	Kalrayan Hills	3041 (8.5)	1393 (3.9)	35760 (100.00)	—	—	32760
1.	Kendikkal	13 (1.78)	2 (0.27)	730 (100.0)	43 (2.94)	6 (0.41)	1464 (100.00)
2.	Vellimalai	47 (4.78)	16 (1.63)	983 (100.00)	34 (7.42)	9 (1.97)	458 (100.00)
3.	Vazhapady	2 (0.24)	0	822 (100.00)	19 (2.61)	2 (0.28)	727 (100.00)
4.	Karialur	292 (26.55)	115 (10.45)	1100 (100.00)	132 (13.54)	76 (7.79)	975 (100.00)
5.	Mavadipattu	72 (9.46)	50 (6.57)	761 (100.00)	3 (0.49)	1 (0.16)	615 (100.00)
6.	Nochimedu	10 (2.32)	4 (0.93)	431 (100.00)	10 (3.72)	3 (1.12)	269 (100.00)
7.	Kundiynatham	26 (10.74)	2 (0.83)	242 (100.00)	3 (0.89)	1 (0.3)	337 (100.00)
8.	Pottiyam	92 (15.81)	49 (8.42)	582 (100.00)	77 (7.26)	40 (3.77)	1061 (100.00)
9.	Malliampady	43 (7.41)	13 (2.24)	580 (100.00)	—	1 (0.09)	1059 (100.00)

(Figures in parentheses are percentage to the total).

Sources: Tamil Nadu census 1981, Part IX, Special Tables for Scheduled Castes and Scheduled Tribes, and Census of India 1991, Rural Data for District: South Arcot-Part II.

population of the district. On the other, land the biggest hills in the State is South Arcot Kalrayan with 600 square kilometers, with 91.56 per cent of tribal population of the Kalrayan hills.

Distribution of Tribal Population in the Sample Villages

As found in Table 4.4, the Kalrayan hills were not surveyed until the 1971 census. Further, the tribal population of the hills increased by 4.8 per cent from 1981 census to 1991 census, whereas, the non-tribal population increased at an alarming rate of 35.72 per cent over the same period. The total population of the hills has increased by 9.16 per cent from 1981 to 1991. The statistics clearly indicate that the non-tribal population is on the increasing trend compared to the increase of native tribals. Moreover, the tribal population in the villages of Kendikkal, Pottiyam, Kundiyanatham and Karialur had decreased from 1981 to 1991. In other sample villages, the increase was minimum except in Vellimalai, where the population increased from 390 persons in 1981 to 797 persons in 1991.

The table further reveals the fact that in Vellimalai, Karialur and Mavadipattu the non-tribal population had increased from 1981 to 1991. The increase in non-tribal population was due to locational advantage of the villages. That is, Vellimalai and Karialur contain Government offices, Banks Schools and Business establishments. On the other hand in other villages the non-tribal population had decreased from 1981 to 1991 census, except in Malliampady where the non-tribal population dropped from 535 persons in 1981 to 42 in 1991. Such, a fall in the population from 1981 census to 1991, was due to migration. That is, on the day of census enumeration if the tribe happened to be outside the area concerned, then as per the Presidential order, they will not be included in Scheduled Tribes.[17] Therefore, the tribal population in many villages showed a decreasing trend over a period of ten years from 1981.

Table 4.6 : Distribution of Categories of Workers in the Study Area as per 1981 Census

Sl. No.	Name of the Village	*Total Worker*						*Cultivators*			*Agricultural Labour*			*Household Industry*			*Main Workers*		
		M	F	Total	M	F	Total	M	F	Total	M	F	Total	M	F	Total	M	F	Total
1.	Nochimedu	108	108	216	83	83	166	24	24	48	-	-	-	1	0	1	0	0	0	30	30	60
2.	Mavadipattu	244	256	500	242	254	496	-	-	-	-	-	-	2	2	4	-	-	-	67	68	115
3.	Karialur	249	141	390	205	13	218	29	121	150	-	-	-	15	7	22	-	-	-	256	329	585
4.	Vellimalai	153	123	276	117	108	225	13	12	25	-	-	-	21	3	24	9	16	25	67	90	157
5.	Vazhapady	194	178	372	190	171	361	3	5	8	1	-	1	-	2	2	37	46	83	140	132	272
6.	Kundiyanatham	98	160	258	78	34	112	17	25	42	-	-	-	3	1	4	2	1	3	69	97	166
7.	Kendikkal	471	478	949	463	476	939	2	-	2	-	-	-	6	2	8	16	26	42	269	212	481
8.	Pottiyam	317	301	618	257	202	459	51	99	150	-	-	-	9	-	9	-	-	-	169	137	306
9.	Malliampady	378	67	445	369	63	432	6	3	9	-	-	-	3	1	4	14	266	280	148	186	334

Household industry: manufacturing, processing, service and repairs. M = Male, F = Female.

Source: Census of India, 1981. Part XIII.B, Village and Town wise Primary Census Abstract, South Arcot District, Services-20, pp. 228-285.

Literacy Level of Tribals

As soon as Jagirs were taken over, along with other massive development programmes, efforts are also made to improve the educational status of the tribals. The major steps began with opening up of 23 Government Tribal Residential Schools and 59 child welfare centres. Such efforts from 1976 improved the literacy level of tribals from total illiteracy.[18]

Table 4.5 reveals that in 1991, the over all literacy rate in the hills was only 12 per cent. This is much below the state's level of 39.47 per cent and the national literacy level of 30.07 per cent.[19] Further, the village wise data portrays that the literacy rate has gone up in all the sample villages except Kendikkal and Vazgapady. Moreover, in Karialur the literacy rate had increased from 21.33 per cent in 1981 to 37 per cent in 1991. This remarkable increase in literacy was due to a well maintained Missionary school located in the village run by the Arcot Luthrane Church. The table also exhibits that in all the sample villages there were wide differences between male and female literacy level. Therefore, the Kalrayan hills have not only lower literacy level than the state and the country levels but also displayed higher gender inequality in the literacy level.

Occupational Characteristics

In Tamil Nadu, as per census 1981 the working population was 47 per cent of the total population. The work force participation rate was more among male population (67) than female population (37.9) in the rural areas of the state.[20] On the other hand, in the Kalrayan hills, for the first time, the demographic distribution of categories of workers were enumerated in both 1981 and 1991 census and presented in Table 4.6 and Table 4.7.

Table 4.6 provides the distribution of categories, of workers as per 1981 census. Among the sample villages, Kendikkal had more workers (949) than all other villages.

Table 4.7 : Distribution of Main Workers in the Sample Villages as per 1991 Census

Sl. No.	Name of the Village	Cultivators			Agricultural Labourers						Livestock, Forestry etc.						Mining & Quarrying			Manufacturing						Construction		
		M	*F*	*T*	*M*	*F*	*T*	*M*	*F*	*T*	*M*	*F*	*T*	*M*	*F*	*T*	*M*	*F*	*T*	*M*	*F*	*T*	*M*	*F*	*T*	*M*	*F*	*T*
1.	Nochimedu	10	0	10	135	26	161	0	0	0	0	0	0	0	0	0	0	0	0	0	0	0	0	0	0	0	0	0
2.	Mavadipattu	172	11	183	22	94	116	1	0	1	0	0	0	0	0	0	0	0	0	1	2	3	1	0	1	7	5	12
3.	Karialur	180	27	207	82	102	184	1	0	1	0	0	0	0	0	0	2	0	2	5	0	5	4	0	4	34	15	49
4.	Vellimalai	0	0	0	274	251	525	0	0	0	1	2	3	0	0	0	0	0	0	3	0	3	3	0	3	13	9	22
5.	Vazhapady	255	219	474	0	33	33	0	0	0	0	0	0	0	0	0	0	0	0	0	0	0	0	0	0	0	0	0
6.	Kundiyanatham	75	3	78	2	55	57	0	0	0	0	0	0	0	0	0	0	0	0	0	0	0	0	0	0	0	0	0
7.	Kendikkal	196	14	210	78	74	152	0	0	0	0	0	0	0	0	0	0	0	0	1	0	1	0	0	0	1	1	1
8.	Pottiyam	77	42	119	61	56	117	0	0	0	0	0	0	7	2	9	0	0	0	0	0	0	0	0	0	9	3	12
9.	Malliampady	148	28	176	72	97	169	0	0	0	0	0	0	0	0	0	0	0	0	0	0	0	0	0	1	1	0	1

M = Male F = Female T = Total.

Source: Census 1991, Rural Data for District: South Arcot - Part 2, p. 2.

The concentration of total workers was more in cultivators than in other categories of workers. Ironically, agricultural labourers were less in number in most of the villages, except in Pottiyam and Karialur. Moreover, only one tribe in Vazghapady village is engaged in household industry. (the household industry includes manufacturing, processing, service and repairs). Therefore, employment in territory sector was the lowest compared to the national data of 6.12 per cent and state's data of 7.94 per cent respectively. Similarly, no tribe was employed in the secondary sector. Thus, the tribal area contains more cultivators and non-workers, than in other categories of work. Perhaps, in 5 years after Jagirs were taken over the achievement was remarkable. The employment condition as per 1991 census is shown in table 4.7.

Table 4.7 depicts that in Vazhapady there were 474 cultivators, the highest of all the sample villages, whereas, in Kendikkal and Karialur it was 210 and 207 respectively. It is important to note that in Vellimalai no cultivator was reported in the 1991 census report. On the other hand the highest numbers of 525 agricultural labourers were estimated in the same village. Here, the enumerators should have added the cultivators to agricultural labourers. To endorse this view, the table shows that in no other sample village the total agricultural labourer exceeded 184. Further, in Vazhapady also extreme statistics of more cultivators (474) and less agricultural labourers (33) were observed in the 1991 census report. Moreover, in the absence of alternative category of employment the concentration in agriculture shows only their primitive condition. Further, such a situation in the midst of changed socio-economic condition would worsen the living conditions of the tribals.

The demographic distribution of categories of main workers in 1981 census and 1991 census as given in tables 6 and 7 for the nine sample villages delineate a crucial employment situation in the hills. The table indicates for an

Table 4.8. Land Use Pattern in Kalrayan Block from 1986 to 1999 (in Hectares)

Sl. No.	*Classification of Land*	*1986-87*	*1987-88*	*1988-89*	*1989-90*	*1990-91*	*1991-92*	*1992-93*	*1993-94*	*1994-95*	*1995-96*	*1996 97*	*1997-98*	*1998-99*
1.	Forest Land	41382	42052	39936	36446	38107	34636	39352	34936	39831	39853	36423	37549	38368
		(72.33)	(73.51)	(69.81)	(63.71)	(66.61)	(60.54)	(68.79)	(61.07)	(69.63)	(69.66)	(63.66)	(65.63)	(67.07)
2.	Land unfit for cultivation	772	397	3166	1736	515	1255	691	2653	691	713	678	714	930
		(1.35)	(0.71)	(5.53)	(3.03)	(0.91)	(2.19)	(1.21)	(4.64)	(1.21)	(1.25)	(1.19)	(1.25)	(1.63)
3.	Land used for purposes other than cultivation	726	580	976	976	767	786	1027	976	1008	986	765	804	856
		(1.27)	(1.01)	(1.71)	(1.71)	(1.34)	(1.53)	(1.8)	(1.71)	(1.76)	(1.72)	(1.34)	(1.41)	(1.49)
4.	Fallow land fit for cultivation	779	119	994	762	762	894	980	894	407	429	534	712	509
		(1.36)	(0.21)	(1.74)	(1.33)	(1.33)	(1.56)	(1.71)	(1.74)	(0.71)	(0.75)	(0.93)	(1.24)	(0.89)
5.	Grazing land	184	115	23	16	14	24	23	23	36	46	38	36	34
		(0.32)	(0.2)	(0.04)	(0.03)	(0.02)	(0.04)	(0.04)	(0.04)	(0.06)	(0.08)	(0.07)	(0.06)	(0.06)
6.	Trees and garden	128	105	60	94	153	85	80	80	107	98	94	517	183
		(0.22)	(0.18)	(0.01)	(0.16)	(0.27)	(0.15)	(0.14)	(0.14)	(0.19)	(0.17)	(0.16)	(0.90)	(0.32)
7.	Current fallows	928	449	1153	2014	2445	1814	1420	2902	1357	1384	1924	2257	1849
		(1.62)	(0.78)	(2.02)	(3.52)	(4.27)	(3.17)	(2.48)	(5.07)	(2.37)	(2.42)	(3.36)	(3.95)	(3.23)
8.	Other fallows	356	340	739	920	1037	894	575	969	475	449	693	653	498
		(0.62)	(0.59)	(1.29)	(1.61)	(1.81)	(1.56)	(1.01)	(1.69)	(0.83)	(0.78)	(1.12)	(1.14)	(0.87)
9.	Net cultivated Land	11954	13052	10162	14245	13409	16731	13061	13676	13297	13251	16660	13967	13982
		(20.91)	(22.81)	(17.86)	(24.9)	(23.44)	(29.26)	(22.82)	(23.90)	(23.24)	(23.17)	(29.12)	(24.41)	(24.44)
	Total	52209	57209	57209	57209	57209	57209	57209	57209	57209	57209	57209	57209	57209
		(100)	(100)	(100)	(100)	(100)	(100)	(100)	(100)	(100)	(100)	(100)	(100)	(100)

Values in parentheses are percentages to the total.

Sources: 1. Government of Tamil Nadu: Divisional Statistical Office, Kallakuruchi.

2. Government of Tamil Nadu: Divisional Statistical Office, Sankarapuram.

exodus of cultivators into agricultural labourers category over ten years period from 1981. Moreover, the transition in the Kalrayan hills had brought more agricultural labourers. That is, cultivators were changed into agricultural labourers in the hills.

Distribution of Land and Cropping Pattern

An analysis of the distribution of land and the cropping pattern of the Kalrayan hills and the sample villages are simultaneously discussed in this section. The secondary data presented in the following 20 tables from 4.8 to 4.27 provides enormous incite for an analysis of not only the land use pattern and cropping pattern but also to study the impact of land reforms in the study area. The land in each village is divided into 9 categories as per A-1 register. First of all, "Forest Land" includes: forest belonging to the Government, and land classified as per Forest Conservation Acts. This category of land also includes forest owned by private people subject to the Acts. However, in the Kalrayan hills the forest land represents only the forest land of the Government and no private forest land is reported in the A-1 register of the Taluk offices.

Secondly, "Land unfit for cultivation", contains hilly or mountainous, desert and other lands. In the study area this category of land includes only hilly land.

Another category of land is the "Land used for purposes other than cultivation". This land includes: roads and lanes, railway lines, rivers, temples, government wells, canals, tanks, ponds and the village site. Such lands are also called the poramboke land.

The fourth category is the "Fallow land fit for cultivation", which contains, all lands fit for cultivation which were left fallow for a few years.

Table 4.9. Cropping Pattern in the Kalrayan Block from 1986 to 1999 (in Hectares)

Sl. No.	Name of Crop	1986-87	1987-88	1988-89	1989-90	1990-91	1991-92	1992-93	1993-94	1994-95	1995-96	1996 97	1997-98	1998-99
1.	Paddy	2690	2921	3055	3055	2831	3558	3140	3058	3183	3246	3352	3573	3438
		(19.52)	(21.00)	(15.86)	(16.51)	(16.96)	(22.96)	(22.5)	(21.17)	(21.8)	(23.14)	(22.83)	(23.13)	(21.56)
2.	Cholam	313	183	238	238	276	203	390	277	332	344	321	364	431
		(2.27)	(1.32)	(1.24)	(1.29)	(1.65)	(1.31)	(2.79)	(1.92)	(2.28)	(2.45)	(2.19)	(2.36)	(2.70)
3.	Sugarcane	310	512	1099	971	922	1071	956	886	720	814	867	890	942
		(2.25)	(3.88)	(5.71)	(5.25)	(5.52)	(6.91)	(6.85)	(6.13)	(4.93)	(5.8)	(5.90)	(5.76)	(5.91)
4.	Ragi	804	525	771	771	962	1300	950	838	1049	1056	1110	1265	1320
		(5.84)	(3.77)	(4.0)	(4.17)	(5.76)	(8.39)	(6.81)	(5.8)	(7.18)	(7.53)	(7.56)	(8.19)	(8.28)
5.	Thinai	280	321	296	296	392	372	509	439	567	616	592	648	717
		(2.03)	(2.31)	(1.54)	(1.6)	(2.35)	(2.4)	(3.64)	(3.04)	(3.88)	(4.39)	(4.03)	(4.19)	(4.5)
6.	Varagu	4025	3783	7956	7956	6415	3231	3856	3965	3242	3199	3325	4635	4519
		(29.21)	(27.19)	(41.31)	(43.00)	(38.42)	(20.85)	(27.63)	(27.44)	(22.21)	(22.8)	(22.64)	(30.00)	(28.34)
7.	Samai	1429	1325	1259	1259	1160	1003	1034	1042	1070	1054	1206	1200	1322
		(10.37)	(9.52)	(6.54)	(6.81)	(6.95)	(6.47)	(7.41)	(7.21)	(7.33)	(7.51)	(8.21)	(7.77)	(8.29)
8.	Tamarind	7	7	2	2	2	2	2	2	2	2	2	2	2
		(0.05)	(0.05)	(0.01)	(0.01)	(0.01)	(0.01)	(0.01)	(0.01)	(0.01)	(0.01)	(0.01)	(0.01)	(0.02)
9.	Fruits, Vegetables & roots	790	810	890	178	315	260	184	193	69	150	164	170	331
		(5.73)	(5.82)	(4.62)	(0.96)	(1.89)	(1.68)	(1.32)	(1.34)	(0.47)	(1.07)	(1.12)	(1.10)	(2.08)
10.	Coconut	3	7	7	7	5	5	5	5	5	5	5	5	5
		(0.02)	(0.05)	(0.04)	(0.04)	(0.03)	(0.03)	(0.04)	(0.03)	(0.03)	(0.04)	(0.03)	(0.03)	(0.03)

(Contd.)

(Table 4.9 Contd.)

Sl. No.	*Name of Crop*	*1986-87*	*1987-88*	*1988-89*	*1989-90*	*1990-91*	*1991-92*	*1992-93*	*1993-94*	*1994-95*	*1995-96*	*1996 97*	*1997-98*	*1998-99*
11.	Gingili	2	6	6	4	2	5	5	3	7	15	16	12	14
		(0.01)	(0.03)	(0.04)	(0.02)	(0.01)	(0.03)	(0.04)	(0.02)	(0.05)	(0.11)	(0.11)	(0.08)	(0.09)
12.	Mulberry	5	10	15	15	-	-	-	-	-	-	-	-	-
		(0.04)	(0.07)	(0.08)	(0.08)	-	-	-	-	-	-	-	-	-
13.	Plantain	12	49	178	178	315	325	380	376	306	323	342	195	223
		(0.09)	(0.35)	(0.92)	(0.96)	(1.89)	(2.17)	(2.72)	(2.62)	(2.1)	(2.3)	(2.33)	(1.26)	(1.4)
14.	Jackfruit	5	5	5	5	5	5	5	5	5	5	5	5	5
		(0.04)	(0.04)	(0.03)	(0.03)	(0.03)	(0.03)	(0.03)	(0.03)	(0.03)	(10.04)	(0.03)	(0.03)	(0.03)
15.	Lemon	20	22	22	20	20	20	20	20	20	20	20	20	20
		(0.15)	(0.06)	(0.11)	(0.11)	(0.12)	(0.13)	(0.14)	(0.14)	(0.14)	(0.14)	(0.14)	(0.13)	(0.13)
16.	Tapioca	672	946	676	676	911	970	810	962	1073	871	893	675	730
		(4.88)	(6.8)	(3.51)	(3.65)	(5.46)	(6.26)	(5.8)	(6.66)	(7.35)	(6.21)	(6.08)	(4.37)	(4.58)
17.	Cumbu	1213	1250	1425	1379	1395	1771	600	954	1648	1477	1536	820	906
		(8.8)	(8.99)	(7.4)	(7.45)	(8.36)	(11.43)	(4.3)	(6.6)	(11.29)	(10.53)	(10.46)	(5.31)	(5.68)
18.	Pulses	988	760	820	673	492	542	471	713	741	396	436	637	647
		(7.17)	(5.46)	(4.26)	(3.64)	(2.95)	(3.5)	(3.37)	(4.93)	(5.08)	(2.83)	(2.97)	(4.12)	(4.06)
	Total	13778	13912	19258	18501	16695	15494	13957	14448	14600	14028	14684	15449	15948
		(100)	(100)	(100)	(100)	(100)	(100)	(100)	(100)	(100)	(100)	(100)	(100)	(100)

Values in parentheses are percentages to the total.

Source: 1. Government of Tamil Nadu: Divisional statistical office, Kallakuruchi.

2. Government of Tamil Nadu: Divisional statistical office, Śankarapuram.

Table 4.10 : Cropping Pattern in Nochimedu from 1989-1999 (in Hectares)

Sl. No.	*Name of Crop*	*1989-90*	*1990-91*	*1991-92*	*1992-93*	*1993-94*	*1994-95*	*1995-96*	*1996 97*	*1997-98*	*1998-99*
1.	Paddy	55.96.0	67.74	50.53.0	29.57.5	45.10.5	38.45.0	39.06.0	55.01.0	43.75.0	33.21.0
		(40.18)	(44.11)	(30.69)	(17.84)	(28.06)	(24.69)	(24.97)	(36.38)	(29.18)	(20.35)
2.	Ragi	9.23.0	4.92.0	12.91.5	13.75.0	12.21.5	24.30.0	14.85.0	10.15.0	12.05.0	24.63.0
		(6.63)	(3.20)	(7.85)	(8.29)	(7.59)	(15.61)	(9.49)	(6.71)	(8.04)	(15.09)
3.	Varagu	27.69.0	25.69.0	35.69.0	46.26.5	54.98.0	36.81.0	37.39.0	44.80.0	42.50.0	46.50.0
		(19.89)	(16.73)	(21.68)	(27.9)	(34.18)	(23.64)	(23.9)	(29.63)	(28.34)	(28.49)
4.	Thinai	0.78.0	2.71.0	2.70.5	-	-	-	8.28.0	-	-	6.28.0
		(0.56)	(1.76)	(1.65)	-	-	-	(5.29)	-	-	(3.85)
5.	Samai	6.04.0	21.13.0	31.33.0	40.10.0	13.34.0	10.97.0	9.26.0	9.75.0	11.73.0	12.20.0
		(4.34)	(13.77)	(19.03)	(24.19)	(8.29)	(7.05)	(5.92)	(6.45)	(7.82)	(7.48)
6.	Horse Gram	0.60.0	-	-	7.45.0	7.54.0	21.78.0	21.39.0	8.64.0	11.68.0	19.61.0
		(0.43)	-	-	(4.49)	(4.69)	(13.99)	(13.68)	(5.71)	(7.79)	(12.02)
7.	Tapioca	38.34.0	30.98.0	31.05.0	25.00	25.00.0	22.33.0	24.85.0	19.25.0	23.50.0	18.50.0
		(27.54)	(20.17)	(18.86)	(15.09	(15.54)	(14.34)	(15.88)	(12.73)	(15.67)	(11.34)
8.	Plantain	0.60.0	0.40.0	0.40.0	3.64.0	2.66.0	1.07.0	1.36.0	3.61.0	4.74.0	2.28.0
		(0.43)	(0.26)	(0.24)	(2.2)	(1.65)	(0.68)	(0.87)	(2.39)	(3.16)	(1.40)
	Total	139.24.0	153.57.0	164.62.0	165.78.0	160.84.0	155.71.0	156.44.00	151.21.0	149.95.0	163.21.00
		(100.00)	(100.00)	(100.00)	(100.00)	(100.00)	(100.00)	(100.00)	(100.00)	(100.00)	(100.00)

Figures in parentheses are percentages to the total.

Source: 1. Government of Tamil Nadu: Divisional Statistical Office, Kallakuruchi.
2. Government of Tamil Nadu: Divisional Statistical Office, Sankarapuram.

Yet another category of land is "grazing land". This land contains all permanent grazing land. Sixthly, "Trees and Garden" lands include all lands fit for cultivation and those lands that are not shown in the net cultivated land. Seventhly, the "current fallow" land contains all lands cultivated in the previous season and left uncultivated in the current season. Further, "other fallow" land consists of all lands left uncultivated to a minimum of one year and a maximum of five years. This classification of land includes only those lands that were cultivated in the previous years. Finally, the "net cultivated land" includes all lands used for cultivation of various crops. These classifications of lands are given as per statistical reports A-1, A-2 and also corroborate with Report "G" of the Taluk office. Such data as are collected in different time periods are presented in the following tables.

Table 4.8 gives the details of distribution of land in Kalrayan Block from 1986 to 1999. In 1986-87, the forest land constituted 72.33 per cent of the total land. While the net cultivated land was 20.91 per cent of the tribal land of the hills. While the total land of the hills remain unchanged with 57209 hectares from 1986 to 1999. The forest varied from 72.33 per cent (1986-87) to 67.07 per cent (1998-99). On the other hand, the net cultivated land had increased from 20.91 per cent in 1986-87 to 24.44 per cent is 1998-99. Moreover, the increase or decrease of net cultivated land in all these years also corroborated with such fluctuations in the forest land. Thus, in the absence of much variation in other types of land, the tribals use of forest land and other types of lands should have changed the extent of net cultivated land. Further, the 69.66 per cent of forest land as reported in the A-1 register of taluk office was much below the 79 per cent of forest land (1995-96) as shown in the Forest Department Records (Table 5.7). This shows a favourable situation in the hills, but, the right of the tribals on forest land is questionable as per the Forest Conservation Policy of the Government.

Table 4.11 : Land Use Pattern in Mavadipattu from 1989-1999 (in Hectares)

Sl. No.	*Classification of Land*	*1989-90*	*1990-91*	*1991-92*	*1992-93*	*1993-94*	*1994-95*	*1995-96*	*1996 97*	*1997-98*	*1998-99*
1.	Forest Land	529.02.5 (57.39)	528.65.0 (57.35)	525.61.5 (57.02)	525.61.5 (57.02)	525.61.5 (57.02)	525.61.5 (57.02)	525.61.5 (57.02)	525.61.5 (57.02)	525.61.5 (57.02)	525.61.5 (57.02)
2.	Land unfit for cultivation	6.43.0 (0.7)	4.80.0 (0.52)	72.92.0 (7.92)	20.92.0 (2.27)	49.74.0 (5.4)	49.74.0 (5.4)	45.07.0 (4.89)	49.74.0 (5.4)	44.45.0 (4.82)	4.80.0 (0.52)
3.	Land used for puposes other than cultivation	45.21.0 (4.9)	45.21.0 (4.91)	- -	- -	- -	5.77.0 (0.63)	2.38.0 (0.26)	- -	5.27.0 (0.57)	45.21.0 (4.91)
4.	Fallow land fit for cultivation	7.90.5 (0.86)	8.40.0 (0.91)	- -	- -	- -	10.44.0 (1.13)	- -	- -	9.50.0 (1.03)	8.40.0 (0.91)
5.	Grazing land	-	-	-	-	-	-	-	-	-	-
6.	Trees and garden	-	-	-	-	-	-	-	-	-	-
7.	Current fallows	38.03.5 (4.13)	58.92.0 (6.39)	20.58.0 (2.23)	25.98.0 (2.82)	- -	12.50.0 (1.35)	51.45.0 (5.58)	- -	30.22.0 (3.28)	58.92.0 (6.39)
8.	Other fallows	-	-	-	-	-	-	-	-	-	-
9.	Net cultivated land	295.16.0 (32.02)	275.79.5 (29.92)	302.65.0 (32.83)	349.25.0 (37.89)	346.41.0 (37.58)	317.70.0 (34.47)	297.26.0 (32.25)	346.41.0 (37.58)	306.71.0 (33.27)	275.79.5 (29.92)
	Total	921.76.5 (100.00)	921.76.5 (100.00)	921.76.5 (100.00)	921.76.5 (100.00)	921.76.5 (100.00)	921.76.5 (100.00)	921.76.5 (100.00)	921.76.5 (100.00)	921.76.5 (100.00)	921.76.5 (100.00)

Values in parentheses are percentages to the total.

Source: 1. Government of Tamil Nadu: Divisional Statistical office, Kallakuruchi.
2. Government of Tamil Nadu: Divisional Statistical office, Sankarapuram.

Table 4.12 : Cropping Pattern in Mavadipattu from 1989-1999 (in Hectares)

Sl. No.	Name of the Crop	1989-90	1990-91	1991-92	1992-93	1993-94	1994-95	1995-96	1996 97	1997-98	1998-99
1.	Paddy	90.32.0	87.17.0	87.17.0	97.52.5	95.47.5	90.03.0	88.85.5	87.17.0	88.35.0	91.25.0
		(28.13)	(29.53)	(31.62)	(31.13)	(27.42)	(27.99)	(29.83)	(29.53)	(28.40)	(30.88)
2.	Ragi	25.29.0	29.19.5	29.19.5	26.65.0	26.64.5	33.42.0	31.51.5	29.19.5	29.25.0	33.64.0
		(7.88)	(9.89)	(10.59)	(8.51)	(7.65)	(10.39)	(10.58)	(9.89)	(9.40)	(11.38)
3.	Thinai	16.44.0	12.50.0	-	3.07.5	-	39.14.0	22.75.5	12.50.0	14.40.0	22.75.0
		(5.12)	(4.23)	-	(0.98)	-	(12.17)	(7.64)	(4.23)	(4.63)	(7.70)
4.	Varagu	96.72.0	66.47.5	66.47.5	88.33.0	106.47.5	59.93.0	60.48.0	66.47.5	66.50.0	59.85.0
		(30.13)	(22.52)	(24.11)	(28.2)	(30.58)	(18.63)	(20.3)	(22.52)	(31.38)	(20.26)
5.	Samai	39.34.0	55.58.0	55.56.5	62.73.5	81.64.5	50.10.0	20.49.5	55.58.0	64.08.0	50.45.0
		(12.25)	(18.83)	(20.16)	(20.03)	(23.45)	(15.58)	(6.88)	(18.83)	(20.60)	(17.07)
6.	Plantain	-	-	-	-	1.46.0	3.33.0	1.83.5	-	1.75.0	2.67.0
						(0.42)	(1.04)	(0.62)	-	(0.56)	(0.90)
7.	Tapioca	47.04.0	37.27.0	37.27.0	32.44.5	31.75.5	26.19.0	19.38.0	37.27.0	37.52.0	22.72.0
		(14.65)	(12.62)	(13.52)	(10.35)	(9.12)	(8.15)	(6.5)	(12.62)	(12.06)	(7.69)
8.	Mulberry	-	-	-	-	2.03.0	-	-	-	-	-
		-	-	-	-	(0.58)	-	-	-	-	-
9.	Pulses	5.90.0	7.05.0	-	2.52.0	2.67.5	19.46.0	52.60.5	7.05.0	9.20.0	12.15.0
		(1.84)	(2.39)	-	(0.8)	(0.76)	(6.05)	(17.65)	(2.39)	(2.96)	(4.11)
	Total	321.05.0	295.24.0	275.67.5	313.28.0	348.16.0	321.60.0	297.93.0	295.24.0	311.05.0	295.48.0
		(100.00)	(100.00)	(100.00)	(100.00)	(100.00)	(100.00)	(100.00)	(100.00)	(100.00)	(100.00)

Values in parentheses are percentages to the total

Source: 1. Government of Tamil Nadu: Divisional Statistical Office, Kallakuruchi.
2. Government of Tamil Nadu: Divisional Statistical Office, Sankarapuram.

In the Kalrayan hills, the tribals cultivated 19 types of crops from 1986 to 1999. The long list of crops presented in table 4.9 clearly indicates that the Kalrayan hills tribes had experience in raising various crops. The major food crops raised by them were Paddy, Varagu, Samai, Ragi, Cumbu and Cholam, whereas, the major commercial crops cultivated by them were Tapioca and Sugarcane.

Further, they also cultivated Groundnut, Gingili, Pulses Mulberry, Jackfruit, Lemon, Fruits, and Vegetables etc. Till 1990-91 Varagu crops topped in the crop pattern with 29.21 per cent in 1986-87 and increased to 38.42 per cent in 1990-91. While Paddy crop was second only in the rank, showed an increasing trend from 1988-89 (15.86 per cent) to 1995-96 (23.14 per cent), but decreased to 21.56 per cent in 1998-99. On the other hand, there was decreasing trend in the cultivation of Varagu from 1990-91 (38.42 per cent) to 1998-99 (28.34 per cent). Moreover, the decreased extent of land for Varagu was allocated with increasing area of land in raising Paddy and commercial crops, i.e., Tapioca and some extent Sugarcane and Groundnut. The gross cultivated land was the maximum of 19,258 hectares in 1988-88 and in other periods, it fluctuated from 13,778 hectares in 1986-87 to 14,028 hectares in 1995-96 and 15,948 hectares in 1998-99. If we compare the net cultivated land as given in table 4.8 and the gross cultivated land as per table 4.9, it is clear that the gross cultivated area of land was more than the net area sown. This shows that the tribals cultivated two crops and adopted crop rotation. It is observed that when Paddy was raised in one season pulses or Ragi or Cumbu was cultivated in the second reason.

The land distribution in Nochimedu is presented in Table 4.10. The total land area of the hills is 561.87.5 hectares and it remains the same from 1989 to 1999. Similar to table 4.8, in Nochimedu also the change in net cultivated land affected the area under forestland to a minimum 22.21 per cent and

Table 4.13 : Land Use Pattern in Karialur from 1989-1999 (in Hectares)

Sl. No.	Classification of Land	1989-90	1990-91	1991-92	1992-93	1993-94	1994-95	1995-96	1996 97	1997-98	1998-99
1.	Forest Land	501.54.0 (51.69)	498.81.0 (51.41)	580.81.0 (59.86)	580.49.5 (59.83)	580.49.0 (59.83)	553.320.5 (57.03)	460.05.0 (47.42)	534.67.0 (55.11)	525.50.0 (54.16)	470.05.0 (48.45)
2.	Land unfit for Cultivation	22.37.0 (2.38)	22.25.0 (2.29)	125.59.5 (12.95)	125.59.5 (12.95)	129.59.5 (12.95)	33.32.5 (3.43)	22.13.5 (2.28)	29.92.0 (3.08)	30.27.0 (3.12)	20.13.0 (2.07)
3.	Land used for purposes other than cultivation	70.20.0 (7.24)	70.19.0 (7.23)	4.10.5 (0.42)	4.10.5 (0.42)	4.10.5 (0.42)	24.56.5 (2.53)	46.2.0 (4.77)	41.30.0 (4.26)	39.50.0 (4.07)	48.29.0 (4.98)
4.	Fallow land fit for cultivation	3.88.0 (0.40)	3.88.0 (0.4)	—	—	—	—	—	—	—	—
5.	Grazing land	—	—	—	—	—	—	—	—	—	—
6.	Trees and garden	—	—	—	—	—	—	—	—	—	—
7.	Current fallows	50.49.0 (5.20)	125.61.0 (12.95)	14.29.0 (1.47)	11.43.0 (1.18)	14.29.0 (1.47)	57.48.5 (5.93)	133.77.0 (13.79)	109.71.0 (11.31)	101.50.0 (10.46)	133.77.0 (13.79)
8.	Other fallows	—	—	—	—	—	—	—	—	—	—
9.	Net cultivated land	321.77.0 (33.16)	249.51.0 (25.72)	245.45.0 (25.30)	248.62.5 (25.62)	245.77.0 (25.33)	301.57.0 (31.08)	305.01.0 (31.44)	254.65.0 (26.25)	273.48.0 (28.19)	295.01.0 (30.40)
	Total	970.25.0 (100.00)	970.25.0 (100.00)	970.25.0 (100.00)	970.25.0 (100.00)	970.25.0 (100.00)	970.25.0 (100.00)	970.25.0 (100.00)	970.25.0 (100.00)	970.25.0 (100.00)	970.25.0 (100.00)

Values in parentheses are percentages to the total.

Source: 1. Government of Tamil Nadu: Divisional Statistical Office, Kallakuruchi.

2. Government of Tamil Nadu: Divisional Statistical Office, Sankarapuram.

Table 4.14 : Cropping Pattern in Karialur from 1989-1999 (in Hectares)

Sl. No.	Name of the Crop	1989-90	1990-91	1991-92	1992-93	1993-94	1994-95	1995-96	1996 97	1997-98	1998-99
1.	Paddy	112.85.0	99.90.0	99.90.0	102.56.0	81.58.5	118.94.0	109.66.0	99.90.0	111.50.0	99.87.0
		(35.78)	(38.16)	(39.27)	(29.36)	(32.65)	(32.03)	(34.81)	(39.27)	(4.25)	(39.57)
2.	Cumbu	1.40.0	0.90.0	1.00.00	0.71.5	1.80.0	2.74.0	0.72.0	1.00.00	1.45.0	2.25.0
		(0.43)	(0.34)	(0.39)	(0.21)	(0.72)	(0.81)	(0.23)	(0.39)	(0.52)	(0.89)
3.	Ragi	18.03.0	16.45.0	16.45.0	15.94.0	11.86.0	22.91.0	46.63.0	16.45.0	19.17.0	15.67.0
		(5.56)	(6.28)	96.47)	(4.57)	(4.75)	(6.75)	(14.80)	(6.47)	(6.92)	(6.21)
4.	Thinai	7.85.0	6.30.0	3.20.0	0.97.5	3.55.0	2.11.0	26.07.0	3.20.0	3.01.0	6.71.0
		(2.42)	(2.41)	(1.26)	(0.27)	(1.42)	(0.62)	(8.28)	(1.26)	(1.09)	(2.66)
5.	Varagu	67.63.5	38.76.0	37.94.0	97.15.0	46.51.5	68.64.0	59.56.0	37.94.0	38.50.0	37.04.0
		(20.76)	(14.80)	(14.91)	(27.81)	(18.61)	(20.21)	(18.92)	(14.91)	(13.90)	(14.68)
6.	Samai	34.80.5	38.15.0	37.23.0	65.95.0	41.68.0	49.02.0	21.34.0	37.23.0	41.02.0	31.75.0
		(10.72)	(14.57)	(14.63)	(18.88)	(16.68)	(14.44)	(6.77)	(14.63)	(14.81)	(12.58)
7.	Plantain	3.62.0	3.10.0	2.90.0	1.52.0	1.42.0	5.07.0	5.26.0	2.90.0	3.17.0	3.64.0
		(1.12)	(1.18)	(1.14)	(0.44)	(0.57)	(1.49)	(1.67)	(1.14)	(1.14)	(1.44)
8.	Mango	0.10.0	0.03.0	0.03.0	0.03.0	0.10.0	0.03.0	0.03.0	0.03.0	0.10.0	0.03.0
		(0.03)	90.10)	(0.01)	(0.001)	(0.01)	(0.008)	(0.009)	(0.01)	(0.01)	(0.01)
9.	Tapioca	76.90.0	56.22.0	54.22.0	65.25.0	58.60.0	67.36.0	42.65.0	54.22.0	57.65.0	53.50.0
		(23.7)	(21.49)	(21.31)	(17.82)	(23.45)	(19.84)	(13.54)	(21.31)	(20.82)	(21.20)
10.	Cholam	1.57.0	2.00.0	1.55.0	2.25.0	2.85.0	2.75.0	3.10.0	1.55.0	1.50.0	1.90.0
		(0.48)	(0.76)	(0.61)	(0.64)	(1.14)	(0.81)	(0.98)	(0.61)	(0.54)	(0.75)
	Total	324.49.0	261.81.0	254.42.0	349.37.0	249.90.0	339.57.0	315.02.0	254.42.0	277.00.00	252.36.0
		(100.00)	(100.00)	(100.00)	(100.00)	(100.00)	(100.00)	(100.00)	(100.00)	(100.00)	(100.00)

Values in parentheses are percentages to the total.

Source: 1. Government of Tamil Nadu: Divisional Statistical Office, Kallakuruchi.
2. Government of Tamil Nadu: Divisional Statistical Office, Sankarapuram.

Table 4.15 : Land Use Pattern in Vellimalai from 1989-1999 (in Hectares)

Sl. No.	Classification of Land	1989-90	1990-91	1991-92	1992-93	1993-94	1994-95	1995-96	1996 97	1997-98	1998-99
1.	Forest Land	645.20.5 (59.66)	690.71.0 (63.88)	645.20.5 (59.66)	645.20.5 (59.66)	645.20.5 (59.66)	688.65.0 (63.68)	697.32.0 (64.48)	686.49.0 (63.48)	659.21.0 960.96)	681.22.0 (62.99)
2.	Land unfit for cultivation	28.35.5 (2.62)	28.35.0 (2.62)	28.35.5 (2.62)	28.35.5 (2.62)	28.35.5 (2.62)	48.64.0 (4.5)	13.15.0 (1.22)	18.75.0 (1.73)	19.57.0 (1.81)	18.40.0 (1.70)
3.	Land used for purposes other than cultivation	18.84.5 (1.74)	18.84.0 (1.74)	18.84.5 (1.74)	18.84.5 (1.75)	18.84.5 (1.75)	7.70.0 (0.71)	8.32.0 (0.77)	9.50.0 (0.88)	10.04.0 (0.93)	17.31.0 (1.60)
4.	Fallow land fit for cultivation	9.81.5 (0.91)	34.92.0 (3.23)	8.96.5 90.83)	14.62.5 (1.35)	14.62.5 (1.35)	10.64.0 (0.98)	5.14.0 (0.48)	4.02.0 (0.37)	6.14.0 (0.57)	11.40.0 (1.05)
5.	Grazing land	0.12.0 (0.01)	— —	0.12.0 (0.01)	0.12.0 (0.01)	0.12.0 (0.01)	0.12.0 (0.01)	0.12.0 (0.01)	—	0.12.0 (0.01)	0.12.0 (0.01)
6.	Trees and garden	—	—	—	—	—	—	—	—	—	—
7.	Current fallows	26.10.5 (2.40)	1.98.0 (0.18)	1.41.5 (0.13)	3.14.0 (0.29)	14.65.5 (1.36)	19.46.0 (1.79)	17.54.0 (1.62)	11.80.0 (1.09)	9.85.0 (0.92)	14.62.0 (1.35)
8.	Other fallows	—	—	26.10.5 (2.41)	34.56.0 (3.2)	28.16.0 (2.6)	28.16.0— 92.6)	—	—	36.56.0 (3.38)	38.50.6 (3.56)
9.	Net cultivated land	352.94.5 (32.66)	306.62.0 (28.35)	352.41.0 (32.59)	336.57.0 (31.12)	331.45.5 (30.65)	278.05.0 (25.71)	339.85.0 (31.42)	350.86.0 (32.44)	339.93.0 (31.44)	299.85.0 (27.73)
	Total	1081.42.0 (100.00)	1081.42.0 (100.00)	1081.42.0 (100.00)	1081.42.0 (100.00)	1081.42.0 (100.00)	1081.42.0 (100.00)	1081.42.0 (100.00)	1081.42.0 (100.00)	1081.42.0 (100.00)	1081.42.0 (100.00)

Values in parentheses are percentages to the total.

Source: 1. Government of Tamil Nadu: Divisional Statistical Office, Kallakuruchi.
2. Government of Tamil Nadu: Divisional Statistical Office, Sankarapuram.

Table 4.16 : Cropping Pattern in Vellimalai from 1989-1999 (in Hectares)

Sl. No.	Name of the Crop	1989-90	1990-91	1991-92	1992-93	1993-94	1994-95	1995-96	1996 97	1997-98	1998-99
1.	Paddy	95.99.0 (27.19)	134.31.0 (37.86)	133.21.5 (37.61)	116.96.5 (32.29)	124.58.0 (36.82)	97.95.0 (31.90)	128.64.0 (37.47)	119.09.0 (35.77)	127.50.0 (31.90)	131.37.0 (35.73)
2.	Ragi	28.02.0 (7.94)	16.47.0 (4.64)	12.86.5 (3.63)	15.04.0 (4.15)	2.05.5 (0.61)	7.75.0 (2.52)	5.10.0 (1.49)	5.25.0 (1.58)	9.05.0 (2.52)	8.58.0 (2.33)
3.	Cholam	0.10.0 (0.03)	0.04.0 (0.01)	—	—	—	10.85.0 (3.53)	6.50.0 (1.89)	—	1.31.0 (3.53)	2.75.0 (0.75)
4.	Thinai	7.04.0 (2.00)	2.90.0 (0.82)	0.56.0 (0.16)	0.45.0 (2.88)	4.60.0 (1.36)	0.63.0 (0.21)	7.32.0 (21.97)	6.17.0 (1.85)	9.30.0 (0.21)	9.25.0 (2.52)
5.	Varagu	118.33.0 (33.52)	29.12.0 (8.20)	114.49.0 (32.32)	107.54.5 (29.69)	129.65.5 (38.32)	103.83.0 (33.82)	75.43.0 (21.97)	92.50.0 (27.79)	99.75.0 (26.05)	97.03.0 (26.39)
6.	Samai	30.71.0 (8.7)	96.67.0 (27.25)	23.61.5 (6.67)	42.08.5 (11.61)	10.05.5 (2.97)	53.35.0 (17.38)	42.42.0 (12.36)	39.75.0 (11.94)	40.00.0 (10.45)	51.30.0 (13.95)
7.	Motchai	0.05.0 (0.01)	—	—	2.48.5 (0.69)	—	25.71.0 (8.38)	—	—	22.15.0 (5.79)	—
8.	Plantain	3.61.0 (1.02)	0.30.0 (0.08)	2.60.0 (0.73)	0.04.0 (0.01)	0.76.5 (0.23)	—	4.60.0 (1.34)	0.96.0 (0.29)	—	0.60.0 (0.16)
9.	Tapioca	68.91.5 (19.53)	72.59.0 (20.46)	60.39.5 (17.05)	57.51.0 (15.87)	38.31.0 (11.32)	0.75.0 (0.24)	68.13.0 (19.84)	61.15.0 (18.37)	55.64.0 (14.53)	58.46.0 (15.90)
10.	Vegetables	0.21.0 (0.06)	2.40.0 (0.68)	6.47.5 (1.83)	10.18.0 (2.81)	28.31.0 (8.37)	6.20.0 (2.02)	5.20.0 (1.51)	8.01.0 (2.41)	9.08.0 (2.37)	8.36.0 (2.27)
	Total	352.97.5 (100.00)	354.80.0 (100.00)	354.22.0 (100.00)	362.30.0 (100.00)	338.33.0 (100.00)	307.02.0 (100.00)	343.35.0 (100.00)	332.86.0 (100.00)	373.78.0 (100.00)	367.70.0 (100.00)

Values in parentheses are percentages to the total.

Source: 1. Government of Tamil Nadu: Divisional Statistical Office, Kallakuruchi.
2. Government of Tamil Nádu: Divisional Statistical Office, Sankarapuram.

Table 4.17 : Land Use Pattern in Vazhapady from 1989-1999 (in Hectares)

Sl. No.	*Classification of Land*	*1989-90*	*1990-91*	*1991-92*	*1992-93*	*1993-94*	*1994-95*	*1995-96*	*1996 97*	*1997-98*	*1998-99*
1.	Forest Land	1139.46.0 (72.17)	1197.71.0 (75.860	1216.14.0 (77.02)	1213.72.0 (76.87)	1187.49.0 (75.21)	1234.73.0 (78.2)	1234.73.0 (78.2)	1216.14.0 (77.01)	1231.43. (77.99)	1142.25.0 (72.35)
2.	Land unfit for cultivation	26.97.0 (1.71)	—	—	—	—	—	—	—	—	—
3.	Land used for purposes other than cultivation	27.32.0 (1.73)	32.71.0 (2.07)	32.71.0 (2.07)	32.71.0 (2.07)	32.71.0 (2.07)	0.40.0 (0.03)	0.40.0 (0.03)	32.71.0 (2.07)	42.25.0 (2.68)	39.03.0 (2.47)
4.	Fallow land fit for cultivation	18.47.0 (1.17)	18.48.0 (1.17)	—	—	—	—	—	—	—	—
5.	Grazing land	—	—	—	—	—	—	—	—	—	—
6.	Trees and garden	—	—	—	—	—	—	—	—	—	—
7.	Current fallows	22.28.0 (1.41)	16.00.0 (1.01)	18.47.5 (1.17)	18.47.0 (1.17)	16.04.5 (1.02)	8.84.0 (0.56)	8.56.0 (0.54)	8.47.0 (0.54)	8.00.0 (0.51)	9.07.0s (0.57)
8.	Other fallows	—	—	—	—	—	—	—	—	—	—
9.	Net cultivated land	344.39.0 (21.81)	313.99.0 (19.89)	311.56.5 (19.74)	313.99.0 (19.89)	342.64.5 (21.70)	334.92.0 (21.21)	335.20.0 (21.23)	321.57.0 (20.37)	297.21.0 (18.82)	388.54.0 (24.61)
	Total	1578.89.0 (100.00)	1578.89 (100.00)	1578.89.0 (100.00)	1578.89 (100.00)	1578.89.0 (100.00)	1578.89 (100.00)	1578.89.0 (100.00)	1578.89 (100.00)	1578.89.0 (100.00)	1578.89 (100.00)

Values in parentheses are percentages to the total.

Source: 1. Government of Tamil Nadu: Divisional Statistical Office, Kallakuruchi.

2. Government of Tamil Nadu: Divisional Statistical Office, Sankarapuram.

Table 4.18 : Cropping Pattern in Vazhapady from 1989-1999 (in Hectares)

Sl. No.	*Name of the Crop*	*1989-90*	*1990-91*	*1991-92*	*1992-93*	*1993-94*	*1994-95*	*1995-96*	*1996 97*	*1997-98*	*1998-99*
1.	Paddy	175.25.0	179.76.0	167.41.0	60.88.0	112.04.0	79.77.0	79.58.0	96.51.0	108.35.0	112.39.0
		(50.89)	(54.47)	(53.73)	(19.39)	(31.7)	(23.75)	(23.57)	(27.24)	(29.14)	(29.38)
2.	Ragi	27.00.0	23.59.0	36.77.	57.37.0	54.13.0	51.67.0	56.94.0	57.34.0	63.04.0	65.42.0
		(7.84)	(7.15)	(11.8)	(18.27)	(15.8)	(15.38)	(16.86)	(16.18)	(16.95)	(17.10)
3.	Varagu	100.75.5	84.10.0	72.30.0	153.85.0	123.53.	180.03.0	176.01.0	167.03.0	169.23.0	171.35.0
		(29.25)	(25.29)	(23.21)	949.00)	(36.05)	(53.59)	(52.12)	(47.14)	(45.52)	(44.79)
4.	Tapioca	41.39.5	42.54.0	35.09.0	41.89.0	52.94.0	24.46.0	25.15.0	33.43.	31.19.0	33.40.0
		(12.02)	(12.89)	(11.26)	(13.34)	(15.45)	(7.28)	(7.45)	(9.44)	(8.39)	(8.73)
	Total	344.40.0	329.899.0	311.57.0	313.99.0	342.64.0	335.93.0	337.68.	354.31.0	371.81.0	382.56.0
		(100.00)	(100.00)	(100.00)	(100.00)	(100.00)	(100.00)	(100.00)	(100.00)	(100.00)	(100.00)

Values in parentheses are percentages to the total.

Source: 1. Government of Tamil Nadu: Divisional Statistical Office, Kallakuruchi.
2. Government of Tamil Nadu: Divisional Statistical Office, Sankarapuram.

Table 4.19 : Land Use Pattern in Kundiyanatham from 1989-1999 (in Hectares)

Sl. No.	*Classification of Land*	*1989-90*	*1990-91*	*1991-92*	*1992-93*	*1993-94*	*1994-95*	*1995-96*	*1996 97*	*1997-98*	*1998-99*
1.	Forest Land	1297.70.0 (85.2)	1297.70.0 (85.2)	1271.94.0 (83.51)	1271.94.0 (83.51)	1280.94.0 (84.09)	1280.77.0 (83.93)	1278.34.0 (83.93)	1199.31.0 (78.74)	1301.12.0 (85.42)	1239.22.0 (81.34)
2.	Land unfit for cultivation	1.99.0 (0.13)	10.00.0 (0.66)	20.26.0 (1.33)	14.26.0 (1.33)	15.28.0 (1.0)	17.66.0 (1.16)	17.66.0 (1.16)	23.05.0 (1.51)	26.31.0 (1.73)	27.50.0 (1.81)
3.	Land used for purposes other than cultivation	2.84.0 (0.19)	2.60.0 (0.17)	6.03.5 (0.4)	4.74.0 (0.31)	3.50.0 (0.23)	0.96.0 (0.06)	0.96.0 (0.06)	0.82.0 (0.05)	1.67.0 (0.11)	2.64.0 (0.17)
4.	Fallow land fit for cultivation	21.84.0 (1.43)	20.60.0 (1.35)	2.34.5 (0.15)	2.34.0 (0.15)	1.02.0 (0.07)	0.80.0 (0.05)	1.05.0 (0.07)	1.02.0 (0.07)	1.26.0 (0.08)	2.65.0 (0.17)
5.	Grazing land	—	—	—	—	—	—	—	—	—	—
6.	Trees and garden	—	—	—	—	—	—	—	—	—	—
7.	Current fallows	—	—	2.10.0 (0.14)	2.10.0 (0.14)	1.00.0 (0.07)	4.51.0 (0.3)	5.92.0 (0.39)	4.16.0 (0.27)	3.15.0 (0.21)	4.64.0 (0.30)
8.	Other fallows	—	—	—	—	—	—	—	—	—	—
9.	Net cultivated land	198.78.0 (13.05)	195.25.0 (12.62)	220.47.0 (14.47)	227.77.0 (14.95)	221.58.0 (14.55)	220.88.0 (14.5)	219.22.0 (14.39)	294.79.0 (19.35)	189.64.0 (12.45)	246.50.0 (16.18)
	Total	1523.15.0 (100.00)	1523.15.0 (100.00)	1523.15.0 (100.00)	1523.15.0 (100.00)	1523.15.0 (100.00)	1523.15.0 (100.00)	1523.15.0 (100.00)	1523.15.0 (100.00)	1523.15.0 (100.00)	1523.15.0 (100.00)

Values in parentheses are percentages to the total.

Source: 1. Government of Tamil Nadu: Divisional Statistical Office, Kallakuruchi.
2. Government of Tamil Nadu: Divisional Statistical Office, Sankarapuram.

Table 4.20 : Cropping Pattern in Kundiyanatham from 1989-1999 (in Hectares)

Sl. No.	Name of the Crop	1989-90	1990-91	1991-92	1992-93	1993-94	1994-95	1995-96	1996 97	1997-98	1998-99
1.	Paddy	36.03.0	25.66.0	33.79.5	20.15.0	30.00.0	55.00.0	63.96.0	53.32.0	59.67.0	61.39.0
		(15.26)	(11.95)	(15.33)	(8.85)	(13.54)	(22.21)	(26.49)	(20.65)	(21.17)	(22.19)
2.	Cholam	4.89.0	3.95.0	3.31.0	2.98.0	6.20.5	7.15.0	5.70.0	5.19.0	9.05.0	8.61.0
		(2.07)	(1.84)	(1.5)	(1.31)	(2.8)	(2.89)	(2.36)	(2.05)	(3.21)	(3.11)
3.	Cumbu	11.16.0	10.50.0	12.22.5	13.44.5	10.20.0	16.77.0	11.87.0	12.33.0	13.45.0	12.07.0
		(4.73)	(4.88)	(5.54)	(5.90)	(4.6)	(6.77)	(4.92)	(4.87)	(4.77)	(4.36)
4.	Ragi	8.40.0	1.67.0	2.69.0	13.52.0	14.89.5	12.85.0	11.04.0	12.77.0	12.85.0	13.04.0
		(3.55)	(0.78)	(1.22)	(5.94)	(6.72)	(5.19)	(4.57)	(5.04)	(4.56)	(4.71)
5.	Thinai	6.60.0	4.62.0	—	5.00.0	8.98.0	8.14.0	6.72.0	6.84.0	6.09.0	6.00.0
		(2.8)	(2.15)		(2.2)	(4.05)	(3.29)	(2.78)	(2.70)	(2.16)	(2.17)
6.	Varagu	116.76.0	98.72.0	111.79.5	73.73.5	56.63.5	49.19.0	41.64.0	56.34.0	57.33.0	53.46.0
		(49.45)	(45.97)	(50.71)	(32.37)	(21.05)	(19.86)	(17.24)	(22.24)	(20.34)	(19.34)
7.	Sama	14.00.0	16.90.0	6.86.5	6.92.0	14.52.5	16.33.0	6.38.0	4.77.0	6.00.0	6.33.0
		(5.93)	(7.87)	(3.12)	(3.04)	(6.55)	(6.59)	(2.64)	(1.88)	(2.13)	(2.29)
8.	Pulses	17.05.0	11.20.0	18.24.0	65.24.0	50.62.0	26.11.0	26.53.0	45.34.0	46.37.0	43.00.0
		(7.22)	(5.22)	(8.27)	(28.64)	(22.85)	(10.55)	(10.99)	(17.90)	(16.45)	(15.54)
9.	Plantain	11.57.0	21.99.0	11.82.0	6.72.5	17.43.	14.66.0	19.11.0	19.95.0	19.72.0	19.23.0
		(4.9)	(10.24)	(5.36)	(2.95)	(7.87)	(5.92)	(7.91)	(7.88)	(6.99)	(6.95)
10.	Tapioca	9.65.0	15.53.0	19.73.0	20.05.0	22.09.0	41.44.0	48.54.0	37.47.0	51.39.0	53.49.0
		(4.09)	(9.1)	(8.95)	(8.8)	(9.97)	(16.73)	(20.1)	(14.79)	(18.23)	(19.34)
	Total	236.11.0	214.74.0	220.47.0	227.76.5	221.58.0	247.64.0	241.49.0	253.32.0	281.92.0	276.62.0
		(100.00)	(100.00)	(100.00)	(100.00)	(100.00)	(100.00)	(100.00)	(100.00)	(100.00)	(100.00)

Values in parentheses are percentages to the total.

Source: 1. Government of Tamil Nadu: Divisional Statistical Office, Kallakuruchi.
2. Government of Tamil Nadu: Divisional Statistical Office, Sankarapuram.

Table 4.21 : Land Use Pattern in Kendikkal from 1989-1999 (in Hectares)

Sl. No.	*Classification of Land*	*1989-90*	*1990-91*	*1991-92*	*1992-93*	*1993-94*	*1994-95*	*1995-96*	*1996 97*	*1997-98*	*1998-99*
1.	Forest Land	1291.30.0 (66.98)	1291.30.0 (66.98)	1248.76.5 (64.78)	1249.77.5 (64.83)	1248.76.5 (64.78)	1347.13.5 (69.88)	1299.25.0 (67.4)	1260.06.0 (65.36)	1247.30.0 964.70)	1265.80.0 (65.66)
2.	Land unfit for cultivation	—	—	—	—	24.00.0 (1.24)	19.20.5 (1.0)	19.25.0 (1.0)	20.32.0 (1.05)	21.05.0 (1.09)	23.20.0 (1.20)
3.	Land used for purposes other than cultivation	—	—	19.55.0 (1.01)	19.55.0 (1.01)	19.55.0 (1.01)	—	122.09.5 (6.33)	39.55.0 (2.05)	—	32.19.0 (1.67)
4.	Fallow land fit for cultivation	13.38.0 (0.69)	13.38.0 (0.69)	0.91.0 (0.05)	1.10.0 (0.06)	1.10.0 (0.06)	1.45.0 (0.08)	10.47.0 (0.54)	9.41.0 (0.49)	7.45.0 (0.39)	9.14.0 (0.47)
5.	Grazing land	—	—	—	—	—	1.00.0 (0.05)	—	—	1.10.0 (0.05)	—
6.	Trees and garden	—	—	—	—	—	1.10.0 (0.06)	—	—	1.10.0 (0.06)	—
7.	Current fallows	—	—	17.31.0 (0.9)	108.88.0 (5.65)	84.88.0 (4.40)	10.47.0 (0.54)	—	44.75.0 (2.32)	31.25.0 (1.62)	—
8.	Other fallows	9.57.0 (0.5)	9.57.0 (0.5)	8.38.0 (0.43)	8.45.0 (0.44)	8.45.0 (0.44)	25.35.5 (1.32)	—	19.50.0 (1.01)	20.19.0 (1.05)	—
9.	Net cultivated land	613.56.0 (31.83)	613.56. (31.83)	632.89.5 (32.83)	539.96.5 (28.01)	541.15.5 (28.07)	522.09.5 (27.07)	476.740 (24.73)	534.22.0 (27.71)	598.47.0 (31.04)	597.48.0 (30.99)
	Total	1927.81.0 (100.00)	1927.81.0 (100.00)	1927.81.0 (100.00)	1927.81.0 (100.00)	1927.81.0 (100.00)	1927.81.0 (100.00)	1927.81.0 (100.00)	1927.81.0 (100.00)	1927.81.0 (100.00)	1927.81.0 (100.00)

Values in parentheses are percentages to the total.

Source: 1. Government of Tamil Nadu: Divisional Statistical Office, Kallakuruchi.
2. Government of Tamil Nadu: Divisional Statistical Office, Sankarapuram.

Table 4.22 : Cropping Pattern in Kendikkal from 1989-1999 (in Hectares)

Sl. No.	Name of the Crop	1989-90	1990-91	1991-92	1992-93	1993-94	1994-95	1995-96	1996 97	1997-98	1998-99
1.	Paddy	370.38.0	305.42.5	360.64.5	190.77.0	196.79.0	182.04.0	113.39.0	113.12.0	112.50.0	121.57.0
		(60.37)	(49.78)	(57)	(35.33)	(36.45)	(34.8)	(23.78)	(23.61)	(23.26)	(23.17)
2.	Ragi	41.81.5	71.88.5	54.29.5	30.14.5	23.74.5	27.45.5	29.13.0	25.42.0	23.51.0	29.32.0
		(6.82)	(11.72)	(8.59)	(5.58)	(4.4)	(5.25)	(6.11)	(5.31)	(4.86)	(5.59)
3.	Thinai	25.21.0	18.29.0	5.40.0	30.85.5	33.65.0	21.09.0	19.47.0	22.50.0	21.09.0	19.47.0
		(4.11)	(2.98)	(0.85)	(5.71)	(6.23)	(4.03)	(4.08)	(4.70)	(4.36)	(3.71)
4.	Samai	19.81.0	27.69.0	14.96.0	48.95.5	45.93.0	45.36.0	41.34.0	43.13.0	49.60.0	45.23.0
		(3.23)	(4.51)	(2.36)	(9.07)	(8.51)	(8.67)	(8.67)	(9.00)	(10.25)	(8.62)
5.	Pulses	4.56.5	0.11.0	2.88.0	1.93.0	2.91.0	3.14.0	11.19.0	12.01.0	13.04.0	13.22.0
		(0.74)	(0.02)	(0.46)	(0.36)	(0.54)	(0.6)	(2.35)	(2.51)	(2.70)	(2.52)
6.	Varagu	92.70.0	112.59.0	148.02.0	183.63.5	163.87.5	147.03.5	155.53.0	159.74.0	157.23.0	159.43.0
		(15.11)	(18.35)	(23.39)	(0.36)	(0.54)	(0.6)	(2.35)	(2.51)	(2.70)	(2.52)
7.	Plantain	0.07.0	0.07.0	0.07.0	—	—	1.00.0	0.07.0	—	1.00.0	2.07.0
		(9.61)	(12.63)	(7.34)			(0.19)	(0.01)		(0.21)	(0.39)
8.	Tapioca	59.01.0	77.50.0	46.46.	53.67.0	73.06.0	95.97.0	106.69.0	103.15.0	105.75.0	134.46.0
		(9.61)	(12.63)	(7.34)	(9.94)	(13.52)	(18.35)	(22.38)	(21.53)	(21.86)	(25.62)
	Total	613.56.0	613.56.0	632.73.	539.96.0	539.96.0	523.09.0	476.81.0	479.07.0	483.72.0	524.77.0
		(100.00)	(100.00)	(100.00)	(100.00)	(100.00)	(100.00)	(100.00)	(100.00)	(100.00)	(100.00)

Values in parentheses are percentages to the total.

Source: 1. Government of Tamil Nadu: Divisional Statistical Office, Kallakuruchi.

2. Government of Tamil Nadu: Divisional Statistical Office, Sankarapuram.

Table 4.23 : Land Use Pattern in Pottiyam from 1989-1999 (in Hectares)

Sl. No.	*Classification of Land*	*1989-90*	*1990-91*	*1991-92*	*1992-93*	*1993-94*	*1994-95*	*1995-96*	*1996 97*	*1997-98*	*1998-99*
1.	Forest Land	785.23.5 (59.25)	786.38.5 (59.33)	786.38.5 (59.33)	786.38.5 (59.33)	786.38.5 (59.33)	786.38.5 (59.33)	920.41.0 (69.44)	860.08.5 (64.89)	871.28.5 (65.74)	892.73.0 (67.36)
2.	Land unfit for cultivation	4.90.5 (0.37)	4.90.0 (0.37)	4.90.0 (0.37)	4.90.0 (0.37)	4.90.0 (0.37)	39.19.0 (2.96)	52.04.5 (3.92)	31.25.0 (2.36)	33.72.0 (2.54)	32.50.0 (2.45)
3.	Land used for purposes other than cultivation	107.79.5 (8.13)	107.79.5 (8.13)	107.79.0 (8.13)	100.79.0 (7.61)	100.21.0 (7.56)	54.00.0 (4.07)	44.76.5 (3.38)	90.11.0 (6.80)	84.12.0 (6.35)	78.67.0 (5.94)
4.	Fallow land fit for cultivation	—	24.18.0 (1.82)	24.18.0 (1.82)	31.18.0 (2.35)	32.23.0 (2.43)	13.19.0 (1.0)	—	12.13. (0.92)	13.00.0 (0.98)	—
5.	Grazing land	—	—	—	—	—	—	—	—	—	—
6.	Trees and garden	—	—	—	—	—	—	—	—	—	—
7.	Current fallows	62.19.0 (4.69)	59.25.0 (4.47)	59.25.0 (4.470	—	—	36.54.0 (2.76)	49.12.5 (3.71)	—	46.37.0 (3.50)	49.12.5 (3.71)
8.	Other fallows	—	—	—	—	—	—	—	—	—	—
9.	Net cultivated land	365.25.0 (27.56)	342.86.5 (25.88)	342.86.5 (25.88)	402.12.0 (30.34)	401.65.0 (30.31)	396.07.0 (29.88)	259.06.0 (19.55)	331.81.0 (25.04)	276.88.0 (20.890	272.35.0 (20.55)
	Total	1325.37.5 (100.00)	1325.37.5 (100.00)	1325.37.5 (100.00)	1325.37.5 (100.00)	1325.37.5 (100.00)	1325.37.5 (100.00)	1325.37.5 (100.00)	1325.37.5 (100.00)	1325.37.5 (100.00)	1325.37.5 (100.00)

Values in parentheses are percentages to the total.

Source: 1. Government of Tamil Nadu: Divisional Statistical Office, Kallakuruchi.

2. Government of Tamil Nadu: Divisional Statistical Office, Sankarapuram.

Table 4.24 : Cropping Pattern in Pottiyam from 1989-1999 (in Hectares)

Sl. No.	Name of the Crop	1989-90	1990-91	1991-92	1992-93	1993-94	1994-95	1995-96	1996 97	1997-98	1998-99
1.	Paddy	71.78.5	77.12.0	77.12.0	81.00.0	81.00.0	99.65.0	92.89.0	94.50.0	98.23.0	101.34
		(18.10)	(20.87)	(21.36)	(19.43)	(19.33)	(22.79)	(22.38)	(18.29)	(21.70)	(21.17)
2.	Cholam	2.46.5	4.98.5	49.85.0	47.05.0	46.03.0	53.50.0	47.00.0	48.25.0	57.39.0	51.09.0
		(0.62)	(1.35)	(13.80)	(11.28)	(10.99)	(12.24)	(11.32)	(9.34)	(12.68)	(10.67)
3.	Plantain	96.05.0	84.30.5	44.30.5	44.30.5	40.25.0	43.17.0	38.30.0	39.17.0	40.03.0	39.20.0
		(24.23)	(22.82)	(12.27)	(10.63)	(9.60)	(9.87)	(9.23)	(7.58)	(8.84)	(8.19)
4.	Tapioca	54.57.0	63.72.0	43.72.0	67.16.0	71.46.0	73.50.0	83.94.0	85.33.0	86.00.0	89.35.0
		(13.76)	(17.25)	(12.11)	(16.11)	(17.06)	(16.81)	(20.23)	(16.51)	(19.00)	(18.67)
5.	Groundnut	53.26.5	42.10.0	26.11.0	30.05.0	29.36.0	35.00.0	28.13.0	31.20.0	37.00.0	43.02.0
		(13.44)	(11.4)	(7.23)	(7.21)	(7.00)	(8.00)	(6.78)	(6.04)	(8.17)	(8.99)
6.	Cumbu	18.22.0	24.35.0	24.35.0	30.00.0	30.00.0	11.55.0	7.74.0	9.04.0	10.01.0	13.34.0
		(4.6)	(6.59)	(6.74)	(7.19)	(7.16)	(2.64)	(1.86)	(1.75)	(2.21)	(2.79)
7.	Horse Gram	25.24.0	23.99.5	23.99.5	20.99.0	20.99.0	16.09.0	15.50.0	14.12.0	15.94.0	15.91.0
		(6.37)	(6.49)	(6.64)	(5.01)	(5.01)	(3.68)	(3.73)	(2.73)	(3.52)	(3.32)
8.	Ragi	18.22.0	9.25.0	22.27.0	27.17.5	28.17.0	10.78.0	12.10.0	12.84.0	11.70.0	14.88.0
		(4.6)	(2.5)	(6.17)	(6.52)	(6.72)	(2.47)	(2.92)	(2.48)	(2.58)	(3.11)
9.	Varagu	41.08.5	15.45.5	15.45.0	22.310	22.31.0	48.01.0	43.60.0	38.46.0	48.01.0	53.90.0
		(10.36)	(4.18)	(4.28)	(5.35)	(5.33)	(10.98)	(10.51)	(7.44)	(10.60)	(11.26)
10.	Vegetables	0.20.0	6.10.0	11.56.0	11.56.0	12.56.0	9.60.0	10.00.0	11.62.0	13.25.0	12.60.0
		(0.05)	(1.65)	(3.2)	(2.77)	(3.0)	(2.2)	(2.41)	(1.18)	(2.93)	(2.63)
11.	Samai	5.50.0	8.48.5	8.48.5	17.11.	16.11.0	7.66.0	2.70.0	6.11.0	8.02.0	9.43.0
		(1.39)	(2.3)	(2.35)	(4.1)	(3.85)	(1.75)	(0.58)	(3.85)	(1.77)	(1.97)
12.	Cashewnut	1.00.0	1.00.0	1.00.0	1.00.0	1.00.0	1.00.0	1.00.0	1.63.0	1.39.0	1.00.0
		(0.25)	(0.27)	(0.28)	(0.24)	(0.24)	(0.23)	(0.24)	(0.32)	(0.30)	(0.21)

(Contd.)

(Table 4.24 Contd.)

Sl. No.	Name of the Crop	*1989-90*	*1990-91*	*1991-92*	*1992-93*	*1993-94*	*1994-95*	*1995-96*	*1996 97*	*1997-98*	*1998-99*
13.	Turmeric	1.10.0	0.77.0	0.77.0	0.77.0	0.77.0	0.77.0	1.99.5	0.77.5	0.77.0	0.99.0
		(0.28)	(0.21)	(0.21)	(0.18)	(0.18)	(0.18)	(0.48)	(0.15)	(0.17)	(0.21)
14.	Mulberry	0.63.0	0.68.0	0.68.0	1.00.0	1.00.0	1.00.0	1.00.0	1.00.0	1.00.0	1.00.0
		(0.16)	(0.18)	(0.19)	(0.24)	(0.24)	(0.23)	(0.24)	(0.15)	(0.17)	(0.210
15.	Mango	0.44.0	0.44.0	0.44.0	0.44.0	0.44.0	0.44.0	0.44.0	0.64.0	0.44.0	0.44.0
		(0.110	(0.12)	(0.12)	(0.11)	(0.11)	(0.1)	(0.11)	(0.12)	(0.10)	(0.12)
16.	Sugarcane	6.70.0	6.70.0	11.02.0	15.05.0	17.50.0	25.50.0	28.98.5	27.61.0	23.57.0	31.00.0
	Total	396.47.0	369.45.0	361.12.0	416.97.0	481.95.0	437.22.0	415.02.0	516.79.0	452.75.0	478.66.0
		(100.00)	(100.00)	(100.00)	(100.00)	(100.00)	(100.00)	(100.00)	(100.00)	(100.00)	(100.00)

Values in parentheses are percentages to the total.

Source: 1. Government of Tamil Nadu: Divisional Statistical Office, Kallakuruchi.
2. Government of Tamil Nadu: Divisional Statistical Office, Sankarapuram.

Table 4.25 : Land Use Pattern in Malliampady from 1989-1999 (in Hectares)

Sl. No.	Classification of Land	1989-90	1990-91	1991-92	1992-93	1993-94	1994-95	1995-96	1996 97	1997-98	1998-99
1.	Forest Land	135.73.5 (66.16)	1081.52.0 (63.0)	984.38.0 957.33)	1081.35.0 (62.99)	984.68.0 (57.36)	1138.48.0 (66.32)	1138.52.0 (66.32)	1084.00.0 (63.15)	1081.35.0 (62.99)	1084.02.0 (63.15)
2.	Land unfit for cultivation	31.60.5 (1.84)	0.50.0 (0.03)	0.50.0 (0.03)	0.50.0 (0.03)	0.50.0 (0.03)	0.98.0 (0.06)	0.98.0 (0.06)	0.50.0 (0.03)	0.50.0 (0.03)	0.50.0 (0.03)
3.	Land used for purposes other than cultivation	117.18.0 (6.83)	0.50.0 (0.03)	0.50.0 (0.03)	0.50.0 (0.03)	0.50.0 (0.03)	—	35.27.0 (2.05)	12.15.0 (0.71)	0.50.0 (0.03)	0.50.0 (0.03)
4.	Fallow land fit for cultivation	53.70.5 (3.13)	37.69.0 (2.2)	38.95.0 (2.27)	37.66.0 (2.19)	38.95.0 (2.27)	35.26.0 (2.05)	—	29.55.0 (1.72)	37.66.0 (2.19)	31.39.0 (1.83)
5.	Grazing land	—	—	—	—	—	—	—	—	—	—
6.	Trees and garden	—	—	—	—	—	—	—	—	—	—
7.	Current fallows	59.45.0 (3.46)	217.11.0 (12.65)	217.11.0 (12.64)	217.11.0 (12.65)	217.11.0 (12.65)	133.34.0 (7.77)	103.06.0 (6.01)	171.78.0 (10.01)	217.11.0 (12.65)	217.11.0 (12.65)
8.	Other fallows	—	—	—	—	—	—	—	—	—	—
9.	Net cultivated land	319.00.5 (18.58)	379.36.0 (22.1)	475.24.0 (27.68)	379.56.0 (22.11)	474.94.0 (27.66)	408.62.0 (23.80)	438.79.0 (25.56)	418.70.0 (24.39)	379.56.0 (22.11)	578.57.0 (33.70)
	Total	1716.68.0 (100.00)	1716.68.0 (100.00)	1716.68.0 (100.00)	1716.68.0 (100.00)	1716.68.0 (100.00)	1716.68.0 (100.00)	1716.68.0 (100.00)	1716.68.0 (100.00)	1716.68.0 (100.00)	1716.68.0 (100.00)

Values in parentheses are percentages to the total.

Source: 1. Government of Tamil Nadu: Divisional Statistical Office, Kallakuruchi.
2. Government of Tamil Nadu: Divisional Statistical Office, Sankarapuram.

to a maximum of 27.36 per cent in the study period. However, the maxmimum percentage of forestland (75.57 in 1998-99) is observed in the village. The land unfit for cultivation and current fallows occupied only small portion of the total village land.

As shown in Table 4.10, in Nochimedu, Paddy, Tapioca and Varagu were predominant crops from 1989 to 1999. With regard to area under these crops, Paddy crop showed a decreasing trend from a maximum of 44.11 per cent in 1990-91 to 24.69 per cent in 1994-95. The Varagu crop was cultivated with the maximum of 34.18 per cent in 1993-94, decreased to 23.64 per cent and 28.49 per cent in 1994-95 and 1998-99, respectively. On the other hand, Tapioca crop was cultivated in the maximum of 38.34 hectares in 1989-90 and gradually decreased to 24.85 hectares in 1995-96. Further, the tribals also cultivated Ragi, Thinai, Samai, Horse gram and Plantain and fluctuation in the area under cultivation was observed in the village. When there were 19 crops cultivated in the whole of Kalrayan hills only 8 crops were raised in the village.

As depicted in Table 4.11, the total extent of land in Mavadipattu was 921.76.5 hectares, during the years from 1989 to 1999. The per capita land availability for the tribals in the village was 1.51 hectares in 1981 and decreased to 1.27 hectares in 1996. Further, the forestland was around 57.02 per cent from 1988 to 1999, whereas the net cultivated land varied between 32.02 per cent in 1989-90 to the maximum of 37.89 per cent in 1992.93. The fluctuation in net cultivated land was effected by changes in current fallows, fallow land fit for cultivation and the land unfit for cultivation. Further, the percentage of forestland of this village (57.02 per cent in 1995-96) was less than the hills percentage of forestland as per forest department records, i.e., 79 per cent.

The crop pattern of Mavadipattu village depicted in Table 4.12 indicates that the tribals raise nine different kinds of

Table 4.26 : Cropping Pattern in Malliampaddy from 1989-1999 (in Hectares)

Sl. No.	Name of the Crop	1989-90	1990-91	1991-92	1992-93	1993-94	1994-95	1995-96	1996 97	1997-98	1998-99
1.	Varagu	53.00.0	75.23.0	104.65.0	124.39.0	202.12.0	96.56.0	106.31.0	123.28.0	133.60.0	137.93.0
		(15.39)	(19.83)	(21.91)	(32.62)	(42.1)	(20.21)	(22.51)	(24.33)	(25.45)	(24.81)
2.	Samai	19.00.0	61.18.0	130.00.0	32.91.0	90.67.0	66.00.0	43.50.0	97.34.0	93.11.0	79.18.0
		(5.52)	(16.29)	(27.21)	(8.63)	(18.88)	(13.81)	(9.21)	(19.21)	(17.74)	(14.24)
3.	Plantain	87.57.5	91.95.0	64.92.0	70.98.0	72.43.0	161.09.0	145.30.0	107.07.0	115.24.0	133.08.0
		(25.42)	(24.24)	(13.59)	(18.61)	(15.09)	(33.72)	(30.77)	(21.13)	(21.95)	(23.52)
4.	Paddy	81.00.0	84.75.0	57.86.5	40.20.0	54.64.0	73.57.0	80.78.0	77.42.0	75.73.0	93.08.0
		(23.52)	(22.54)	(12.11)	(10.54)	(11.38)	(15.4)	(17.11)	(15.28)	(14.43)	(16.74)
5.	Turmeric	2.30.0	6.00.00	15.13.0	8.10.0	15.99.0	20.82.0	21.71.0	29.00.0	30.20.0	31.60.0
		(0.67)	91.58)	(3.17)	(2.12)	(3.33)	(4.36)	(4.6)	(5.72)	(5.75)	(5.68)
6.	Sugarcane	9.02.0	10.43.0	11.64.5	15.80.0	9.41.0	31.08.0	46.84.0	39.26.0	41.17.0	41.23.0
		(2.62)	(2.75)	(2.44)	(4.14)	(1.96)	(6.51)	(9.92)	(7.75)	(7.84)	(7.42)
7.	Ragi	1.00.0	4.50.0	10.00.0	12.00.0	0.98.0	2.00.0	3.05.0	2.85.0	2.99.0	3.05.0
		(0.29)	(1.19)	(2.09)	(3.15)	(0.2)	(0.42)	(0.65)	(0.56)	(0.57)	(0.55)
8.	Cholam	4.00.0	4.00.0	3.50.0	2.00.0	3.40.0	4.00.0	3.50.0	3.40.0	3.37.0	3.59.0
		(1.16)	(1.05)	(0.73)	(0.52)	(0.71)	(0.84)	90.74)	90.67)	(0.64)	(0.65)
9.	Tapioca	87.54.5	40.69.0	80.00.0	75.00.0	30.50.0	22.65.0	21.20.0	27.17.0	29.50.0	33.27.0
		(25.41)	(10.73)	(16.75)	(19.67)	(6.35)	(4.73)	(4.49)	(5.36)	(5.62)	(5.98)
	Total	344.44.0	379.36.0	477.71.0	381.38.0	480.14.0	477.77.0	472.19.0	506.79.0	524.91.0	556.01.0
		(100.00)	(100.00)	(100.00)	(100.00)	(100.00)	(100.00)	(100.00)	(100.00)	(100.00)	(100.00)

Values in parentheses are percentages to the total.

Source: 1. Government of Tamil Nadu: Divisional Statistical Office, Kallakuruchi.

2. Government of Tamil Nadu: Divisional Statistical Office, Sankarapuram.

crops in the village. Like other villages, Varagu, Paddy and Tapioca were the predominant crops, while Samai, Ragi and Thinai were also cultivated in a considerable extent of land in this village. The area under Tapioca crop was decreasing from 14.65 per cent in 1989-90 to 7.69 per cent in 1998-99. The same plight was observed for Varagu crop, but area under paddy showed an increasing trend from 1994-95 after a drop in 1991-92. On the other hand, the tribals have experimented mulberry and plantain in 1993-94.

Yet another village in the hills that has low percentage of forestland is Karialur, where it varied from 51.69 per cent in 1989-90 to 48.45 per cent in 1998-99. Table 4.13 depicts that in this village comparatively more net cultivated land was observed during the study period. Further, land unfit for cultivation decreased from 12.95 per cent in 1991-92 to 3.43 and 2.07 per cent in 1994-95 and 1998-99 respectively. In addition, land used for purposes other than cultivation and current fallows have also increased in 1994-95 and 1998-99. The net cultivated land has decreased due to fall in the forestland. Since, this village is a progressive village with more literates and also accessible to the Government offices and also located near the main road, such a remarkable picture of land distribution is observed.

In Table 4.14, the crop pattern in Karialur is given, which shows that the majority of land was used for cultivation of Paddy, Varagu and Tapioca. The tribals of this village experimented Cumbu in few hectares of land, while more land was allotted for Paddy i.e., 109.66 hectares in 1995-96. Similarly, Mango and Cholam crops were raised in the sample villages. Among the crops, the percentage of land was increasing in the case of Paddy where as for Varagu and Tapioca, the percentage of land under cultivation was decreasing after 1994.

The distribution of land in Vellimalai is given in table 4.15. Though Vellimalai is also an important village like

Karialur with more Government offices, schools, bus stand etc., the land used for purposes other than cultivation was only 0.71 per cent and 0.77 per cent is 1994-95 and 1995-96 respectively. Further, grazing land reported only in Vellimalai. Similarly, land unfit for cultivation fluctuated from 2.62 per cent in 1989-90 to 1.70 per cent in 1998-99. The forestland has varied between 59.66 per cent and 64.48 per cent from 1989 to 1999. The fluctuation in the forestland and the other categories of land had actually changed the net cultivated land in the study period as seen in the table.

It is clear from table 4.16, that in Vellimalai also the predominant crops were Paddy, Varagu and Tapioca. In 1990-91, 1994-95 and 1995-96, the emphasis was also given to Samai crop cultivated in 27.25 per cent, 17.38 per cent and 12.36 per cent of land respectively. Further, the increase of land on Samai crop was at the expenses of land under Varagu crop. In 1994-95 Tapioca was cultivated to the lowest of 0.75 hectares due to poor rainfall and the land was used in experimenting Motchai and Cholam crops.

The forestland in Vazhapady as found in table 4.17 was the maximum of 78.2 per cent in 1994-95 and 77.99 per cent in 1997-98. The 1.71 per cent of land unfit from cultivation disappeared after 1989-90 and the land used for purposes other than cultivation had decreased from 2.07 per cent in 1990-91 to 0.03 per cent in 1994-1995 and 1995-1996.

Further, even with decreasing extent of current fallows, the net cultivated land fluctuated from 19.74 per cent (1991-92) to 24.61 per cent (1998-99). Unlike, the previous villages, the variation in the forest land did not change the net cultivated land. Since, the village is an inaccessible tribal area more extent of forestland was reported in the table.

According to Table 4.189, in Vazhapady, the tribals cultivated only four crops. It is the only sample village where tribals have raised a few crops from 1989 to 1999. The table shows that Varagu became the predominant crop from 1992, while Paddy, Tapioca and Ragi crops were also cultivated with considerable fluctuation of land.

In Kundiyanatham, a vast area of forestland is reported in the study period as seen in Table 4.19. The net cultivated land varied between 12.62 per cent and 14.5 per cent during 1989 to 1995. Moreover, this is the village with lesser extent of land used for cultivation compared to other sample villages. As observed in the table, the land unfit for cultivation was increasing form 0.13 per cent in 1989-90 to 1.16 per cent in 1994-95 and 1.81 per cent in 1998-99.

It is evident from table 4.20 that in Kundiyanatham also about 10 types of crops were raised by the tribals. Here again, Paddy and Varagu formed the major crops and the other 8 crops as shown in the table were cultivated in a distributed manner. Another interesting feature was that more area of land was used for raising pulses in the village with the maximum of 65.24 hectares in 1992-93. Further, in the same year, the lowest extent of 20.15 hectares was used for cultivating Paddy. On the other hand, in 1995-96 about 48.54 hectares of land was brought under Tapioca, which shows that the transition was in favour of raising commercial crops in the village.

Kendikkal is one of the interior and inaccessible villages of the hills. The distribution of land of this village as given in Table 4.21 shows that the total village land was 1927.81 hectares in all the years from 1989. The forest land was 69.88 per cent and 67.4 per cent in 1994-1995 and 1995-1996 respectively. Further, the variation in the forestland influenced the extent of net cultivated land from 1989 to 1999. The current fallow and other fallow lands were brought under use in 1995-96.

In Table 4.22, the crop pattern in Kendikkal is presented. This depicts that Varagu, Paddy and Tapioca were the predominant crops of the eight crops cultivated by the tribals. However, only in 1989-90, about 60.37 per cent of land was under Paddy crop and after that it showed only a decreasing trend. On the other hand, more area of land was used to grow Varagu and Tapioca in 1995-96.

In Table 4.23, the distribution of land of Pottiyam village is presented. The data in the table delineates that the forestland fluctuated from 59.25 per cent of the total land from 1989-90 to 67.36 per cent in 1998-99. Of all the villages of the hills, Pottiyam is important, because it is the village of the erstwhile Jagirs and also located close to the Gomugidam. With all these, the net cultivated land was 27.56 per cent in 1989-90 and 20.55 per cent in 1998-99. Further, the variation in the net cultivated land was due to the change in the forest land. Moreover, in this village more land was used for purposes other than cultivation, compared to other sample villages. In addition, the current fallows and land unfit for cultivation had also affected the area under cultivation. Even though, the village is located in the lower hills slopes of the hills, nothing about grazing land and trees and garden land was reported.

The Crop pattern in Pottiyam as shown in Table 4.24 portrays that the tribals of the Village are the progressive farmers who cultivated the maximum numbers of 16 crops in the Kalrayan hills. Since, the village is located very near to the Gomugi Dam; Paddy was cultivated, in more area of land. Further, Groundnut, Plantain, Tapioca, and sugarcane were also cultivated in more land area of the village. Moreover, the distribution of land in other crops also shows their advanced farming method adopted by the farmers in the village. It is very important to note that the gross area sown was more than the net cultivated land as shown in Table 4.24. Therefore, the crop rotation and cropping pattern from 1989 onwards indicates that the Pottiyam tribals are the model tribals of the hills in agriculture.

The distribution of land in various categories of land in Malliampady from 1989 to 1999 is presented in Table 4.25. The village is located in the lower hills slopes of Kalrayan hills. The forestland varied from 57.33 per cent (1991-92) to 63.15 per cent (1998-99). This table portrays that current fallows and fallow land fit for cultivation were responsible for a comparatively lower percentage of net cultivated land. However, the net cultivated land showed an increasing trend from 23.80 per cent in 1994-95 to 33.70 per cent in 1998-99.

The crop pattern in Malliampady shown in Table 4.26 portrays that only nine different crops were raised from 1989 to 1999, of the crops, Varagu, Paddy and Plantain were the major crops raised with considerable variation in the use of land. Unlike the other villages discussed above, tribals in this village had attempted Turmeric and they have use of land increased from 0.67 per unit in 1989-90 to 5.68 per cent in 1998-99. Moreover, the area under plantain was also more than all other sample villages, but, land under tapioca was decreasing after 1992-93 and more land was used for raising Plantain.

It is clear from the distribution of land in the Kalrayan hills as well as in all the nine sample villages that the tribals encroached into forest and the forest land was influenced by the cultivated lands of the tribals. This is much against the Forest Conservation Act of the State. Further, when the forest officials deny the entry of tribal into forest area the fluctuation was found in the forest area. It is inferred from the official sources that the tribals entry in to deep forest is prohibited while the use of forest and located near the village site is not that much controlled. However, there were cases booked against tribals using such lands in the hills. The cropping pattern in the Kalrayan hills and the sample villages, explains that the type of distribution of land is favourable to raise dry crops. In the hills, commercial crops are cultivated in dry land condition and hence the return is not attractive as explained in chapter VI of the thesis. However, the farming system evolved by the native tribals and the number of crops raised by them indicate their farm skills. Obviously, this analysis should form the basis for implementing any agricultural programme in the hills area. Presently, the tribals in the upper hills cultivate on average 10 crops, in which paddy, Varagu, Samai and Tapioca occupy the prime position, while in the lower hills slopes in addition to the four crops mentioned above, and they grow plantain, groundnut and pulses.

References

1. Government of Tamil Nadu: A Note on the Achievements under Tribal Sun-Plan in Kalrayan Hills 1976-77 to 1984-85, (Issued by Director of Adi-dravidar and Tribal Welfare, Ezhilagan, Chennai) p. 2.
2. Madras Institute of Development Studies, *Tamil Nadu Economy: Performance and Issues,* (Oxford and IBH Publishing Co. Pvt., Ltd., New Delhi; 1988), p. 5.
3. *Ibid.*, p. 6.
4. Manual of South Arcot District, Compiled by J.H.Garstin M.C.S. Collector of South Arcot (Lawrence Asylum Press, Madras; 1878), p. 375
5. Government of Tamil Nadu: A Note on the Achievements *op. cit.*, p. 6.
6. Ramanathan, S. *Tribal Welfare in Kalrayan hills (SADt.) Role of Government and Voluntary Welfare Agencies* (Madras Institute of Development studies, Chennai, 1977) p. 14.
7. Government of Tamil Nadu: A Note on the Achievements, *Ibid.*, p. 7.
8. Manual of South Arcot District, *op. cit.*, pp. 374-76.
9. Government of Tamil Nadu: A Note on the achievements, *op. cit.*, p. 8
10. Government of Tamil Nadu: Report of the Committee on Welfare of Scheduled Tribes, February 1976, p. 11 and 12.

11. Ramanathan, S. *op. cit.*, p. 15.

12. The Sundary Standard (Special setup for Kalrayan hills development) Published from Chennai, August 22, 1976, p. 5.

13. The Hindu (New Life for Tribes of Kallakuruchi Taluk) Published at Chennai, August 22, 1976.

14. District Census Handbook 1972, South Arcot District, Vol. 11, pp. 284-85, Census 1961, Vol. IX, Part V, A (11) and the area map as per 1971 and 1981 census are given in annexure.

15. According to Article 342 (1) of the Constitution of India, "The President (may with respect to any state [or Union Territory], and where it is a state after consultation with the Governor there of) by public notification, specify the tribes or tribal communities or parts of or groups within tribes or tribal communities which shall for the purpose of this Constitution be deemed to be Scheduled Tribes in relating to that State (or Union Territory, as the case may be), as quoted in The Constitution of India, p. 218 and 219.

16. Census reports of 1981 and 1991.

17. Ramanathan, S. *op.cit.* p. 2 and according to Census of India, 1961, Vol. IV (Madras) Part V-A (i), p. 19, "If the tribals migrate to some other area during the Census enumeration works, they will not be included in the census. Hence these people disappear and reappear from census after census.

18. Government of Tamil Nadu: A note on the Achievements, *op. cit.* pp. 14-17.

19. Census of India, Series-1, Paper-2 of 1991, Final Population Totals.

20. Madras Institute of Development Studies, *op. cit.*, p. 56.

5

Progress of Land Reforms in the Kalrayan Hills

As discussed in the previous chapter, the situation in the Kalrayan hills demanded, drastic remedial measures. Perhaps this is to establish an egalitarian social order in pursuance of the National Goal as enshrined in the Constitution of India. To quote the Report of the Commissioner, "Equity for the weaker sections of the society, therefore, is the moving spirit of the Constitutional schema and permeates the same. The founding fathers realised the intrinsic culpability of iniquitous forces embedded in the social systems, economic institutions and also political organisations, both old and new, particularly in relation to certain vulnerable sections of the society. They, therefore, considered it necessary to provide specific safeguards in the constitution in their favour."[1] Under this, predestine steps are taken by the Government of Tamil Nadu to put an end to all disabilities, exploitation, social and economic injustices, that was persisting for centuries in the Kalrayan hills. Such of those measures are (1) Land Reforms (2) Abolition of bondage and (3) Package measures to supplement land reforms.

Land Reform Measures

The principal acts on land reforms in Tamil Nadu are :

1. The Tamil Nadu Land Reforms (Fixation of Ceiling on Land) Act, 1961 (Tamil Nadu Act 58 of 1961).

2. The Inam Estate (Abolition and Convertion in to Ryotwari) Act of 1963 and the Madras Inam (Supplementary) Act, 1963 (Madras Act 31 of 1963).

These Acts are commonly applied to solve land issues in both non-tribal and tribal areas of the state. The Inam Estate (Abolition and Convertion into Ryotwari) Act of 1963 was used to take over the Kalrayan hills from the Jagirdars in 1976. This is, "An Act to provide for the determination of questions whether any non-ryotwari area in the State of Madras is or is not an existing inam estate, a part of village inam estate, a minor inam or a whole inam village in Pudukottai".[2] Further, "It shall come into force on such date as the State Government may, by notification, appoint... It applies to all non-ryotwari areas in the State of Madras except the Kanyakumari district and the Shencottah taluk of the Tirunelveli District".[3]

Modus Operandi of the Act

The Government of Tamil Nadu, after declaring an area as "Inam area", appoints a Settlement Officer/Officers and who in accordance with the relevant Clauses of the Act issue orders to the concerned parties and publishes it in the District Gazette. Then, the affected party may be Government, landholder, or inamdar, should apply to the settlement officer within three months from the date of issue of the order or from the date of publication in the District Gazette.

Further, "on receipt of an application under sub-section (1) the settlement officer shall after giving notice in the prescribed manner to the applicant, to the State Government, if the State Government is not the applicant, to the landholder or the inamdar, as the case may be, and if the applicant is the landholder or the inamdar, as the case may be, to the person in occupation of the land in the area concerned, and after publishing the notice in the prescribed manner in the village and after giving the parties who appear before him an opportunity to be heard and to adduce their evidence, give his decision whether the non-ryotwari area concerned is an existing inam estate, or a part village inam estate or a minor inam or a whole inam village in Pudukottai".[4]

The aggrieved party, on the nature of the decision of the Settlement Officer, may go for an appeal i.e., within three months from the date of the decision or order. The appeal is to be made before the Tribunal. The Tribunal in its discretion may allow further time not exceeding two months for the filing of any such appeal.[5] The tribunal shall follow such procedure as may be prescribed, while deciding on the appeal. However, the order of the Tribunal shall be liable to revision by the High Court. Thus, "Every decision of the Settlement Officer, subject to any decision of the Tribunal or of the High Court, and every decision of the Tribunal subject to any decision of the High Court shall be binding on all persons claiming an interest in any land in the non-ryotwari area concerned notwithstanding that any such person has not preferred any application or filed any statement or adduced any evidence or appeared or participated in the proceedings before the Settlement Officer, the Tribunal or the High Court, as the case may be".[6]

The said Act was promulgated in the Kalrayan hills and orders were issued to the Jagirdars, stating that the Jagirs are taken over by the Government and they have no jurisdiction over the collection of revenue or on the ownership of land. Such eviction had enkindled a legal battle between the tribal chieftains and the State Government[7] However; the Jagirdars withdrew the case against the Government,[8] and accordingly on 25.8.1976 entire Kalrayan hills was brought under Government's direct administration.

Survey and Settlement of Land

In the post-land reform period, fresh survey and settlement operations were carried out by the Survey and Settlement Department, Government of Tamil Nadu, in accordance with the provisions contained in the Tamil Nadu Survey and Boundaries Act, 1923 (Tamil Nadu Act VIII of 1923). Before implementing the recommendations of Survey and Settlement Team and the decision of the Government, let us see, how allotment of land was made to the tribals in the Kalrayan hills.

Usually in the non-tribal areas, during the land settlement, lands will be assigned in accordance with the extent of acquired land and number of applications from the needy people. The allotment of land according to the Act, "Notwithstanding anything contained in any judgments, decree or order of any court or other authority, all acts done and proceedings taken by any officer or authority under the Principal Act before the date of the publication of this Act in the Tamil Nadu Government Gazette, on the basis that a person who had a right to enjoy the land during his lifetime but had no power to alienate the land was a limited owner under the principal Act and shall, for all purposes be deemed to be and to have always been validly done".[9] Therefore, sale of allotted land is prohibited and the allottees can only enjoy the fruits of the land.

In the tribal areas, land alienation is the issue before the Government of Tamil Nadu. There is no specific Act available in Tamil Nadu to prohibit land alienation in the tribal areas. However, order Numbers 40 and 41 of the Revenue Standing Order, underlines pre-condition for allotment of land and on alienation of tribal land.[10] According to Order Number 40 of the Revenue Standing Order, the allotment of land to the hill tribes is only "conditional assignment". That is, "In the following cases the assignment of land to Malayalis or Sholagas, as the case may be, shall be subject to the condition that the land shall not be transferred by the assignees to any person outside the class to which they belong without the express sanction of the Divisional Officer, and that, if land is transferred without such sanction or is attached and sold by any legal process, it shall be liable to resumption by the Divisional Officer without payment of any compensation whatever.[11] Similarly, Order Number 41 and Clause (III), empowers the Government to re-enter in case of violation of conditions. For instance, if the condition of non-alienation is violated or if the land ceases to be owned by the assignee or his legal heirs or the members of their class after ten years, sale of land or default in payment of tax to the Government,[12] then the Government may re-enter and take possession of the assigned land. Therefore, it is the conditional assignment of land to the tribals. The crucial recommendation of the Survey Team on the distribution of land in the Kalrayan hills is given in Table 5.1.

Table 5.1 : Progress of Land Reform in the Kalrayan Hills-1979-80 (in hectares)

Sl. No.	*Categories of Land*	*Extent of Land*	*Percentage*
1.	Land distributed	8153.02.0	14.22
2.	Land declared as forest	10112.95.0	17.64
3.	Old forest land	35395.06.0	61.72
4.	Poramboke land	1862.34.0	3.25
5.	Fallow land	1104.02.0	1.93
6.	Unrecognised fallows	716.21.0	1.24
	Total	57343.60.0	100.00

Source: Government of Tamil Nadu: Taluk office of Vellimalai located at Kallakuruchi.

The Table 5.1 reveals that, the total land allotted to the tribals was 8153.02 hectares (14.22 per cent). On the other hand, the forestland including the land declared as forestland comes to 79.36 per cent of the total land. Moreover, the allotted land to the tribals included their habitation also. Hence, the immediate effect of land reform was shrunk in the moving area of the tribals and land available for cultivation. The plight is that in the new land tenure system, the tribal's entry into forestland is restricted by the forest officials and has resulted in the conflict between the tribals and the forest department.

Table 5.2 : Distribution of Land in the Kalrayan Hills as per Forest Department Records (in hectares)

Sl.No.	*Categories of Land*	*Extent of Land*	*Percentage*
1.	Actual Forest	45225	79.19
2.	Wet land	997	1.75
3.	Dry land	7052	12.35
4.	Other paramboke land	1842	3.23
5.	Assessed waste-dry	1205	2.10
6.	Assessed waste-wet	12	0.02
7.	Un-assessed land	778	1.36
	Total	56111	100.00

Source: Government of Tamil Nadu: Forest Department, Kalrayan hills.

The distribution of land as per revenue records (Table 5.1) and forest department records (Table 5.2) shows little variation. The total land according to the revenue records is 57343.60 hectares, while it is 57111 hectares in the forest department records. Further, forestland in the Forest

Table 5.3 : Progress of Land Reforms in the Sample Villages from 1979 to 1996 (in Hectares)

Sl. No.	*Name of the Village*	*Area distributed*		*Area declared as forest*		*Old forest land*		*Total forest land*		*Total village land*	
		1979-80	*1988-89**	*1979-80*	*1988-89***	*1979-80*	*1988-89***	*1979-80*	*1988-89***	*1979-80*	*1988-89***
1.	Kendikkal	246.82.0	296.20.0	326.01.0	—	1249.62.0	—	1575.63.0	1631.61.0	1928.81.0	1927.81.0
		(12.80)	(15.36)	(16.91)		(64.82)		(81.73)	(84.64)	(100.00)	(100.00)
2.	Vellimalai	112.44.0	233.63.0	105.84.0	—	750.19.0	—	865.03.0	847.79.0	1081.42.0	1081.42.0
		(10.4)	(21.6)	(9.79)		(69.37)		(79.99)	(78.4)	(100.00)	(100.00)
3.	Vazhapady	177.78.0	179.46.0	178.05.0	—	1028.18.0	—	1353.14.0	1380.96.0	1578.89.0	1578.9.0
		(11.26)	(11.37)	(11.28)		(65.12)		(85.7)	(87.46)	(100.00)	(100.00)
4.	Karailur	25185.0	351.43.0	150.27.0	—	455.63.0	—	605.90.0	580.49.0	955.25.0	955.25.0
		(26.36)	(36.79)	(15.73)		(57.7)		(63.43)	(60.77)	(100.00)	(100.00)
5.	Movadipattu	153.45.0	152.51.0	190.66.0	—	495.43.0	—	686.09.0	619.44.0	921.77.0	921.77.0
		(16.65)	(17.63)	(20.68)		(53.75)		(74.43)	(67.21)	(100.00)	(100.00)
6.	Nochimedu	32.52.0	34.25.0	105.54.0	—	402.71.0	—	508.24.0	518.53.0	561.88.0	561.88.0
		(5.79)	(6.1)	(18.78)		(71.67)		(90.45)	(92.28)	(100.00)	(100.00)
7.	Kundiyanatham	111.70.0	112.64.0	203.49.0	—	1166.77.0	—	1370.26.0	1386.8	1523.15.0	1523.15.0
		(7.33)	(7.4)	(13.36)		(76.6)		(89.96)	(91.04)	(100.00)	(100.00)
8.	Pottiyam	273.34.0	260.41.0	105.00.0	—	733.32.0	—	838.32.0	957.116.0	1325.88.0	1325.88.0
		(20.62)	(19.64)	(7.92)		(55.31)		(63.23)	(72.19)	(100.00)	(100.00)
9.	Malliampady	390.15.0	290.54.0	105.05.0	—	1028.18.0	—	1136.23.0	1252.92.0	1716.88.0	1716.88.0
		(22.72)	(16.92)	(6.12)		(59.89)		(66.18)	(72.97)	(100.00)	(100.00)

Values in parentheses are percentages to the total.

Source: 1. Government of Tamil Nadu: Taluk Office, Kallakuruchi for 1979-80 and 1988-89.

2. Government of Tamil Nadu: Taluk Office, Sankarapuram after the bifurcation of District for 1995-96 period.

**The extent of land found for the year 1988-89 is also same for the year 1998-99.

Department records does not have any classification of land as in the Revenue record that is land declared as forest and old forestland. However, the total land in forest is about 79 per cent in both the records. Thus, the disputed land in the Revenue records (17.64 per cent) is not taken into account by the Forest Department. Therefore, after the abolition of Jagirs, land alienation in different form (by the Government) is observed in the Kalrayan hills.

Thus, the recommendations of Survey and Settlement Team were implemented in an arbitrary manner. It is because of unscientific and illogical approach of the Survey Team while handling the tribal's land use pattern. That is, they should have studied the land use pattern that prevailed in the pre-reform period, before taking such a crucial decision on land allotment. It is observed during the primary data collection that, the Kalrayan hill tribes classified their land into there viz., Vuzhavu Kadu (plough land), Mettu Kadu (Upper hill land) and Punal Kadu (Land for shifting cultivation). Vuzhavu Kadu was the lands located in the lower hill slopes, i.e., near the village settlement. While, Mettu Kadu was located in between Vuzhavu Kadu and Punal Kadu lands, whereas, Punal Kadu was located on the upper hill slopes adjoin to the forest area. The tribals cultivated these lands by paying specific taxes to the erstwhile Jagirdars. Further, the Jagirdars under the supervision of their ministers regulated those lands. However, such lands were confined to a particular tribal area and tribal families.

The Survey Team should have probed the classification of lands before the recommendation as given in Table No. 5.1. However, the Survey Team mistook the English equivalence of Kadu (Kadu means forest) and subsequently most of the land is reserved as forestland.[13] Further, the Government of Tamil Nadu should have taken into account what had happened in some other tribal areas[14] before proceeding with reform process in the hill.

Yet another hurdle in solving the land issue of the Kalrayan hills is the latest Government Order which totally prohibit further assignment of land to the tribals in order to prevent deforestation, land slide and soil erosion.[15] Ironically, it is not a burning problem in the Kalrayan hills, but it had happened in other hill area and so the order is passed. Therefore, the tangled land issue had created an awful situation in the Kalrayan hills area. This can be solved only by restoring their inherent rights of tribals on land and forest.

Progress of Land Reforms in the Sample Villages

The progress of land reform to the sample villages for the periods 1979, 1989 and 1996 would provide material for the post-reform measures undertaken by the Government. After the initial allotment of land in 1979, lands were assigned to the tribals from 1979 to 1989 and no allotment of land is possible after 1989 due to the Government of Tamil Nadu order. Therefore, the three years chosen here will be sufficient to compare the progress of land reforms in the sample villages, and the data is presented in Table 5.3.

Table 5.3 reveals that land allotted to the tribals was more in Karialur (26.36 per cent), Malliampady (22.72 per cent) and Pottiyam (20.62 per cent) than the other six sample villages for the year 1979-80. The villages have been classified into two:

First, in 1979-80, the land allotted to the tribals was less than the land under dispute between the tribals and the Government. Such villages are Kendikkal (area distributed 246.82 hectares and disputed land 326.01 hectares), Mavadipattu (land distributed 153.45 hectares and disputed land 190.66 hectares), Nochimedu (land distributed 32.53 hectares and disputed 105.54 hectares), and Kundiyanatham (land distributed 111.70 hectares and disputed land 203.49 hectares).

Secondly, in 1979-80, the other sample villages had relatively more land allotted by the Government and lesser extent of disputed land between the tribals and the Government. Those villages were Vellimalai (112.44 hectares) of allotted land and 105.84 hectares of disputed land. In Karialur, land allotted was 251.85 hectares, area under dispute was 150.27 hectares, and Malliampady (land distributed 390.15 hectares and land under dispute 105.05 hectares).

Further, in the first group of villages, the total forestland was more than the second group of villages. Moreover, the villages in the second group are relatively advanced villages than the first group of villages. That is, Vellimalai contains the headquarters of Block Development Office, LAMP Society, market place and bus stand. Pottiyam is located in the lower hill slope near the Gomuki Dam and the village of one of the erstwhile Jagirdars. Karialur village has a good school run by Arcot Luthrane Church and many Government Offices. Finally, Malliampady village is located in the lower hill slopes of the hill. Thus, the disputed land was more in the other five villages because these villages are inaccessible and relatively less advanced in socio-economic conditions.

In relation to this, the land situation in 1988-89 and 1995-96 was improved in most of the villages. The land area declared as forest was totally nil in 1988-89 and 1995-96 respectively. On the other hand, the area allotted also increased in village like Kendikkal, Villimalai, Vazhapady, Karialur, Mavadipattu, Nochimedu and Kundiyanatham. In Pottiyam and Malliampady, the area under dispute had decreased and the total forestland has increased in 1988-89 and 1995-96. Similarly, the old forestland had totally disappeared in all the sample villages. Therefore, in order to put an end to the disputed land the Government of Tamil Nadu allotted fresh land here and there in the villages and simply added the rest of the land into the forest land. This is vividly seen in the increase of forestland in the villages except for a marginal decrease in Vellimalai, Karialur and Mavadipattu.

Abolition of Bondage

The special situation of the Kalrayan hills, demanded the removal of hereditary bondage to implement welfare measures in the hill. Therefore, the Government of Tamil Nadu released about 24,945 tribals from slavery and hereditary bondage, by using The Bonded Labour System (Abolition) Act,1976 (Central Act 19 of 1976). According to the report of the Government, as on 25.8.1976, "the tribal population was not under any obligation or compulsion to render their services of labour to the Jagirdars".[16]

Package Measures

Land reform measures would be successful, only if it is followed by package measures to support the allottees, financially and technically. Such measures are very much needed for the tribals, because, they have to start cultivation afresh in the lands allotted by the Government. The package measure that are implemented in the Kalrayan hills are schemes relating to agriculture, forest, cooperatives, land reforms, minor irrigation, soil conservation, education, minimum needs programme, village and small industries and ecology and environment.[17] The Special Central Assistance from the Tribal Sub-Plan outlay and from the State Plan schemes funds these schemes.

Agricultural programmes contain distribution of improved seeds of paddy, millets, pulses and wheat, matched with a programme of education process to adopt the new technology with new chemical fertilizer, pesticide and new farm protection measures.[18] These inputs were distributed to the tribals from 1976 to 1980, on an ad hoc manner. Whereas, from 1980-81 onwards the inputs are supplied to the tribals based on individual family needs.

Table 5.4 : Development Programmes for Agriculture in the Kalrayan Hills from 1976 to 1999

Sl. No.	Year	Seed in Acres	Fertilizers in Acres	Pesticide in Acres	Fruit Plants		Agricultural Implements Distributed	Training	Tour	Subsidy (per cent)
					Number Distributed	Area Covered in Acres				
1.	1976-77	281	25	Nil	10294	225	700	Nil	Nil	100
2.	1977-78	1243	196	220	46470	382	600	400	154	100
3.	1978-79	1995	340	700	85075	Nil	2055	Nil	Nil	90
4.	1979-80	2145	744	Nil	35600	300	85	400	151	75
5.	1980-81	3522	1010	1700	Nil	Nil	1000	500	150	75
6.	1981-82	360	480	440	Nil	Nil	Nil	300	147	75
7.	1982-83	360	380	480	Nil	60	Nil	150	150	75
8.	1983-84	195	240	480	Nil	60	Nil	300	150	75
9.	1984-85	145	145	1200	Nil	60	Nil	300	150	75
10.	1985-86	600	600	1200	Nil	60	Nil	300	150	75
11.	1986-87	600	600	1200	Nil	60	Nil	300	150	75
12.	1987-88	600	600	1200	Nil	60	Nil	300	150	75
13.	1988-89	600	600	1200	Nil	Nil	Nil	200	100	75
14.	1989-90	600	600	1200	Nil	Nil	Nil	200	100	75
15.	1990-91	600	600	1200	Nil	Nil	Nil	200	100	75
16.	1991-92	600	600	1200	Nil	Nil	Nil	200	100	75

(Contd.)

(Table 5.4 Contd.)

Sl. No.	*Year*	*Seed in Acres*	*Fertilizers in Acres*	*Pesticide in Acres*	*Fruit Plants*		*Agricultural Implements Distributed*	*Training*	*Tour*	*Subsidy (per cent)*
					Number Distributed	*Area Covered in Acres*				
17.	1992-93	600	600	1200	Nil	Nil	Nil	200	100	75
18.	1993-94	600	600	1200	Nil	Nil	Nil	200	100	75
19.	1994-95	600	600	1200	Nil	Nil	Nil	200	100	75
20.	1995-96	600	600	1200	Nil	Nil	Nil	200	100	75
21.	1996-97	600	600	1200	Nil	Nil	Nil	200	100	75
22.	1997-98	600	600	1200	Nil	Nil	Nil	200	100	75
23.	1998-99	600	600	1200	Nil	Nil	Nil	200	100	75
24.	1999-2000	600	600	1200	Nil	Nil	Nil	200	100	75

Source: Government of Tamil Nadu: Annual Tribal Sub-Plans from 1976-1996, Director of Adi-Dravidar and Tribal Welfare, Chennai.

Table No. 5.4 depicts all the assistance provided by the Government to the tribals from 1976 onwards. The financial and other assistance of the Government to the tribals with 100 per cent subsidy from 1976 to 1978, then 90 per cent subsidy from 1978 to 1979 and 75 per cent from 1980 onwards.

In order to increase the agricultural production, high-yielding varieties of seeds are supplied to the tribals. The quantity of seed distributed to the tribals was 983 kilograms in 1976 and increased to 22,914 kilograms in 1980. It is an achievement to the Government, but it is observed during the primary data collection that these seeds are not suitable for cultivation in the Kalrayan hills, because most of the lands are rain fed. Therefore, the tribals continued to sow only the Punal Kadu Nellu (local paddy seed).

Similarly, fertilizers and pesticide distributed, covered 25 acres to 1200 acres of land. This extent of coverage is very negligible and the method of identification of needy tribals is not clearly explained. Further, distribution of fruit plants, and agricultural implements were stopped after 1980. Similarly, the demonstration plots, tour and visit system failed to achieve the desired result. It is because, "No Government has accepted boldly the adverse effects of malfunctioning of the system with the result that there has been ambivalence in the State's policies, programme and action".[19]

Large Size Multipurpose Societies

In December 1971, a study team was appointed under the chairmanship of K.S. Bawa to review the co-operative structure in tribal development project areas. The committee recommended organising of a Large-size Multipurpose Societies (LAMPS) in the tribal areas. The LAMPS are to function on the line of both co-operative credit and non-credit societies in the tribal areas They will provide term loans for agriculture, consumption needs of the tribals, technical advice, to help the tribals to market their produce at a very profitable price, sericulture, animal husbandry, poultry, piggery etc.[20] The LAMPS are meant to provide such facilities for the tribals to reduce the possibility of exploitation by contractors and others in the tribal areas.

In Tamil Nadu, there are 18 such LAMP Co-operative Societies in nine Integrated Tribal Development Project (ITDP) areas. These societies are providing single window service for production, consumer credit, supply of agricultural inputs, marketing of agricultural and allied minor forest products, supply of essential commodities, primary processing, encouraging through savings and providing technical services.[21] In the Kalrayan hills only in 1980-81, three such LAMP Societies were formed at Vellimalai, Kilakkadu and Mottampatti. The working of LAMP cooperatives in Kalrayan hills, clearly indicate that there is a large-scale violation of admitting non-tribals as members into the LAMPS. The LAMPS at Mottampatti, the lower hill group of the Block Development Offices, registered more non-tribals (639) than the other two societies (i.e. 138 in Kilakkadu and 95 in Vellimalai). The financial assistance to LAMPS through ITDP schemes also benefited the non-tribals. Such policies would attract the entry of non-tribals in large numbers and usurp all the benefits that are for tribals.

LAMPS in the study area perform the functions of co-operative credit societies and non-credit societies, just like the co-operative credit societies in the non-tribal areas of the State. It is observed during the primary data collection that the tribals are willing to avail only the loans and facilities provided by the LAMPS. The total loan outstanding from 29.9.1987 to 31.3.1996 for the LAMP society at Vellimalai was Rs. 29, 87,119. The special officer of the Society informed that, event though the Revenue Standing Order No. (41) Clause (IV) empower the authority to attach the lands of defaulting tribes, who could not do so because of the Government order prohibiting the authorities to precede any legal action against the defaulting tribals. It is also noted that the tribals prefer to sell their produce to the contractors and outsiders rather than to the LAMPS, because, they get not only more price but also credit and money on time. Further, the LAMPS cannot fix up a higher procurement price due to official reasons and Societies Acts. Therefore, revamping LAMPS is essential. Accordingly, a committee to review the working of LAMPS was formed under the Chairmanship of B.Sivarman and he submitted the report in 1981. The main observations are: Non-LAMPS Primary Societies and LAMPS simultaneously perform and confuse the tribals; the performance of LAMPS lags behind the functioning of service co-operatives in the non-tribal areas; and coverage of tribal members is inadequate and in some states, the average working capital for LAMPS is minimum.[22] With an average working capital earmarked, LAMPS continue to function in the tribals with the same problems mentioned above.

The Tribal Co-operative Marketing Federation of India Limited

In addition to LAMPS, The Tribal Co-operative Marketing Development Federation of India Limited (TRIFED) is organised under the auspicious of the Ministry of Welfare, Government of India, since 1988. It is providing marketing support to the State Tribal Co-operative Federation of Forest Corporation, for marketing and in export of minor forest products and surplus agricultural produce of the tribals, to protect them from exploitation by the private traders. The objectives of TRIFED are : to ensure full utilisation of natural products of tribal areas by improving their marketability; to ensure higher earning and employment opportunities through suitable economic schemes; to provide marketing support to State Co-operative Federation or Forest Cooperation and boost-up their economic and commercial viability; to identify the minor forest produce in different states for taking them up for co-operative marketing; and to recommend fixation of uniform procurement price of minor forest products by each state.[23]

The objectives of TRIFED resemble some of the functions of LAMPS. Even though the scheme was introduced in 1988, the effective functioning is yet to begin in the tribal areas. However, it is a major step taken by the Government to decentralise LAMPS from performing cooperative non-credit functions.

Cooperative Farming

In addition to LAMPS and TRIFED, Cooperative farming is also a prevailing system in the tribal areas. Cooperative farming as understood today is an organisation of the farmers, which comes into existence because of the serious efforts to effect certain socio-economic changes by extending the principles of co-operation to agriculture. In a co-operative farming society of substantial size it is possible to eliminate several wasteful operations and to ensure better planning of the use of land, including selection of crops, rotation, soil conservation, development of irrigation and introduction of improved techniques. Economies that cannot be availed of by small farms are available to large ones.[24] Co-operative farming of general type is implemented in the tribal areas.

The working of co-operative farming is part of ITDP and LAMPS in the Kalrayan hills. However, it is not implemented as suggested[25] by the policy makers. Co-operative farming in the hill is implemented under the Control of the Registrar of Cooperative Societies, Government of Tamil Nadu. The apex body invites the proposal for cooperative farming from each area and on approval sanctions money through ITDP and LAMP schemes. Table 5.5 gives information about the cooperative farming in the Kalrayan hills.

Table 5.5 : Cooperative Farming in Kalrayan Hills-1994-95 (in Rupees)

Sl. No.	*Purpose of Grant*	*LAMPS* *Velli-malai*	*Killa-kadu*	*Nottam-patti*
1.	Share capital subsidy		20400	
2.	Interest-subsidy	3960	20830	13100
3.	Transport subsidy	10000	10000	10000
4.	Subsidy for drivers pay and maintenance of vehicles	19000	19000	s19000
5.	Managerial subsidy	18000	18000	18000
6.	Employment of Managing Director	45000	45000	45000
7.	Subsidy for construction of strong room	12055	12055	120055
	Total	108015	145285	117155

Source: Government of Tamil Nadu: Office of the Registrar of Co-operative Societies, Madras.

The co-operative farming outlay as portrayed in Table 5.5 shows only the items of expenditure as found in the outlays of LAMPS. Further, in the hill, practically the tribals reported no such scheme during the primary data collection and during the subsequent visits of the researcher. Moreover, the purpose of grant listed in Table 5.5 Projects that majority of the grant is used for the maintenance of the office and vehicles and not the scheme.

The progress of land reforms in the Kalrayan hills explains that the Government was successful while taking over the hill, but failed miserably at the time of implementing the programme. On the other hand, the procedure and various sections of the Acts had only confused the illiterate tribals and resulted in the incomplete post-reform measures. The extent of disputed land between the Government and the tribals is absent in the records of the Government, but, it is not so when the tribals reported about the disputed land, during the primary data collection (details are given in

Chapter VI of the book). Hence, all these facts affirm only for the incomplete implementation of land reforms in the hill. Similarly, the package schemes are not need-based and merely an extension of state plan schemes meant for non-tribals.

References

1. Government of India: Report of the Commissioner for Scheduled Castes and Scheduled Tribes, (Manager of Publication, New Delhi, 28th Report, 1986-1987) p. 1.

2. Government of Tamil Nadu: The Madras Inams (Supplementary Act of 1963).

3. *Ibid.*

4. *Ibid.*, p. 3.

5. *Ibid.*, p. 3 and as per Section 115 of the Code of Civil Procedure, 1908 (Central Act V of 1908).

6. *Ibid.*, p. 3.

7. Government of Tamil Nadu: A Sub-Plan for Tribal Development (For Implementation in the Fifth Five Year Plan), published in August 1974, p. 53. According to the report, "another contributory factor to tribal indebtedness is the unsettled land tenure in some of the areas particularly in places like the Kalrayan Hills, for as the Kalrayan Hill concerned the Court, and the parties to the dispute are the Jagirdars on the one side and the Government on the others", and also refer chapter IV.

8. Government of Tamil Nadu: A Note on the Achievements of Tribal Sub-Plan, *op. cit.*, p. 10.

9. Government of Tamil Nadu: The Tamil Nadu Land Reforms (Fixation of Ceiling on Land) Act, 1961 (Tamil Nadu Act 58 of 1961), (As modified up to the 31st August 1980), p. 113.

10. Government of Tamil Nadu: Standing Orders of the Board of Revenue (Land Revenue, Settlement and Miscellaneous),

issued under the authority of the Board of Revenue, Vol. 1 and Chapter I.

11. *Ibid.*, p. 110.

12. *Ibid.*, p. 115.

13. First hand information from the tribals during the primary data collection.

14. Government of Tamil Nadu: Report of the Commissioner, *op. cit.*, p. 27. "The most notable example is that of Mirzapur in Uttar Pradesh in which case the Supreme Court has ordered fresh proceedings from the very beginning. In the case of ex-jagirdari forests, reservation orders were issued on the premise that the State had stepped into the shoes of the erstwhile owners, disregarding the informal arrangements under which the people had been cultivating the lands-same on payment of token rent or some for nominal services to the chief. The most notable example is that of 'warkas' and 'dali' lands in Maharashtra which have not even been formally taken note of by the State Government. These people subsisting on land in forests have been deemed to be in unauthorised possession. Thirdly, the decision of the State Governments from time to time to regularise unauthorised occupations in forests and reach an amicable solution got invariably enmeshed in the procedural issues, delays and admissibility of evidence regarding possession on a specified date".

15. The Government of Tamil Nadu Order, *op. cit.*

16. Government of Tamil Nadu: Revenue Department letter No. 220053/Y1/76-2 dated 299.3.1976 and No. A7/8350/76 dated 5.12.1977, as taken from the Note on the Achievements of Tribal Sub-Plan, *op. cit.*, p. 11.

17. Government of Tamil Nadu: A Note on the Achievements of Tribal Sub-Plan, *op. cit.*

18. Government of Tamil Nadu: Director of Adi-Dravidar and Tribal Welfare, Chennai, Annual Tribal Sub-Plan 1988-90.

19. Government of India: Report of the Commissioner, *op. cit.*, p. 95.

20. Gupta, Dipankar. "Integrated Tribal Development Programme: An Evaluation of ITDP in Birbhm District, West Bengal" in M.L. Dantwala *et al.*, *Asian Seminar on Rural Development: The Indian Experience*, (Oxford and IBH Publishing Co. Pvt. Ltd., New Delhi, ed. 1986) p. 101.

21. Government of Tamil Nadu: Annual Tribal Sub-Plan, 1992-93 and 1995-96.

22. Government of India: Report of the Commissioner *op. cit.*, p. 392.

23. Government of Tamil Nadu: Annual Tribal Sub-Plan, 1992-93.

24. Government of India: Progress of Land Reform (Planning Commission, New Delhi, 1963) p. 225.

25. Government of India: Second Five Year Plan-Draft Framework, (Planning Commission, New Delhi), "while organising cooperative farming: Ownership of land may be retained by a member. The member must-accept the decision of the co-operatives and he will be compensated in the form of dividend; ownership of land may be transferred to the co-operatives, but share representation value of the land may be given to the members; and the land may be leased to the cooperatives for a specified period and the rent payment may be prescribed by the Law" p. 202.

6

Analysis of the Tribal Economy of Kalrayan Hill

In India, the variation in the socio-economic conditions of the people is a serious issue before the planners and policy makers. Any package programme for the uplift of the weaker section is aimed with dual goal of achieving social as well as economic development. Further, such programmes for the tribals should be framed, by taking cognisance of the special situation of the tribal people and tribal areas. Moreover, these schemes meant for their economic development and not to distort their cultural and social institution. Keeping these in view, a study of their socio-economic situation is all the more essential to asses the path of the tribal development schemes implemented in the tribal areas. To quote Barraclough, "If we are really serious about wanting to encourage development policies that benefit the low-income rural classes, a great deal more attention must be paid to the analysis of social structures and political processes. Development is not just economics or sociology or technology but history. How it proceeds depends to a large extent on how power is distributed among different social groups.... Rural development for the low-income majorities requires fundamental and often revolutionary reforms in social institutions...."[1]

In this chapter, an attempt is made to examine the prevailing socio-economic conditions, statistical analysis of agricultural production of the tribals and test of hypotheses.

Analysis of Socio-economic Conditions

Social Characteristics

The social features of the sample population analysed here are the size of family, age, caste, occupation-wise distribution of sample tribals and finally the literacy level of the tribals.

Size of Family

The size of family to a large extent influences employment, income, savings, investment and also determines the production activity of the households. The size of family represents the average number of persons per tribal family. As per 1981 census, in India the size of family was 4.71 in general and 4.61 in the rural areas in particular. On the other hand, it was much below the country's data of 5.55 and 5.59 respectively. On the other hand, in Kalrayan Hills, the family size was 5.63 as per 1981 and 3.91 in 1991 census. The decrease in the family size from 5.63 to 3.91 was due to an increase in the number of households i.e., from 5820 (1981) to 7550 (1991), with a slow growth of population and higher degree of nucleation of families. The following table 6.1 portrays the size of family in the sample villages.

The size of family depicted in table 6.1 resembles the size of family as reported in the 1991 census report. That is, as per 1991 census the family size was 4.8 in the hill. The firsthand information gathered from the tribals shows that the average size of family was 5.1 and it concentrated more in 3 to 5 (93) and 5 to 7 (39) category than the other groups of up to 3, and 7 to 12 size of family in the hill.

Table 6.1 : Size of Family of the Tribals in the Sample Villages of Kalrayan Hills

Sl. No.	*Name of the Village*	*Size of family upto 3*	*Size of family 3 to 5*	*Size of family 5 to 7*	*Size of family 7 and above*	*Total House holds*	*Total Sample Population*
1	Kendikkal	1	18	10	3	32	163
2	Vellimalai	2	10	4	1	17	78
3	Karialur	2	10	4	5	21	112
4	Mavadipattu	-	9	1	1	11	53
5	Nochimedu	1	2	3	-	6	29
6	Kundiyanatham	-	5	3	1	9	83
7	Vazhapady	1	8	7	2	18	96
8	Pottiyam	2	22	5	2	31	141
9	Malliampady	3	9	2	-	14	56
	Total	12	93	39	15	159	811

Source: Computed.

Further, if we look into the size of family in the sample villages, in the first group (up to 3) there were 3 households in Malliampady, two in Vellimalai, Pottiyam and Karialur. It was only one in other villages and nil in Mavadipattu and Kundiyanatham. On the other hand, in 3 to 5 group it was maximum of 22 in Pottiyam, followed by Kendikkal (18), Karialur (10), and Vellimalai (10) respectively. With regard to 5 to 7 family size, the highest number was Kendikkal (10) while it ranges from 2 to 7 in other villages. Ironically in the 7 to 12 size group, the maximum households were found in Karialur.

The average size of family was high in Kundiyanatham (9.2) and it was 5.3 in Karialur and Vazhapady, 5.1 in Kendikkal, 4.8 in Nochimedu and Mavadipattu, 4.6 in Pottiyam and Vellimalai and 4 in Malliampady. Moreover, no difference in the family size between lower and upper was found in the study.

Age Structure of Sample Tribals

In India, the percentage of children (0-14 years) decreased from 1980 (39.72 per cent) to 1990 (36 per cent). Whereas, the percentage of adults in the working age group (15 to 59 years) increased from 54.07 per cent (1980) to 57.50 per cent (1990). Similarly, the increase was also seen in the old age-group (60 years and above) from 6.21 per cent (1980) to 6.50 per cent (1990). Thus, the national data shows that the dependents comprised 42.50 per cent of the total population in 1990, while the working age-group comprised 57.50 per cent in the same year.[2] The distribution of sample population in age-groups is presented in Table 6.2.

As depicted in table 6.2, a high percentage of population was found in 15-59 age group (50.55 per cent) than the dependents i.e., 0-14 age group (39.59 per cent) and 60 and above (9.86 per cent). Unlike, the other areas of the state, it was peculiar that children in 0-14 age group in the Kalrayan hills were born after the Jagirs were taken over by the Government in 1976. On the other hand two age-groups experienced the effects of pre and post land reform period soil and economic conditions. Further, the 15-59 age groups was predominant in all the sample villages except in Malliampady (0-14 age-group was 50 per cent while 15-59 age-group was 42.86 per cent) and in Kendikkal 0-14 age-group 47.85 per cent and 15-59 age-group was (44.76 per cent). Since, a high percentage of tribals were found in 0-14 age group, if Government declares elementary education as the fundamental right, then it would increase the literacy level of the hill in the future. Similarly, the 15-59 age-group which is considered as "work-force", also demanded a need-based employment policy to improve their living conditions.

Caste

Caste still remains as one of the pivotal factors in the socio-economic structure of people. In those days, caste was associated with a particular craft or occupation. But, presently that system has changed due to social, economic and political awareness of the people. This study is pertaining to tribes and hence the classification of different castes does not arise. According to the Manual of South Arcot, "The hill men are sudras of one caste. There are no Brahmans or Pariahs among them."[3] As already explained the hill men are classified as "Malayali tribes" and constitute 86 per cent of the total population of the hill.[4]

Table 6.2 : Distribution of Sample Population in Different Age Groups (Age in years)

Sl. No.	*Name of the Village*	*0-14*	*15-59*	*60+*	*Total*
1.	Kendikkal	78 (47.85)	73 (44.79)	12 (7.36)	163 (100.00)
2.	Vellimali	28 (35.9)	41 (52.56)	9 (11.54)	78 (100.00)
3.	Vazhapady	41 (42.71)	43 (44.79)	12 (12.5)	96 (100.00)
4.	Karialur	31 (27.68)	68 (60.71)	13 (11.61)	112 (100.00)
5.	Mavadipattu	19 (35.85)	29 (54.72)	5 (9.43)	53 (100.00)
6.	Nochimedu	13 (44.83)	13 (44.83)	3 (10.34)	29 (100.00)
7.	Kundiyanatham	28 (33.73)	43 (51.81)	12 (14.46)	83 (100.00)
8.	Pottiyam	55 (39.09)	76 (53.9)	10 (7.09)	141 (100.00)
9.	Malliampady	28 (50.00)	24 (42.86)	4 (7.14)	56 (100.00)
	Total	321 (39.59)	410 (50.55)	80 (9.86)	811 (100.00)

(Figures in parentheses are percentages to the total).
Source: Computed.

Occupation of Tribals

Occupation of tribals is divided into two viz., farm and non-farm occupation, of which, farm occupation contains employment in agriculture, sericulture and horticulture and the non-farm employment includes works in construction, industries, service sector, off-season non-farm works, employment in Government prospects etc. The details of occupation of tribes are presented in Table 6.3.

Table 6.3 : Occupation Wise Distribution of Sample Tribes in the Kalrayan Hills

Sl. No.	*Name of the Village*	*Farm Occupation*	*Non-Farm Occupation*	*Dependents*	*Total sample Population*
1.	Kendikkal	132	1	30	163
		(8098)	(0.61)	(18.40)	(100.00)
2.	Vellimali	73	—	5	78
		(93.59)		(6.41)	(100.00)
3.	Vazhapady	89	—	7	96
		(92.71)		(7.29)	(100.00)
4.	Karialur	106	—	6	112
		(94.64)		(5.36)	(100.00)
5.	Mavadipattu	46	—	7	53
		(86.79)		(13.21)	(100.00)
6.	Nochimedu	22	—	7	29
		(75.86)		(24.14)	(100.00)
7.	Kundiyanatham	69	—	14	83
		(83.13)		(16.87)	(100.00)
8.	Pottiyam	121	—	20	141
		(85.82)		(14.18)	(100.00)
9.	Malliampady	49	—	7	56
		(87.5)		(12.5)	(100.00)
	Total	707	1	103	811
		(87.18)	(0.12)	(12.7)	(100.00)

(Figures in parentheses are percentages to the total).
Source: Computed.

Table 6.3 indicates that only 0.12 per cent of tribals were engaged in non-farm occupation, 87.18 per cent were in farm occupation, and 12.7 per cent were dependents. Farm occupation occupied the, maximum percentage of the total occupation because it included children, female population and male population in the farm occupation. The village-wise data also shows that more people were engaged in farm occupation. i.e., maximum of 94.64 per cent in Karialur and relatively lower percentage of 75.86 in Nochimedu.

Further, table 6.3 reveals that the non-farm occupation was very meagre (only one tribe was working as a sub-staff in a nationalised bank at Attur). Hence, the tribes mostly take the traditional farm occupation which results in the concentration of more labour in agriculture and it would lead to disguised unemployment in the hill.

Table 6.4 : Literacy Level of Sample Tribals in the Kalrayan Hills

Sl. No.	*Name of the Village*	*Literates*	*Illiterates*	*Total Population*
1.	Kendikkal	20 (12.27)	143 (87.73)	163 (100.00)
2.	Vellimali	12 (15.38)	66 (84.62)	78 (100.00)
3.	Vazhapady	3 (3.13)	93 (96.88)	96 (100.00)
4.	Karialur	25 (22.32)	87 (77.68)	112 (100.00)
5.	Mavadipattu	3 (5.66)	50 (94.34)	53 (100.00)
6.	Nochimedu	5 (17.24)	24 (82.76)	29 (100.00)
7.	Kundiyanatham	18 (21.69)	60 (78.31)	83 (100.00)
8.	Pottiyam	21 (14.89)	120 (85.11)	141 (100.00)
9.	Malliampady	14 (25.00)	42 (75.00)	56 (100.00)
	Total	121 (14.92)	690 (85.08)	811 (100.00)

(Figures in parentheses are percentages to the total).
Source: Computed.

Educational Status of Tribals

Education is an essential component of socio-economic development of any community. Galbraith says that, "education is not something that economic development affords, it is the experience of the older industrial lands that economic development is what education allows".[5] Several studies [6] on the subject expressed the view that the level of education attained is related to such dimensions of development and agricultural productivity. Usually, education is termed as attainment of literacy by schooling or through non-formal education. In the census reports, literacy is defined as the ability to read and write with understanding and this can be achieved only by schooling.

In India, the literacy level of tribals had increased from 11.30 per cent (1971 census) to 23.63 per cent (1991 census). Similarly, in Tamil Nadu the literacy level of tribals showed an increasing trend from 1971 census (9.02 per cent) to 1991 census (23.35 per cent).[7] The literacy levels of the sample tribals are depicted in Table 6.4.

It is vividly seen in Table 6.4 that of the 811 tribals contacted only 15.01 per cent were literates which was much below the percentage of literacy in the state. The village-wise data explains that the literacy was more in Malliampady (25 per cent), Kundiyanatham (27.69 per cent) and Karialur (22.32 per cent) compared to the other sample villages. It was very low in Vazhapady (3.13 per cent) because the village is located in the inaccessible areas of the hill.

Some of the social features of tribals analysed in this section clearly delineates the fact that the tribals of the hill represent the general characteristics of the tribals of the state. Further, the hill area is in transition from Jagir's regime to the Government's direct administration. In such a transitional tribal economy, preservation of their age-old internal structure, cultural and economic system, should be accorded with priority

Table 6.5 : The Total Value of Wealth Composition of Sample Tribals in the Study Area (in Rs.)

Sl. No.	Name of the Village	Value of House	Value of Land	Value of agricultural Implements	Value of Livestock	Value of Consumer Durable	Total Value of Wealth
1.	Kendikkal	90060	192064	17300	109775	98182	5077381
		(17.75)	(37.85)	(3.41)	(21.64)	(19.35)	(100.00)
2.	Vellimali	56675	178806	30230	33000	19768	318479
		(17.8)	(56.14)	(9.49)	(10.36)	(6.21)	(100.00)
3.	Karialur	22525	432243	23539	50650	34145	563102
		(4.00)	(76.76)	(4.18)	(8.99)	(6.06)	(100.00)
4.	Mavadipattu	50750	67496	41936	30100	6850	197132
		(25.74)	(34.24)	(21.27)	(15.27)	(3.47)	(100.00)
5.	Nochimedu	13750	58752	5750	9050	8245	95547
		(14.39)	(61.49)	(6.02)	(9.47)	(8.63)	(100.00)
6.	Kundiyanatham	32325	76302	830	31815	22770	164042
		(19.71)	(46.51)	(0.51)	(19.39)	(13.88)	(100.00)
7.	Vazhapady	60800	207378	6875	67800	49555	392408
		(15.49)	(52.85)	(1.75)	(17.28)	(12.63)	(100.00)
8.	Pottiyam	568.20	626789	74350	75870	67310	901139
		(6.31)	(69.56)	(8.25)	(8.42)	(7.47)	(100.00)
9.	Malliampady	42100	284844	49500	43155	46355	465954
		(9.04)	(61.13)	(10.62)	(9.26)	(9.95)	(100.00)
	Total	425805	2124674	250310	451215	353180	3605184
		(11.81)	(58.93)	(6.94)	(12.52)	(9.8)	(100.00)

(Figures in parentheses are percentages to the total).
Source: Computed.

Analysis of Economic Characteristics of Tribals

The economic features of the tribals, examined here are, wealth composition, land use pattern, cropping pattern, employment, income, expenditure and loans outstanding.

Wealth Composition

A study of wealth distribution of tribals is important, because, it provides information about the type of wealth possessed by the tribals. Further, economic status of an individual varies in accordance with the volume and type of asset owned by him. Moreover, wealth in the form of assets promises a future stream of income. Possession of such wealth is very common in the tribal areas, due to monetization, penetration of market mechanism and all other forces that accentuate the wealth composition of the tribal. The total wealth is computed by taking the money value of those assets at the market rate prevailing in the hill. The wealth composition of the sample tribals are depicted in Table 6.5.

The wealth composition of the sample tribals as given in Table 6.5 reveals that the value of land forms the major proportion of wealth (58.93 per cent) compared to the value of livestock (12.52 per cent), value of house (11.81 per cent), value of consumer durables (9.8 per cent) and value of agricultural implements (6.94 per cent). The high value of land which draws the attention of non-tribals, always attempt all tricks to alienate the valuable land from the tribals as seen in Table 6.6.

Similarly, village wise wealth composition reveals that value of land constitutes more proportion of the total wealth of the tribals than the other forms of wealth. The village-wise data provided in Table 6.5, depicts that the value of land was high in villages located near the main road viz., Karialur or the village with very fertile land like Pottiyam. The value decreased when the villages are located far away from the main road or inaccessible villages like Kendikkal.

Table 6.6 : Land use Pattern of Land among Sample Tribals in the Selected Villages of Vellimalai Taluk (in acres)

Sl. No.	*Name of the Village*	*Area allotted by the Government*	*Area Under Dispute*	*Area sold to*		*Land leased in*	*Total operational area*
				Tribe	*Non-Tribe*		
1	Velliamalai	44.70 (38.63)	66 (57.04)	—	—	5 (4.32)	115.70 (100.00)
2	Karialur	61.75 (48.34)	66 (51.66)	—	—	—	127.75 (100.00)
3	Mavadipattu	27 (26.73)	74 (73.27)	—	—	—	101 (100.00)
4	Kendikkal	76.82 (50.77)	58.5 (39.32)	15 (9.91)	—	—	152.32 (100.00)
5	Vazhapady	82.95 (89.00)	8.25 (8.85)	2 (2.15)	—	—	93.2 (100.00)
6	Kundiyanatham	38.15 (90.51)	4 (9.49)	—	—	—	42.15 (100.00)
7	Nochimedu	23.5 (68.12)	11 (31.88)	—	—	—	34.5 (100.00)
8	Pottiyam	78.35 (62.38)	42.86 (34.12)	—	—	4.40 (3.50)	125.61 (100.00)
9	Malliampady	31.65 (27.31)	40.25 (34.73)	—	44 (37.96)	—	115.9 (100.00)
	Total	464.87 (51.25)	371.86 (40.99)	(1.87)	44 (1.85)	9.40 (1.04)	907.13 (100.00)

(Figures in parentheses are percentages to the total).
Source: Computed.

Further, the value of livestock varies from 21.64 per cent Kendikkal to 8.42 per cent Pottiyam. Since land and livestock constitute more percentage of the total wealth of the sample tribals, these assets are capable of generating more employment and income to the tribals.

Land Use Pattern

Farmers can be easily identified on the basis of their land holding. These lands could be hereditary land, leased-in-land, purchased or land allotted by the Government. Moreover, the struggle for land and for the right to use the land and the emotional attachment on land is ever-recurring concept in the history of mankind. Further, whoever owns land will be proud to own it and whoever owns more land will be accorded high social and economic status.

In the Kalrayan hills, during the Jagir's regime, no individual ownership of land was present, but, as soon as Jagir's were taken over, lands were assigned to the tribals. There is controversy over the allotment of land, as discussed in chapter V of the thesis. However, a real picture of land distribution in the sample villages would provide actual position of tribals in the event of large-scale land reform measures undertaken in the hill. The first hand information gathered from the tribals on land is presented in Table 6.6.

Land allotted by the Government constituted 51.25 per cent of the total land. But the land under dispute between the Government and the tribals was 40.99 per cent of the total land. According to the records of the State, there are no disputed land (as discussed in Chapter V), but the firsthand information as depicted in table 6.6 provides support for the existence of disputed land. This fact clearly endorses the view that in the Kalrayan hills, land reform measures are incomplete. Further, the village wise details of allotted land and disputed land, show that in Vellimalai, land allotted by the government (38.63 per cent) was less than the disputed

Table 6.7 : Cropping Pattern of the Sample Tribals in the Vellimalai Taluk (in acres)

Sl. No.	*Name of the Village*	*Paddy*	*Ragi*	*Varagu and Samai*	*Plantain*	*Groundnut*	*Tapioca*	*Total*
1	Kendikkal	34	4	73.5	1	1	11.5	125
		(27.2)	(3.2)	(58.8)	(0.8)	(0.8)	(9.2)	(100.00)
2	Vellimalai	26	10.5	45	0	0	11	92.5
		(28.1)	(11.35)	(48.65)			(11.89)	(100.00)
3	Karialur	33.5	14.5	46	0	1	13.25	108.25
		(30.95)	(13.39)	(42.49)		(0.92)	·(12.24)	(100.00)
4	Mavadipattu	19.5	19	25.5	0	0	8	72
		(27.08)	(26.39)	(35.42)			(11.11)	(100.00)
5	Nochimedu	10	0	22.5	0	0	1	33.5
		(29.85)		(67.16)			(2.99)	(100.00)
6	Kundiyanatham	10-	1	25	0	0	1	37
		(27.03)	(2.70)	(67.57)			(2.70)	(100.00)
7	Vazhapady	35	0	54	0	0	1	90
		(38.89)		(60.00)			(1.110	(100.00)
8	Pottiyam	48.25	3.5	36.50	7.70	11	5.65	112.6
		(42.85)	(3.11)	(32.42)	(6.84)	(9.77)	(5.02)	(100.00)
9	Malliampady	12	2	44	3	0	2	63
		(19.05)	(3.17)	(69.84)	(4.76)		(3.17)	(100.00)
	Total	228.25	54.5	372.00	11.70	13	54.4	800.25
		(31.11)	(7.43)	(50.69)	(1.59)	(1.77)	(7.41)	(100.00)

(Figures in parentheses are percentages to the total).
Source: Computed.

land (57.04 per cent), Mavadipattu (allotted land (26.73 per cent) and disputed land (73.27 per cent), Malliampady (27.31 per cent of allotted land and 34.73 per cent of disputed land) and Karialur (48.34 per cent of allotted and 51.66 per cent of disputed land). On the contrary, in Pottiyam allotted land (62.38 per cent) was more than disputed land (34.12 per cent), in Vazhapady (89.00 per cent of allotted land and 8.85 per cent of disputed land, in Kendikkal. Allotted land 50.77 per cent and 39.32 per cent of disputed land), in Kundiyanatham (90.51 per cent of allotted land and 9.49 of disputed land) and in Nochimedu government. Allotted land was more than the disputed land. However, in both the groups of villages there were disputed lands. Further, land alienation was seen in Malliampady, Kendikkal and Vazhapady, wherein the land alienation is illegal as per the Revenue Standing Order. Therefore, it is right time that Government should solve this problem, other-wise; it will permeate into other villages of the hill.

Cropping Pattern

Earlier in Chapter IV, the cropping pattern of the Block is discussed. Table 6.7 portrays the cropping pattern of the sample tribals in the Kalrayan Hill.

The principal crops cultivated by the tribals were Varagu and Samai (50.69 per cent), Paddy (31.11 per cent), Ragi (7.43 per cent), Tapioca (7.41 per cent), Groundnut (1.62 per cent) and Plantain (1.33 per cent). The village wise crop pattern shows that Varagu and Samai, Paddy and Tapioca crops were cultivated in all the sample villages. Since, Varagu and Samai are the normal food of tribals both the crops is cultivated in all the villages. Further, both the crops were cultivated simultaneously and the cost of cultivation is also comparatively cheaper than any other crop raised by the tribals. In those days, these two crops were cultivated under shifting cultivation. However, now the tribals were restricted to cultivate such crops in the allotted land and this restriction stopped the shifting cultivation in the hill.

Further, paddy crop was the principal crop in Pottiyam (42.85 per cent), because, the village is located in the lower hill slopes and nearer to the Gomugi dam. The tribals sow the paddy seed called "punal kattu nellu", which is suitable to the hill area. Hence, high-yielding varieties of seed and technology provided through Tribal Sub-Plan were not accepted by the tribals. In this context, instead of routine extension of such programmes, it is ideal to introduce technology that is suitable for raising rainfed crops.

The commercial crops like Tapioca, Plantain and Groundnut were raised by the tribals, immediately after the monsoon. Of the three crops,-Tapioca was cultivated in all the villages, because of the demand for Tapioca by the Sago industries located in the nearby district. Thus, crop pattern and choice of crops show their skills and also indicate them as progressive farmers among the tribals of the country.

Employment Details of Sample Tribals

Of the 811 sample population of the hill, only one tribe of Kotaputhur habitation is working in the service sector. Therefore, the remaining 811 are either workers or dependents. The 1991 census defines the main workers as "a person who had worked for the major part of the year i.e., 6 months (183 days) or more." Further, "A worker is usually deemed to be a person engaged in 'economically productive work' including work that is remunerated and certain categories of work in family farms and enterprises for which no separate, distinct payment is made"[8] The tribals are engaged in their own farm. They also work in other's farm for wage or on exchange of labour or reciprocal labour. Further, they are also employed in other works like building construction, non-farm works etc., sometime, they also move out of their habitation to seek employment elsewhere in the low country.

Therefore, considering all these facts, the tribal's employment particulars were collected on 'day' basis i.e., which over put 8 hours of labour in such category of work was termed as employed for a 'day'. The collected details are presented village-wise in table 6.8.

Table 6.8 reveals that the male tribes work on an average 277 days in a year, of which 179 days in farm and 98 days in other works. Whereas, female labour work for 148 days in a year, of which 105 days in farm and 43 days in other works. Further, both male and female on an average work for 425 days in farm and other work. The average number of days employed is more in Vazhapady (555 days in a year) than other villages. Further, female labour work more number of days in farm works than in other works compared to male population. Moreover, in the absence of alternative employment, the tribals had to work more number of days in their own field.

Table 6.8 : Average Number of Days Employed by Sample Tribals in the Study Area

Sl. No.	*Name of the Village*	*Male*		*Female*		*Total*
		Farm Labour	*Other works*	*Farm Labour*	*Other works*	
1.	Kendikkal	206	131	93	48	478
2.	Vellimalai	124	57	81	46	308
3.	Karialur	153	115	78	54	400
4.	Mavadipattu	195	76	94	44	409
5.	Nochimedu	173	68	83	39	363
6.	Kundiyanatham	172	108	142	26	448
7.	Vazhapady	213	155	140	47	555
8.	Pottiyam	160	76	112	43	391
9.	Malliampady	209	99	120	43	471
	Total	1605	885	943	390	3823

Source: Computed.

Table 6.9 : Total Income of the Sample Households in the Study Area (in Rs.)

Sl. No.	Name of the Village	Income from Crops	Income from Employment	Income from Livestock	Income from Forest Products	Income from Trees	Income from Development Programmes	Total Income
1.	Kendikkal	1,53,130 (31.23	2,08,755 (42.57)	25,200 (5.14)	17,120 (3.49)	75,020 (1.53)	11,100 (2.26)	4,90,325 (100.00)
2.	Vellimalai	73,635 (42.28)	46,850 (26.9)	12,765 (7.33)	29,760 (17.09)	3,967 (2.28)	7,200 (4.13)	1,74,177 (100.00)
3.	Karialur	78,500 (29.95)	1,26,450 (48.25)	5,485 (2.09)	37,700 (14.39)	4,200 (1.6)	9,735 (3.71)	2,62,070 (100.00)
4.	Mavadipattu	41,195 (39.76)	39,050 (37.69)	6,420 (6.2)	15,150 (14.62)	1,800 (1.74)	—	1,03,615 (100.00)
5.	Nochimedu	35,240 (62.29)	8,500 (15.04)	4,630 (8.18)	8,200 (14.49)	—	—	56,570 (100.00)
6.	Kundiyanatham	51,650 (41.56)	30,710 (24.71)	14,760 (11.88)	26,245 (21.12)	907 (0.73)	—	1,24,272 (100.00)
7.	Vazhapady	1,17,950 (35.01)	1,42,910 (42.42)	15,060 (4.47)	60,980 (18.1)	—	—	3,36,900 (100.00)
8.	Pottiyam	2,66,810 (58.67)	1,76,150 (38.74)	5,550 (1.22)	5,925 (1.3)	300 (0.07)	—	4,54,735 (100.00)
9.	Malliampady	90,650 (46.22)	89,580 (45.48)	11,290 (5.73)	—	—	5,450 (2.77)	1,96,970 (100.00)
	Total	9,08,760 (41.31)	8,68,955 (39.50)	1,01,160 (4.6)	2,01,080 (9.14)	86,194 (3.92)	33,485 (1.52)	21,99,634 (100.00)

(Figures in parentheses are percentages to the total).
Source: Computed.

Table 6.10 : Annual Total Household Expenditure Pattern of Sample Tribals in the study area (in Rs.)

Sl. No.	*Name of the Village*	*Cost of Cultivation*	*Expenditure Livestock*	*Expenditure on Machinery*	*Household expenditure*	*Interest on Loans*		*Total*
						Organised Sector	*Non-Tribals*	
1.	Kendikkal	153056	13728	1792	418977	112	—	587932
		(26.05)	(8.34)	(0.3)	(71.29)	(0.02)		(100.00)
2.	Vellimalai	51221	7993	4641	251957	420	12780	329012
		(15.57)	(2.43)	(1.41)	(76.58)	(0.13)	(3.88)	(100.00)
3.	Karialur	73374	9765	1197	277536	942	4320	367134
		(19.99)	(2.66)	(0.33)	(75.60)	(0.26)	(1.18)	(100.00)
4.	Mavadipattu	31031	5632	1782	73865	1890	4032	118232
		(26.25)	(4.76)	(1.51)	(62.47)	(1.6)	(3.41)	(100.00)
5.	Nochimedu	14550	4020	—	29538	1162	4320	53590
		(27.15)	(7.5)		(55.12)	(2.17)	(8.06)	(100.00)
6.	Kundiyanatham	24992	12231	—	85392	280	7560	130455
		(19.16)	(9.36)		(65.46)	(0.21)	(5.8)	(100.00)
7.	Vazhapady	42858	18594	—	231552	840	3672	297516
		(14.41)	(6.25)		(77.83)	(0.28)	(1.23)	(100.00)
8.	Pottiyam	217186	16523	5208	433659	2782	8460	683818
		(31.76)	(2.42)	(0.76)	(63.42)	(0.41)	(1.24)	(100.00)
9.	Malliampady	100912	7434	—	113204	861	5220	227631
		(44.33)	(3.27)	—	(49.73)	(0.38)	(2.29)	(100.00)
	Total	709180	95920	14620	1915647	9289	50364	2795020
		(25.37)	(3.43)	(0.52)	(68.54)	(0.33)	(1.81)	(100.00)

(Figures in parentheses are percentages to the total).
Source: Computed.

Income Level of the Tribals

Table 6.9 depicts that the per capita income of the sample tribals was Rs. 2712, Whereas, the per capita income of the sample villages was Rs. 3008 in Kendikkal, Rs. 2233 in Vellimalai, Rs. 2340 in Karialur, Rs. 1955 in Mavadipattu, Rs. 1951 in Nochimedu, Rs. 1497 in Kundiyanatham, Rs. 3509 in Vazhapady, Rs. 3225 in Pottiyam and Rs. 3517 in Malliampady. The per capita income of the sample villages portrays that it was more in lower hill villages than in the upper hill villages. On the other hand, the percapita income was high in Vazhapady, because of more income from employment (42.42 per cent). Further, as in table 4.8, only in this village, more tribals were engaged in farm occupation and the income of the bank employee of the village should have increased the per capita income of the village.

The distribution of income in various categories, as given in 6.9, indicates that income from crops (41.31 per cent) was more than income from employment (39.50 per cent). Even though, it is a hill area, the income from forest produce (9.14 per cent) and trees (3.92 per cent) was not encouraging to the tribal. This was the outcome of Government controlling the tribals in the use of forest and forest land.

Expenditure Pattern of the Tribals

The pattern of expenditure by the sample tribals is presented in table 6.10. The per capita household expenditure including expenditure on cultivation, maintenance of livestock etc. of the sample tribals was Rs. 12048 per annum, whereas, their per capita annual household income was Rs. 13834. It was because the sample tribals spent more on household expenditure (i.e., 68.54 per cent) than on cultivation (25.37 per cent) and other types of expenditure. Perhaps, expenditure on machineries, (0.52 per cent) was very little to the total expenditure because, most of the tribals are small farmers. The notable point is that their expenditure by way of interest payment to non-tribals (1.81 per cent) was more than the interest payment to organised sector (0.33 per cent). Such interest payment was high in Nochimedu and Kundiyanatham i.e., 8.06 per cent and 5.8 per cent respectively. The tribals expenditure pattern and income shows only their deficit economy and resulted in indebtedness among the tribals.

Table 6.11 : Total Loans Outstanding of Sample Tribals to the Organised Sector and Moneylender in the Sample Villages (in Rs.)

Sl. No.	*Name of the Village*	*Loans borrowed from Government Agencies*	*Loans borrowed from money lenders*	*Total Loans outstanding*
1.	Kendikkal	3860	17200	21060
		(18.32)	(81.67)	(100.00)
2.	Vellimalai	3600	35800	39400
		(9.14)	(90.86)	(100.00)
3.	Vazhapady	6800	12700	19500
		(34.87)	(65.13)	(100.00)
4.	Karialur	6200	22600	28800
		(21.53)	(78.47)	(100.00)
5.	Mavadipattu	13500	11200	24700
		(54.66)	(45.34)	(100.00)
6.	Nchimedu	8300	19600	27900
		(29.75)	(70.25)	(100.00)
7.	Kundiyanatham	6700	21800	28500
		(23.51)	(76.49)	(100.00)
8.	Pottiyam	19870	23500	43370
		(45.82)	(54.18)	(100.00)
9.	Malliampady	6150	24500	30650
		(20.07)	(79.93)	(100.00)
	Total	74980	188900	263880
		(28.41)	(71.59)	(100.00)

(Figures in parentheses are percentages to the total).
Source: Computed.

Indebtedness Among the Tribals

Indebtedness in the hill was due to moneylenders and traders from the nearby non-tribal areas. These people actually take advantage of poverty and large deficit between income and expenditure of the tribals and lend money on an exorbitant rate of interest. The details of loans outstanding are presented in Table 6.11.

Table 6.11 portrays the loans borrowed from moneylenders constitute the major proportion which (71.59 per cent) and the percentage of loan borrowed from the organised sector constitutes 28.41 per cent of the total loan. In the Government Agencies, it was 28.41 per cent of the total loan. Similarly the village wise data also shows that the loans outstanding were more to the moneylenders than to the Government agencies. The loan outstanding to moneylenders was maximum of 90.86 per cent in Vellimali, because the village was exposed to the non-tribals due to its locational advantage. Table 6.11 clearly explains that the tribals borrowed heavily from the moneylenders. Therefore necessary steps are essential to the tribals, from such indebtedness.

In the economic system of tribals, the land occupies a prominent place. Since forest land is in the hands of the government, the tribals continue to depend more on land than the forest resources. Perhaps, this is the change that took place in the Kalrayan hill in course of the transition by the entry of Government.

Analysis of Agricultural Production

Agriculture in Tribal areas and that too in areas like Kalrayan hill is different from rest of the State. According to RBI report, "the basic parameters of planning for the national economy as a whole (based on labour-surplus hypothesis) will not necessarily hold good for tribal areas, because they have limited manpower relative to natural resources, particularly forests.[9] The study area is gifted with cultivable

Table 6.12 : Average Cost of Cultivation (per acre) of Paddy Crop by Tribal Farmers in the Selected Villages (Value in Rupees)

Sl. No.	Name of the Village	Seed Cost	Ploughing Cost	Manure and Fertilzer cost	Labour cost	Total Cost
1	Kendikkal	81	141	105	320	647
		(12.52)	(21.79)	(16.23)	(49.46)	(100.00)
2	Vellimalai	84	155	199	384	822
		(10.22)	(18.86)	(24.21)	(46.72)	(100.00)
3	Vazhapady	97	171	136	401	805
		(12.05)	(21.24)	(16.89)	(49.81)	(100.00)
4	Karialur	97	168	130	306	701
		(13.84)	(23.97)	(18.54)	(43.65)	(100.00)
5	Mavadipattu	94	254	82	343	773
		(12.16)	(32.86)	(10.61)	(44.37)	(100.00)
6	Nochimedu	117	170	167	430	884
		(10.91)	(17.85)	(13.6)	(57.65)	(100.00)
7	Kundiyanatham	77	126	96	407	706
		(10.91)	(17.85)	(13.6)	(57.65)	(100.00)
8	Pottiyam	113	187	123	248	671
		(16.84)	(27.87)	(18.33)	(36.96)	(100.00)
9	Malliampady	96	161	125	295	677
		(14.18)	(23.78)	(18.46)	(43.57)	(100.00)
	Total	856	1533	1163	3134	6686
		(12.80)	(22.93)	(17.39)	(46.87)	(100.00)

(Figures in parentheses are percentages to the total).

Source: Computed.

lands in the hill slopes and in plains. In the total absence of shifting cultivation, they cultivate a number of crops, like Paddy, Varagu, Samai, Ragi, Tapioca, Groundnut, Sugarcane and Plantain. In this Chapter an analysis is of the input-output-relationship with multiple regressions, simple regression and simple Karl Pearson's correlation coefficient technique for crops like Paddy, Varagu, Samai, Ragi and Tapioca is attempted. The result of each crop is explained as below.

Paddy Crop

Paddy is an important crop, cultivated by tribals in two seasons. The first crop is called Kuruvai, cultivated during the months from May to August of every year in villages where ground water is available. The first crop is cultivated by a few tribals in the lower hills slope villages like Pottiyam and Malliampady. The Second crop is called "Samba" cultivated during August to January, of every year and also cultivated by all the tribals of Kalrayan hills. Since, all the tribals do not uniformly cultivate the first crop; our present analysis is confined to only Samba crop.

In order to analyse the inter-tribal input use and output, the sample villages are divided into two groups' viz., Villages in the lower slopes and villages in the Upper slopes of the hill. The first group consists of Pottiyam and Malliampady and the second group includes all the other seven sample villages. The tribals generally use a special paddy seed called "Punal Kattu Nellu", cultivated during Samba season, the rainy days during which the best seed is preserved for the next crop. At the same time, some progressive farmers of Pottiyam Village cultivate paddy with new technology. The cost of cultivation of Paddy by the sample farmers (per acre) is given in the following table.

Per acre total cost of cultivation was Rs. 671 and Rs. 677 in Pottiyam and Malliampady. In the second group, it was

Table 6.13 : Results of the Multiple Regression Analysis of Paddy Crop by Sample Farmers in the Study Area

Sl. No.	Name of the Village	Constant (B_0)	Seed Cost (B_1)	Ploughing Cost (B_2)	Variable Labour (B_3)	Manure Cost (B_4)	Fertilzer (B_5)	R^2
1.	Kendikkal	–97.864	3.3819**	0.031524^{NS}	0.075215*	0.011148^{NS}	—	0.8816
			(1.6533)	(0.046524)	(0.022863)	(0.029792)		
2.	Vellimalai	137.16	1.0505*	0.04882	0.040830*	0.048062*	—	0.9465
			(0.03194)	(0.015888)	(0.0140452)	(0.011003)		
3.	Karialur	–68.658	0.075176^{NS}	0.054193*	0.070631*	0.044727*	—	0.9402
			(0.072848)	(0.011792)	(0.003133)	(0.02861)		
4.	Mavadipattu	–30.487	0.033765^{NS}	0.054288*	0.049779	0.080179	—	0.9980
			(0.019907)	(0.0081515)	(0.002387)	(0.009219)		
5.	Nochimedu	116.16	0.099134*	.029046*	0.058276*	0.016842*	.049927^{NS}	0.9677
			(0.03439)	(0.013235)	(0.023458)	(0.052418)	(0.024400)	
6.	Kundiyanatham	–159.40	4.0299**	0.061194**	0.056119**	–1.1194^{NS}	—	0.9999
			(0.03653)	(0.04894)	(0.005719)	(0.02457)		
7.	Vazhapady	27.833	–0.02637^{NS}	1.0036*	.049972*	0.14695^{NS}	—	0.7633
			(1.3096)	(0.01828)	(0.016705)	(0.05889)		
8.	Pottiyam	–13.588	0.090838NS	0.044056^{NS}	0.53693*	0.052185*	0.040460*	0.9493
			(0.080020)	(0.024634)	(0.013133)	(0.017629)	(0.012494)	
9.	Malliampady	7.1763	1.1960*	0.09411*	0.004756^{NS}	0.05215**	—	0.9906
			(0.03604)	90.0228)	(0.008157)	(0.08761)		

(Values in parentheses are standard errors).
NS—Statistically not significant.
* —Significant at 5% level of significance.
** —Significant at 10% level of significance.

Rs. 647 in Kendikkal, Rs. 822 in Velliamalai Rs. 701 in Karialur, Rs. 773 in Mavadipattu, Rs. 804 in Nochimedu, Rs. 706 in Kundiyantham, and Rs. 805 in Vazhapady. The total cost of cultivation of paddy shows that per acre cost varies more in the second group of villages than in the first group of villages.

The cost of seed varies from Rs. 81 to Rs. 117 in the second group of villages, while it was Rs. 113 for Pottiyam and Rs. 96 for Malliampady. The variation in Seed cost was observed because the seed cost was more when it was purchased from other tribals or from open market.

The ploughing cost was the cost that was incurred in the process of preparing the land for sowing the seed and replanting the saplings. The cost of ploughing includes cost of hiring bullock labour or cost incurred in hiring power tiller or tractor by the tribals. The cost of ploughing (per acre) varied from a minimum of Rs. 126 to the maximum of Rs. 254. It was Rs. 187 in Pottiyam and Rs. 161 in Malliampady. Ploughing cost is maximum (Rs.254) in Mavadipattu. It was observed from the data that the cost of ploughing is high if the soil is rocky.

The third input was Green Manure and Chemical Fertilizer. Both the inputs were combined because the tribals apply manure while preparing the land for cultivation and apply chemical fertilizer during the growth of the crop. The range for cost of manure and fertilizer varies from Rs. 82 (minimum) in Mavadipattu and Rs. 199 (maximum) in Vellimalai. The variation was found high in the hill areas than in the lower hill areas (Rs.123 in Pottiyam and Rs. 125 in Malliampady). The reasons were : The cost of own manure was less than the purchased one the unit cost of manure or fertilizer was more when the land was far away from the village and the use of chemical fertilizers also increased the cost of cultivation.

Finally, the labour cost includes only the cost incurred in the use of human labour. The human labour is both family labour and hired labour. The value of cost of labour has been computed by taking into account all type of family labour used in the cultivation by calculating the total number of days employed in various farm operations plus the hired human labour. Per acre cost of labour in Pottiyam and Malliampady was Rs. 248 and Rs. 295 respectively. But, the cost of labour was more in the second group of village viz., Rs. 430 in Nochimedu, Rs. 407 in Kundiyanatham, Rs. 401 in Vazhapady, Rs. 384 in Vellimalai, Rs. 343 in Mavadipattu, Rs. 320 in Kendikkal and Rs. 306 in Karialur. The cost of labour was high in the second group of villages because the lands are in the slopes and mostly rocky.

To analyse the input use and the output, Multiple Regression Technique of the following form has been used.

$$Y = A + B_1 \times 1 + B_2 \times 2 + B_3 \times 3 + B_4 \times 4 + B_5 \times 5$$

Where

Y is per acre paddy output in kilograms.

A_1 is constant.

X_1 is per acre cost of seed in rupees.

X_2 is per acre cost of ploughing in rupees.

X_3 is per acre cost of labour in man days.

X_4 is per acre cost of manure and fertilizer in rupees, and

X_5 is per acre cost of pesticide in rupees.

B_1 to B_5 are partial regression co-efficients. The data for the analysis is the primary data directly collected from the tribals and the result is drawn by using computer. The results of the model are given in the table 6.13.

In Kendikkal Village, the R^2 value is 0.8816, hence the model is appropriate, which means that about 88 per cent variation in the output is explained by the four variables viz., X_1, X_2, X_3 and X_4. The partial regression coefficients of cost of Seed and Unit of labour are statistically significant at 10 and 5 per cent levels of significance respectively. The other two partial regression co-efficient are not statistically significant. The partial regression coefficient of cost of Seed is 3.38 which indicates that an increase of Seed cost by one rupee would increase the paddy output by 3.38 kilograms. The tribals in this village use the traditional variety of seeds. The cultivation of paddy is undertaken in the hill slopes and hence they have to invest some more quantity of seed to increase the output. The contribution of other variables to output is meagre and therefore, in this village the tribals should concentrate more on Seed input to increase the output.

The R^2 value of Vellimalai Village is 0.9465. It explains that about 95 per cent variation in the output is explained by the four variables. The values of all the partial regression coefficients of the variables are statistically highly significant and are positive. Like the previous village, the partial regression coefficient of variable $X_1 = 1.05$, means that an increase of one rupee on Seed cost would increase the output by 1.05 kilograms. With regard to other three variables, the contribution to output would be meagre for any incremental investment on these inputs.

The Pottiam Village is located in the lower hill slopes and it is the native village of one of the three Jagirdars, i.e., the Pottiyam Jagirdar. The village is located away from the Kallakurichi and Vellimalai bus route. The village has poor mud roads, surrounded by forests and Gomugi dam. The R^2 value is 0.9493, means that 95 per cent of the variation is explained by the fit. The partial regression coefficients of Seed Cost (X_1) and Ploughing Cost (X_2) are not statistically significant. None of the regression coefficients of the model are negative. The values of coefficients are meagre; hence any amount of additional investment would increase the output nominally under the present technology.

The R^2 value for Karialur Village is 0.9402. The table shows that the partial regression coefficients are positive. The partial regression coefficient of Seed Cost (X_1) is not statistically significant, while for the other variable the coefficients are statistically significant. The coefficient of the variable X_1 is insignificant because, the tribal farmers adopt traditional method of cultivation and the village is located in the hill slopes. Therefore, they cannot prove any increase in paddy output with the present type of farming. They should adopt terraced farming method and modern methods of irrigation (like drop irrigation) to increase the output.

Mavadipattu Village is located in the hill slopes of the Kalrayan hills. The tribal farmers adopt traditional method of cultivation and their agriculture is totally rained. The R^2 value is 0.9980, which reveals that 99.8 per cent of the variation is explained by the regression fit. The partial regression coefficient of the seed cost is statistically insignificant. The partial regression coefficients of ploughing cost (X_2), Labour Unit (X_3) and Manure Cost (X_4) are statistically highly significant. Of the four variables, only for the Manure Cost, the regression coefficient is 0.08 which means that an increase of one rupee on Manure Cost would increase the output by 0.08 kilograms. With regard to other variables the partial regression coefficients are positive and would contribute positively to the output, if any additional investment is made on these variables.

Nochimedu Village is a small village. The R^2 value of the model is 0.9672, means that about 97 per cent of variation in paddy output is explained by the fit. The partial regression coefficients are positive. The coefficients of Seed Cost (X_1), Ploughing (X_2) and Labour (X_3) are statistically significant at five per cent level of significance. The partial regression

Table 6.14 : Results of the Multiple Regression Analysis of Varagu and Samai Crops in the Study Area

Sl. No.	*Name of the Village*	*Constant* (B_0)	*Seed Cost* (B_1)	*Ploughing Cost* (B_2)	*Variable Labour* (B_3)	*Manure Cost* (B_1)	*Name of the Crop*	R^2
1.	Kendikkal	5.9609	2.3531** (0.041329)	2.0980** (0.013132)	1.9645** (0.01043)	1.9493** (0.006745)	Varagu	0.9946
2.	Vellimalai	31.10	1.5118** (0.2445)	–0.030403^{NS} (0.041392)	–0.04953^{NS} (0.046315)	2.2070*** (0.013958)	Samai	0.9974
3.	Karialur	–22.418	1.9475^{NS} (0.08224)	–0.07659^{NS} (0.084365)	1.3622** (0.049335)	0.075065** (0.029856)	Varagu	0.4928
4.	Mavadipattu	80.658	0.03117NS (0.0406)	0.30282** (0.02048)	–0.25945** (0.051853)	0.050426** (0.009206)	Varagu	0.9331
5.	Nochimedu	86.721	2.2321* (0.1068)	1.1015^{NS} (2.2734)	2.5533^{NS} (0.06679)	2.9031*** (0.035366)	Samai	0.9921
6.	Kundiyanatham	–99.483	3.4498** (0.9806)	2.6740** (0.055266)	2.5321** (0.033265)	1.5966** (0.017632)	Samai	0.9932
7.	Vazhapady	–44.879	–0.0739^{NS} (.043467)	0.081685** (0.021547)	0.081003** (0.020422)	0.076009** (0.0095801)	Samai	0.9233
8.	Pottiyam	81.676	3.5587** (6.0241)	0.073644^{NS} (0.050046)	1.3380^{NS} (0.0192633)	2.3670** (0.047662)	Varagu	0.7999
9.	Malliampady	–23.678	0.69021*** (0.034005)	0.058375** (0.0117)	0.043445** (0.0085914)	0.057807** (0.0074574)	Samai	0.9523

(Values in parentheses are standard errors).
NS — Not Significant.
** — Statistically significant at 5% level of significance.
*** — Significant at 10 per cent level of significance.

coefficients of Manure Cost (X4) and pesticide Cost (X5) are statistically insignificant. Even though, partial regression coefficients of the five variables are positive, the tribals would get more output (0.09 kilograms) by an additional investment of one rupee on Seed Cost and for other variables the increase in output is only nominal.

For Kundiyanatham R^2 value is 0.9999, the highest of all the Villages in this analysis. The R^2 value is statistically highly significant. Nearly 100 per cent of the variation in paddy output is explained by the regression fit. The regression coefficient are positive for Seed Cost (X_1), Ploughing Cost (X_2) and Labour (X_3) and negative (–1.1194) for Manure Cost (X_4). The regression coefficients of X_1, X_2 and X_3 are statistically significant at 10 per cent level of significance. The partial regression coefficient of Seed Cost (X_1) is 4.0299, means that an increase of one rupee on Seed would increase the output by 4.03 kilograms. Hence the tribal farmers should use more of Seeds of high quality with utmost care. The partial regression coefficient of Manure Cost is negative, because of either over use of the input or application of the input at inappropriate time or with low quality manure. Thus, they should use more Seed of good quality and right quantity of manure to increase the paddy output.

The R^2 value of Vazhapady village is 0.7633, the lowest of the nine villages studied in this analysis. The partial regression coefficients of Seed Cost (X_1), and manure Cost (X_4) are not statistically significant. The partial regression coefficient of Labour (X_3) and ploughing cost (X_2) are statistically significant at 5 per cent level of significance.

The R^2 value for Malliampady Village is 0.9906 explains that about 99 per cent variation in the output is explained by the fit. The partial regression coefficients are positive and statistically significant except for the Labour. The tribals can increase the output by increasing their investment on all the four variables, but the return would be higher if they invest more on Seed and Ploughing.

So far the impact of input use on output of paddy is analysed Village-wise. Now, let us analyse the same group wise. In the first group, the R^2 value of Pottiyam and Malliampady is 0.9493 and 0.9906 respectively. Only in Malliampady B_1 is 1.196 and the regression coefficients other inputs in both the villages are very meagre. The partial regression coefficients are positive and the values show that the inputs are generally used at the optimum level not leaving much scope for investing any more on these inputs. Whereas in the second group of Villages, it is observed from the result of the model that the cost of seed can be increased in Vellimalai (B_1 = 1.0505), Kendikkal (B_1 = 3.3819) and Kundiyanatham (B_1 = 4.0299) to increase the paddy output. Similar to the first group of Villages, these villages too do not leave much scope for incremental investment on these inputs as discussed in the village wise analysis previously.

Results of Multiple Regression Analysis for Varagu and Samai Crops

In the previous analysis, we have discussed the results of multiple regression analysis for paddy cultivation in Kalrayan hills. Now, let us analyse the results of the similar model for Varagu and Samai cultivation by the tribals in the study area. These two crops are millets and are cultivated in the slopes of the hill. Samai and Varagu crops are totally rained and cultivated in similar seasons. These millets are delicious but in case of over eating would lead to drowsiness. The tribals usually take this food in the morning, because, this will sustain their appetite for a longer time. Samai and Varagu supplement the paddy and hence, the tribals get food throughout the year. The result of the model is given in Table 6.14. Now let us analyse the results for each village.

The R^2 value of Kendikkal Village is 0.9946. Hence, the four variables, Seed Cost (X_1), Ploughing Cost (X_2), Labour

(X_4) and Manure cost (X_5) effectively contributed to the changes in the Varagu output by 99 per cent. All the partial regression coefficients are statistically significant at 5 per cent level of significance. The farmers would get 2.35 kilograms of Varagu output by increasing one rupee investment on Seed. Similarly, the Varagu output would increase by 2.1 kilograms, 1.96 kilograms and 1.95 kilograms, respectively, if they increase one rupee investment on the three variables viz., Ploughing Labour and Manure cost respectively. Thus, the village is more suitable for the cultivation of Varagu due to its soil conditions.

In Vellimalai, the R^2 value is 0.9974, means that about 99.7 per cent variation in the output is explained by the four variables, X_1, X_2, X_3, and X_4. The partial regression coefficients, for Seed cost (X_1) and Manure Cost (X_4) are statistically insignificant. The partial regression coefficient of Seed Cost is-1.51 and also significant. Therefore, they should be careful in using the input. For other variables X_2 and X_3, the partial regression coefficients are negative and the values also-0.03 and-0.05 respectively, hence any more investment on these inputs would yield negative returns on the Samai output.

The R^2 for Pottiyam Village is 0.7999, explains that about 80 per cent variation in the Varagu output is explained by the four variables X_1, X_2, X_3 and X_4. All the regression coefficients are positive. The regression coefficients Ploughing Cost and Labour are not statistically significant. The regression coefficient of Manure Cost (X_4) is significant. This explains that by increasing one rupee on Manure Cost would increase the output by 2.37 kilograms. The R^2 value of Paddy Crop is (0.9493) and it is very encouraging to cultivate paddy crop in the village.

The R^2 value for Karialur village is the lowest of all the villages, i.e., 0.4928. The partial coefficients of Seed Cost (X_1), Labour (X_3) and Manure Cost (X_4) are statistically significant at 5 per cent level of significance and also positive. The regression coefficients of Seed Cost (X_1), Ploughing Cost (X_2) are statistically not significant and also negative. The partial regression coefficients of Seed Cost and Labour are 1.95 and 1.36, which indicate that by an additional one rupee investment on these two inputs would increase the Varagu output by 1.95 and 1.36 kilograms, respectively. The negative value of ploughing cost is due to rocky soil that needed more human and bullock labour to prepare the land for the cultivation of varagu crop.

The tribals of Mavadipattu village cultivated varagu crop. The R^2 value 0.9331 means that about 93 per cent variation in Varagu output is influenced by the four variables X_1, X_2, X_3 and X_4. The partial regression coefficients of seed cost (X_1), is not statistically significant. But it is significant for manure cost (X_4) at 5 per cent level of significance. The partial regression coefficient of X_3 is –0.26 that is over use of family and hired labour for cultivation of the crop. The chances of increasing the output by increasing the input are also very meagre, i.e., less than one kilogram for every one rupee investment on the inputs.

The R^2 value of 0.9921 of Nochimedu village explains that about 99 per cent variations in the Samai output is influenced by the four variables viz., X_1, X_2, X_3 and X_4. The partial regression coefficient of Manure cost which is 2.9031 implies that an additional one rupee investment on Manure cost would increase the Samai output by 2.9 kilograms. Therefore, tribals should concentrate on optimum use of manure to improve the output. The other two variables viz., ploughing cost and Labour are not statistically significant.

Like Kendikkal village, the results of the model are very encouraging in the cultivation of Samai crop by the Kundiyanatham tribals. The R^2 value is 0.9932 means that about 99 per cent variation in Samai output is explained by

Seed Cost, ploughing Cost, Labour and Manure Cost. The regression coefficients of these variables are statistically highly significant. If they increase their investment on these inputs, the Samai output also increase from 1.5 kilograms to 3.5 kilograms. Hence, the opportunities of improving the output are possible for the Kundiyanatham tribals.

The R^2 value of Vazhapady village is 0.9233. The tribals of Vazhapady village cultivate Samai crop. The partial regression coefficient of Seed Cost is-0.07 and not statistically significant. The partial regression coefficients of Ploughing Cost, Labour and Manure Cost are statistically significant at five per cent level of significance. The values of these coefficients are also less than one; hence, any additional investment would yield Samai Output at less than one kilogram.

The tribals of Malliampady Village cultivate Samai Crop. The R^2 value is 0.9523, which means that about 95 per cent variations in the output is explained by the four variables. The partial regression coefficient of the variables X_1, X_2, X_3 and X_4 are statistically significant. Any additional investment made by the tribals would increase the output from 0.05 to 0.6 kilograms.

Ragi

The crop was cultivated in the hill slopes and it was a rained crop. Ragi is cultivated without new technology and the seed preserved from the previous crop was used for the next season. It was cultivated by the tribals of Mavadiapattu, Karialur, Pottiyam and Vellimalai. The relationship between the total cost of cultivation and Ragi output was analysed with simple regression technique, which is of the form given below:

$$Y = A+bX$$

Where, Y is per acre output of Ragi in kilograms

A is intercept and X is the per acre total cost of cultivation which includes all cost incurred in the whole process of cultivation of Ragi, and b is the regression coefficient.

The result of the simple regression technique is given in the following table.

Table 6.15 : Results of Simple Regression Analysis of Ragi Crop in the Study Area

Sl. No.	*Name of the Village*	*Constant A*	*Regression Coefficient b*	R^2
1.	Mavadipattu	-161.44	1.22*	0.81
2.	Karialur	30.08	0.77*	0.6724
3.	Pottiyam	85.51	0.86*	0.5625
4.	Vellimalai	82.68	0.68*	0.64

* Statistically significant at 5 per cent level of Significance.

As shown in table 6.15 the regression coefficients are statistically significant at five per cent level of significance. The regression coefficient explains that any additional investment on Ragi would not be profitable to the tribals of Karialur (0.77), Pottiyam (0.86) and Vellimalai (0.68), because the regression coefficients are less than one. Whereas the regression coefficient of Mavadipattu Village is 1.22 which explains that for every additional one rupee investment, would increase the Ragi output by 1.22 kilograms. Similarly, the R^2 value is high (0.81) for this village compared to the other three villages.

Tapioca

Tapioca is a commercial crop. This crop has from the Sago producers of the nearby Salem district. The tribals with little water available cultivated tapioca just after the rainy season. It was raised by the tribals of Mavadipattu, Kendikkal, Vellimalai and Karialur. Like the other crops, the cultivation of Tapioca also needed proper preparation of land.

The cost of cultivation included, cost of ploughing the land, labour cost, manure and fertilizer cost and other costs incurred while raising the crop. To test the relationship between per acre cost of cultivation and per acre output of Tapioca, Karl Pearson's simple correlation coefficient technique of the form given below is used:

$$r = \frac{\Sigma xy}{N\sigma x\ \sigma y}$$

Where r Karl Pearson's correlation coefficient

X = (X-X)

Y = (Y-Y)

σX = Standard Deviation of series X

σY = Standard Deviation of series Y

N = Total number of observations.

The results of Karl Pearson's correlation coefficient between cost of cultivation and output is given in the following Table 6.16.

Table 6.16 : Results of Simple Karl Pearson's Correlation Coefficient for Tapioca Crop

Sl. No.	*Name of the Village*	*Correlation Coefficient*
1.	Mavadipattu	0.97*
2.	Karialur	0.81*
3.	Kendikkal	0.93*
4.	Vellimalai	0.81*

* Values are highly significant.

The correlation coefficient of Mavadipattu, Karialur, Vellimalai and Kendikkal were 0.97, 0.81, 0.89 and 0.93

respectively. These correlation coefficients are statistically highly significant. The correlation coefficient explains a very close relationship between cost of cultivation and output in the cultivation of Tapioca in the study area. Such a relationship attracts the tribals to raise Tapioca in more extent of land.

The cost of cultivation and output of different crops like Paddy, Varagu or Samai, Ragi and Tapioca has been analysed with multiple regression, simple regression and Karl Pearson's correlation co-efficient techniques. For other crops like Groundnut and Plantain, statistical technique is not applied because very few numbers of tribals cultivated the crops. From the statistical analysis of various crops, it is inferred that given the soil condition, cost of cultivation, it favoured raising Varagu and Samai crop rather than Paddy crop. If water resources are strengthened, then Paddy, Ragi, Groundnut, Tapioca, Groundnut crop would be raised in the hill. However, in the present circumstances, the hill is suitable for raising only millets. The commercial crops, cultivated by few tribals are only with old technology.

Further, the inputs supplied through the package schemes failed to reach the tribals and the tribals also gave only discouraging information about the programme during the primary data collection. It is appropriate hereto quote: "It appears that certain visible gain to small groups are taken as evidence of general advancement and highlighted as such which create a wrong impression and sense of complacency. It is perhaps this psychological make-up that explains why even after formulation of workable strategy, there are serious lapses in their follow-up over a period of time and even simple operational details remain unattended"[10]. Therefore, such package schemes should be tailored to the needs of the Kalrayan hill tribes. For instance, in the analysis, it has been observed that the tribals use only the local paddy seed and mostly cultivated crop like Varagu and Samai. Hence, one could question the rationale of distributing high yielding varieties of paddy seed to the tribals of the hill. Thus agricultural package schemes should be evolved as need-based scheme in improving the living conditions of the tribals and also achieving economy in the financial outlay earmarked for the purpose.

Test of Hypothesis

I. Land reforms of the conventional type had resulted in the land disputes between the government and the tribals.

The following test procedure has been followed:

1. HO : There is no significant variation in land dispute due to distribution of land by the Government.

H1 : There is significant variation in land dispute due to distribution of land by the Government.

2. Level of Significance : $\alpha = 5\%$

3. Statistics used :

$$\text{Spearman's } r = 1 - \frac{6\,\Sigma d_i}{n(n^2-1)}$$

4. Critical region:

Reject H_0 Lf $P \geq = p^2$ value with (n-1) df at 5% level of significance.

P = Critical value

Spearman's rank correlation coefficient is calculated for the data presented in Table 5.6 between the disputed land and total land of the sample villages. For the data, percentages were calculated and ranks were assigned. Spearman's rank correlation coefficient is 0.8796 and the critical value at 5 per cent level of significance is 0.7143. Since, the calculated 'r' is outside the limit of accepted region; we reject the null hypothesis and accept the alternate hypothesis. Therefore, it can be concluded that there is significant land dispute in the villages of Kalrayan hill. For instance as per Table 5.6 land under dispute was 43.95 per cent of the total land of the sample tribal population.

II. Land reform measures have not significantly changed the land use pattern in the post land reform period

To test the hypothesis, the data pertaining to different categories of land from 1986-87 to 1995-96 was considered. The percentages were calculated and ranks were assigned to the data. The total change in the land use pattern in various categories of land for the period has been examined with concordance coefficient.

Test Procedure

1. H_0 : There is no significant change in the land use pattern.

H_1 : There is significant change in the land use pattern.

2. Level of significance $\alpha = 5\%$

3. Statistic used: $\chi^2 = M(n-1)W$

M = number of years

n = number of observation

w = concordance coefficient

$$w = \frac{\Sigma dif^2}{\frac{1}{2}m^2(n^3-n)-nt)}$$

m = number of years

n = number of years

c = number of observations in a group tied for a given rank.

4. Critical region : Reject H_0 lt $\chi^2 \geq \chi^2$ value with (n-1) df at 5% level of significance.

5. Computed value : $\chi^2 = 10\ (19\text{-}1) \times 0.948$

$= 75.84$

$\chi^2 = 28.869$

$\therefore H_0$ is rejected.

From the study it is concluded that there is significant change in the land use pattern in the post-land reform period. The variation was due to change in the net cultivated area, forest land and the other types of land used by the tribals.

III. There is no significant variation in the cropping pattern inspite of land reforms measurer undertaken in the study area.

Test Procedure

1. H_0 : There is no significant change

H_1 : There is significant change in the cropping pattern.

2. Level of significance : $\alpha = 5\%$

3. Statistic used : As in hypothesis II

4. Critical Region : Reject H_0 if Rank Correlation coefficient falls outside critical limits.

To test whether there is a change in the cropping pattern from 1986-87 to 1995-96, Spearman's rank correlation coefficient method and test of concordance were used. For the data, percentages well calculated and ranks were assigned. Then for each pair of years, Spearman's rank correlation coefficients are estimated and presented in Table 6.17.

Table 6.17 : Spearman's Rank Correlation Coefficient for the Vellimalai Block

Sl. No.	*Pairs of years Between*		*Rank Correlation Coefficient*	*Critical Values*
1.	1986-87	1987-88	0.8771	0.4716
2.	1987-88	1988-89	0.9587	0.4716
3.	1988-89	1989-90	0.9469	0.4716
4.	1989-90	1990-91	0.9444	0.4716
5.	1990-91	1991-92	0.9916	0.4716
6.	1991-92	1992-93	0.9928	0.4716
7.	1992-93	1993-94	0.9939	0.4716
8.	1993-94	1994-95	0.9964	0.4716
9.	1994-95	1995-96	0.9967	0.4716

All the rank correlation coefficients are statistically significant at 5 per cent level of significance. The total change over the period from 1986-87 to 1995-96 has been examined with the concordance coefficient. The concordance coefficient is 0.8303 and $\chi^2 = 149.45$. The critical value at 5 per cent level of significance is 28.869. The coefficient is highly significant. Therefore, it can be concluded that there has been significant change in the cropping pattern over a period in the Vellimalai Block.

For the sample villages Spearman's rank correlation coefficient (for the pairs of years) and test of concordance have been used to test the hypothesis by the same procedure adopted for the Vellimalai Block. The results are presented village wise:

Table 6.18 : Results of Spearman's Rank Correlation Coefficient for Kendikkal Village

Sl. No.	*Pairs of years Between*		*Rank Correlation Coefficient*	*Critical Values*
1.	1989-90	1990-91	0.996	0.7450
2.	1990-91	1991-92	0.996	0.7450
3.	1991-92	1992-93	0.8492	0.7450
4.	1992-93	1993-94	1.000	0.8236
5.	1993-94	1994-95	0.8968	0.7450
6.	1994-95	1995-96	0.994	0.7450

All the correlation coefficients are found to be statistically significant at 5 per cent level of significance. The concordance coefficient is 0.6769 and χ^2 is 33.17. It can be concluded that in the village from 1989-90 to 1995-96 significant change has occurred in the crop pattern.

Table 6.19 : Results of Spearman's Rank Correlation Coefficient for Karialur Village

Sl. No.	*Pairs of years Between*		*Rank Correlation Coefficient*	*Critical Values*
1.	1989-90	1990-91	1.000	0.6833
2.	1990-91	1991-92	0.9979	0.6833

(Contd.)

(Table 6.19 Contd.)

Sl. No.	*Pairs of years Between*		*Rank Correlation Coefficient*	*Critical Values*
3.	1991-92	1992-93	0.9879	0.6833
4.	1992-93	1993-94	0.9838	0.6833
5.	1993-94	1994-95	0.9798	0.6833
6.	1994-95	1995-96	0.9768	0.6833

All the correlation coefficients for the pairs of years are statistically significant at 5 per cent level of significance. The test of concordance for the village is 0.9424 and χ^2 is 59.37. Since the value is highly significant it is concluded that there is significant change in the crop pattern for the period from 1989-90 to 1995-96.

Table 6.20 : Results of Spearman's Rank Correlation Coefficient for Vellimalai Village

Sl. No	*Pairs of years Between*		*Rank Correlation Coefficient*	*Critical Values*
1.	1989-90	1990-91	0.8828	0.6833
2.	1990-91	1991-92	0.8834	0.7143
3.	1991-92	1992-93	0.9104	0.7143
4.	1992-93	1993-94	0.9006	0.7143
5.	1993-94	1994-95	0.8455	0.6833
6.	1994-95	1995-96	0.8525	0.6833

The rank correlation coefficients given in Table 6.20 for Vellimalai village are statistically significant at 5 per cent level of significance. Further, the concordance coefficient is 0.5849 and $\chi^2 = 36.8483$. There is significant variation in the crop pattern from 1989-90 to 1995-96.

Table 6.21 : Results of Spearman's Rank Correction Coefficient for Nochimedu Village

Sl. No.	*Pairs of years Between*		*Rank Correlation Coefficient*	*Critical Values*
1.	1989-90	1990-91	0.8839	0.7450
2.	1990-91	1991-92	0.9825	0.7450
3.	1991-92	1992-93	0.9045	0.7450
4.	1992-93	1993-94	0.9861	0.8236
5.	1993-94	1994-95	0.9796	0.8236
6.	1994-95	1995-96	0.8849	0.7450

Spearman's rank correlation coefficients for the pairs of years given in Table 6.21 indicate that they are highly significant. Further, the concordance coefficient is 0.6194 and the χ^2 value is 30.3506. Therefore, it can be concluded that there is significant variation in the crop pattern in the village from 1989-90 to 1995-96.

Table 6.22 : Results of Spearman's Rank Correction Coefficient for Mavadipattu Village

Sl. No.	*Pairs of years Between*		*Rank Correlation Coefficient*	*Critical Values*
1.	1989-90	1990-91	0.994	0.7450
2.	1990-91	1991-92	0.9028	0.7450
3.	1991-92	1992-93	0.8313	0.7450
4.	1992-93	1993-94	0.7956	0.7450
5.	1993-94	1994-95	0.9544	0.7450
6.	1994-95	1995-96	0.9742	0.7450

The rank correletion coefficients for the pairs of years given in Table 6.22 indicate that they are highly significant. Further, the concordance coefficient is 0.5096 and the χ^2 value is 24.97. Therefore, it can be concluded that there is significant variation in the crop pattern in the village from 1989-90 to 1995-96.

Table 6.23 : Results of Spearman's Rank Correlation Coefficient for Kundiyanatham Village

Sl. No.	*Pairs of years Between*		*Rank Correlation Coefficient*	*Critical Values*
1.	1989-90	1990-91	0.9778	0.6833
2.	1990-91	1991-92	0.9131	0.6833
3.	1991-92	1992-93	0.897	0.6833
4.	1992-93	1993-94	0.9838	0.6833
5.	1993-94	1994-5	0.9697	0.6833
6.	1994-95	1995-96	0.9778	0.6833

All the correlation coefficient values are statistically significant for the pairs of years given in Table 6.23. The coefficient of concordance is 0.7479 and χ^2 47-12. It explains significant variation in the crop pattern over a period from 1989-90 to 1995-96 in Kundiyanatham Village.

All the rank correlation coefficients are statistically significant at 5 per cent level. The concordance coefficient for the village = 0.8874 and χ^2 = 93.177, indicate that there is significant change in the crop pattern in the village from 1989-90 to 1995-96.

Table 6.24 : Results of Spearman's Rank Correlation Coefficient for Pottiyam Village

Sl. No.	*Pairs of years Between*		*Rank Correlation Coefficient*	*Critical Values*
1.	1989-90	1990-91	0.9908	0.5179
2.	1990-91	1991-92	0.9743	0.5179
3.	1991-92	1992-93	0.9989	0.5179
4.	1992-93	1993-94	0.9877	0.5179
5.	1993-94	1994-95	0.9952	0.5179
6.	1994-95	1995-96	0.9938	0.5179

Table 6.25 : Results of Spearman's Rank Correlation Coefficient for Malliampady Village

Sl. No.	*Pairs of years Between*		*Rank Correlation Coefficient*	*Critical Values*
1.	1989-90	1990-91	0.975	0.7143
2.	1990-91	1991-92	0.9528	0.7143
3.	1991-92	1992-93	0.9694	0.7143
4.	1992-93	1993-94	0.9625	0.7143
5.	1993-94	1994-95	0.9458	0.7143
6.	1994-95	1995-96	0.9972	0.7143

The Results of Spearman's Correlation coefficient is are statistically significant. Similarly, the concordance coefficient is 0.5840 and χ^2 = 32.70 indicate that there is significant variation in the crop pattern for the given period.

IV. The production possibilities with inputs use and output of various crops favour cultivating traditional crops rather than the newly introduced agricultural package schemes under the Tribal Sub-Plan.

As explained in Chapter VI, Tables 6.13-6.16, the results of multiple regression Karl Pearson's correlation coefficient and simple regression, with relevant tests conducted, show that the tribal areas is more suitable for cultivating millets rather than the schemes implemented through the TSP.

References

1. Barraclough, Solon. "Politics First", Ceres, 1974, No. 41, pp. 24-28, as quoted in Joan P. Mencher's Agriculture and social structure in Tamil Nadu: Past Origins, Present Transformations and Future Prospects, [Allied Publishers Pvt. Ltd., Madras 1978] p. 2.

2. Government of India: Seventh Five Year Plan, Vol. I, p. 12, as taken from I.C. Dhingra, The Indian Economy Resources Planning Development and Problems [Sultan Chand and Sons, New Delhi, 1992], p. 87.

3. Manual of South Arcot, compiled by J.H. Garstin M.C.S. Collector of South Arcot (Lawrence Asylum Press, Madras 1878), p. 375.

4. Government of Tamil Nadu: Annual Tribal-Sub-Plan, 1995-1996, p. 3.

5. Galbraith, J.K. The Voice of the Poor: Essays in Economic, and political persuasion [Harvard University Press, 1983).

6. Jamison and Marlaine, Lockeed E, "Participation in Schooling; Determinants and learning outcomes in Nepal", Economic Development and Cultural Change, Vol. 35, No. 2, Jan.1987, pp. 279-306, and Ahuluwalia, Montek. "Inequality, Poverty and Development", Journal of Development Economics, Vol. 3, 1976, pp. 307-342.

7. Census Reports of 1971 and 1991.

8. Madras Institute of Development Studies: Tamil Nadu Economy : Performance and Issues (Oxford and IBH Publishing Co. Pvt. Ltd., New Delhi, 1988) p. 55.

9. Reserve Bank of India: Report of the Committee on Agricultural Productivity in Eastern India, (Publication Division of Bombay, Vol. I, 1984).

10. Government of India: Report of the commissioner *op. cit.* p. 48.

7

Summary and Suggestions

The New Economic Policy of the Government of India with a newer approach to economic development does not explicitly say anything about the future of land reforms in the country. However, in India, there is a need for land reforms, because of wide and unequal distribution of land and surplus agricultural labourers. Scarcity of capital among small and marginal farmers is yet another problem. Further, in all these years the "trickle down" process and poverty alleviation policies and programmes have not substantially improved the economic conditions of the rural poor. Hence, to initiate rural development, an appropriate and comprehensive land reform measures are inevitable to put the unproductive resources to more productivity. It is true that such reform measures are capable of generating more purchasing power, eradicate poverty and also transfer surplus factors toward agricultural as well as industrial development.

In India, land reform is a State subject. It is uniformly applied both in tribal as well as non-tribal area. But, land reform measures should differ in tribal areas from non-tribal areas, because, of the subtle distinction between these two areas. Introducing land reform measures in the tribal areas are simple as well as complex. It is simple, because, the allotment of land is only to the tribals of a particular locality.

While it is complex due to: insufficient land records owing to heritage ownership, socially, culturally, economically diverse tribal groups and the tribal areas are generally inaccessible. This situation is indeed tragic, for all the tribal people, since they were land owners in the beginning and their right on land was not recognised and there was total absence of official agencies or legal authorities in the tribal areas.

Adding to these the extension of the formal system from the non tribal areas had disturbed their right over forest and land. The ingress of non-tribals as contractors, moneylenders and businessmen had resulted in indebtedness and land alienation. The reservation of forests under the Forest Conservation Act prohibits the tribals to collect the Minor Forest Produce. This is to arrest the deleterious deforestrating effect of shifting cultivation, land slide and soil erosion.

The land reforms for agrarian reconstruction are considered to be of paramount importance than any other development programme for rural development. Therefore, an attempt has been made in the thesis, to study "Land Reforms and Tribal Development: A Case Study of Kalrayan Hills, Tamil Nadu".

In Kalrayan hills of Tamil Nadu, the inhabitants are called "Malayalis' who are the homogenous single tribal group. The hill was under three Jagirdars viz., The Ariya Goundan Jagir, The Kurumba goundan Jagir and The Jadaya Goundan Jagir. They were appointed by the King Krishna Devaraya to collect the revenue from the tribals. But, they slowly took over the hill's administration and ruled their respective villages till 1976. They obtained a Court order and stalled all the land measures in the Kalrayan Hills. However, in order to free the tribals from the clutches of Jagirdars, on 25.8.1976, the Government of Tamil Nadu took over the hill from the Jagirdars by applying the Inam Estate (Abolition and Conversion into Ryotwari) Act of 1963 and the Bonded Labour System (Abolition) Act of 1976.

In the hill, fresh survey and settlement operations were carried out and lands were assigned to the tribals. Along with the land reform measures, several package measures were implemented in the Kalrayan hill from the Fifth Five Year Plan onwards. But, the resultant condition of tribals due to these reform processes is too complex and intricate. The tribals are passing through a unique phase from Jagirdar's administration to the direct Government's administration.

The objectives of this study were: to study the origin and present conditions of the Kalrayan hill tribes; to review the land reforms and tribal development measures implemented in the various five year plans; to study the method and progress of land reform measures undertaken in the study area; to study the socio-economic conditions of tribals in the post-reform period; to study the inputs used and output of various crops cultivated by the beneficiary tribals, and to suggest an alternative strategy for tribal development.

This study was conducted with the documents available about the hill spanning over 200 years. As regards primary data Vellimalai Taluk was chosen for an in-depth analysis. In the taluk, of the 25 villages, 9 villages have been chosen for the study, representing lower hill villages (3 villages) and upper hill villages (6 villages). The sample villages have been chosen in such a way that the result drawn from the study will be representative of the other villages. The nine villages have 1537 households of which 10 per cent of the households were contacted with a specially prepared pre tested questionnaire. Karl Pearson's correlation coefficient, multiple regression, and Spearman's rank correlation coefficient were used in the thesis. Finally, to test the hypotheses 'F' test 'χ^2' test, test of concordance and test for Spearman's' correlation co-efficient were adopted and discussed in the thesis. The research study is presented in seven chapters.

A review of fifty seven studies on the major aspects and problems of the tribals like shifting cultivation, settled cultivation, land alienation and indebtedness were discussed in chapter II. The notable studies were B. Sridharan, S.A. Radhakrishnan, Katar Singh, K.M.B. Rahim, Naresh Chandra, R.P. Singh, Peter Dorner, Tirath Gupta, Shreekant Sambrani, Durgeswar Borah, Mohammed Hasan, Ashok R. Basu, Roy Burman, S.L. Dubey, Ratna Murdia, U.K. Roy, Vinod Jha, Rekha Bandyopadhyay, B.S. Sindhu, E.H. Jacoby, C.F. Jacoby, Keith Griffin, P.J. Dooren, Keith Sutton,Charles C. Geisher, Frank J. Popper, Nrendra K. Sethi, Arthur Macewan, Katar Singh etc. The studies revealed that the States have controlled shifting cultivation by imposing a ban on such practices in the tribal areas. Few studies portray that shifting cultivation came to an end when permanent plough land was assigned to the tribals. It also discussed that the entry of forest department into the tribal areas had also displaced tribals from doing shifting cultivation. The studies on tribals' indebtedness proved that indebtedness resulted in land alienation in the tribal areas. Several studies on land alienation and indebtedness expressed that the legislative measure taken up by the government show only a partial success in controlling such problems in the tribal areas due to bureaucratic and administrative factors.

A study of land reforms and various tribal development measures undertaken during the Five Year Plans were examined in Chapter III of the thesis. The approaches of the Plan show that the thrust on land reform was slowed down from the Sixth Plan onwards. Further, the land reform policies reiterated the same objectives of achieving social justice along with economic development as mentioned in the previous plan policies. Similarly, it is observed that in States like Tamil Nadu, no special law has been enacted to solve the tribals land problems.

The major tribal development measures implemented in the Five Year Plans were discussed in the Third Chapter of this thesis. The First Plan had suggested uniform land reform measures for the whole country. It includes the abolition of intermediaries, ceiling on land holdings, tenancy reform and consolidation of holdings. During the Plan 20 million cultivators were brought under ryotwari system and 57.7 lakhs hectares of land was distributed to the landless agriculturists. The total compensation paid to the erstwhile zamindars was Rs. 670 crore.

In the Second Plan, abolition of intermediaries like Zamindars, Jagirdars and Inamdars was completed in more than 40 per cent of the total area of the country. The total compensation paid to the intermediaries was Rs. 2250 million. Land reform measure in the Second plan included consolidation of land holdings and legislation to prevent fragmentation of land holding under the agrarian reorganisation programme.

Land reforms measures in the Third Plan were abolition of intermediary tenures, reduction of rents, security of tenure, resumption of tenancies rights of ownership for tenants, ceiling on agricultural holdings schemes of resettlement and consolidation of holdings. 20 million of tenants were brought into direct relationship with the State. In the total amount of Rs. 670 crore the compensation amount was Rs. 520 crores and the for interest charges Rs. 150 crore.

In the Fourth Plan, the land reform measures received attention in the recommendations of the Land Reforms Implementation Committee of the National Development Council. In this Plan, about 9, 64,800 hectares of land had been declared as surplus and 6,40,000 hectares have been taken possession of by the State Governments for distribution. In the tribal areas, protection to the tribals in problems like land alienation, scaling down of debts, regulating money lending and control of rate of interest charged by moneylenders and reforming the existing administrative machinery. Multi-Purpose Co-operative Societies, Forest Labour Co-operatives and Tribal Development Blocks were not successful in the tribal areas.

Therefore, by replacing all these schemes a Tribal Sub-Plan approach was evolved and implemented from the Fifth

Plan onwards. This is designed for displaced tribal areas of seventeen states and two Union Territories. However, the studies show that even the Tribal Sub-Plan is merely an extension of schemes meant for the non-tribals.

In the Fifth Plan, the introduction of Tribal Sub-Plan; and the Kalrayan hills were brought under the direct rule of the Government in 1976. The TSP was implemented in 17 States and 2 Union Territories. The other tribal population wise dominated States had regular Plans for tribal development. The Integrated Tribal Development Projects (ITDP's) comprising generally administrative units like sub-division/Tahshils/Taluks with 50 per cent or more Scheduled Tribe Population; 284 pockets of tribal concentration (MADA Pockets) having a total population of 10,000 or more and a Scheduled Tribe population of 50 per cent or more, and 73 Primitive Tribal Group Projects. Like the earlier plans, the Fifth Plan also gave emphasis to land reforms and the same procedure. Laws pertaining to ceiling on land holdings were enacted in all the states except Punjab areas of Haryana and Punjab. During this Plan, Land Reform Tribunals was formed as the core of the implementation machinery in the new strategy of land reforms.

In the Sixth Plan, land reforms and TSP were the major schemes. The Tribal Sub-Plan during the plan concentrated on shifting cultivation, horticulture, credit-cum-marketing, minor irrigation, forestry oriented programme, programme for landless tribals, animal husbandry and education. During the Seventh Plan, the total plan outlay for Tribal Sub-Plan was Rs. 5832.27 lakhs and the expenditure was Rs. 5380.06 lakhs in Tamil Nadu. The plan was to build up the economic base for about 30 lakhs tribal families under beneficiary oriented programmes, human resource development and infrastructure development.

The Eighth Plan focused on the problems like landlessness, unirrigated and poorly developed lands, agricultural worker and bonded labour system. The major ameliorative activities undertaken in the plan were towards the welfare of the tribal population by providing education, employment and housing. The important Acts passed in Tamil Nadu were, The Tamil Nadu Cultivations Tenants Protection Act, 1955; The Tamil Nadu Cultivating Tenants (Payments of Fair Rents) Act, 1956; The Tamil Nadu Land Reforms (Fixation of ceiling on Land) Act, 1961; The Tamil Nadu Public Trusts (Regular Administration of Agricultural Lands), Act, 1961; The Tamil Nadu Agricultural Lands Records of Tenancy Rights Act, 1969; and The Scheduled Castes and the Scheduled Tribal (Prevention of Atrocities) Act, 1989.

In the Ninth Plan, 37,876 families were assisted for their economic betterment under various programmes of TSP as against the Ninth Plan target of 51,382 families. The objective of the Tenth Plan is to reduce the percentage of SC/ ST families living below poverty line to less than 10 per cent and to raise their economic status.

Further, in all these Five Year Plans more emphasis was repeatedly laid on the major problems of the tribals like shifting cultivation, land alienation, indebtedness and tribals right on forest and forest produce. Therefore, it indicates only under achievement or incomplete implementation of tribal development programmes in the Five Year Plans.

Historical, administrative and economic background of the tribes of the Kalrayan Hill has been discussed in Chapter IV. The study revealed that the Kalrayan Hill was controlled by three Jagirdars. The tribal chieftains had a virtual control over the hill for over many centuries from the period of the King Krishna Devaraya of Vijayanagar Kingdom. Moreover, during the British colonial rule the Jagirdars got right over the hill land under the "Inam settlement in the Madras Presidency", for a small "quit-rent" payable to the Government. The present study observed that the economic and social exploitation by the Jagirdars forced the Government to take over the hill from the Jagirs. During the Jagirs regime no land record was maintained and the tribals were deprived of all basic amenities that were available to their counterparts in the other tribal areas of the State. Therefore, as soon as the Kalrayan hill was taken over in 1976, fresh survey and settlement operations were carried out and facilities were extended to the tribals. It was observed that due land settlement operations, shifting cultivation was displaced from the area.

The different category of land classified during is the post-land reform period was also discussed in the chapter. The Sample Villages in the Kalrayan block show that the forest land occupied the vast area of land varying from a minimum of 60 per cent to the maximum of 80 per cent of the total land, in all the sample villages. The variation in the forest land, net cultivated and the other types of land given in tables portray only incomplete land reforms in the Kalrayan Hills.

The Crop pattern in the Kalrayan hill and in the sample villages show that varagu and samai crops were extensively cultivated followed by paddy crop in the nineteen crops cultivated by the tribals. It was observed in the study that the commercial crops were grown under monsoon conditions and also by using traditional methods of cultivation.

The modus operandi of the land reforms act in Tamil Nadu discussed in chapter V, portrayed that "Survey and Settlement" operations were carried out in the Kalrayan hill without probing into the actual land use pattern during the pre-land reform period. The crucial recommendations of the "Survey Team" depicted in Table 5.1. Show that only 14.22 per cent of and was distributed to the tribal and more extent of land was declared as forest land (79.19) per cent). It was estimated in the study the per capita land distributed was only 0.28 hectares. Therefore, the study felt that in the post-land reforms period land alienation in different form was found in the Kalrayan Hill.

In the study area, the financial and technical assistance were provided to the tribals under the package schemes through the Tribal Sub-Plan from 1976 onwards. If is found in the study that the package measures were only an extension of programmes from the usual state plan model. Further, through TSP high yielding varieties of paddy seed have been distributed to the tribals, but, the hill area is suitable for raising crops under monsoon conditions. Therefore the high yielding varieties of paddy seed was not accepted by the hill tribals.

Similarly, through package schemes pesticides have been distributed it covers constantly 1200 acres from 1985-86 to 1995-96, which is a very negligible area of the total land. The performance of LAMPS as discussed in Chapter V show that a large number of non-tribals were allowed to become members of the society. On the other hand, LAMPS also includes both the co-operative credit and non-credit functions. The LAMPS is an extension of co-operative Credit Society, functioning in the non-tribal areas of the state. Incidentally, it is worth noting that in the study area the tribals are more willing to borrow money from the LAMPS rather than disposing their marketable surplus to the society. This is also because of not only delay in the payment to the procured products but also LAMPS offers a low price compared to the private buyers. The high price offered by the private buyers also draws Government's intervention to safeguard the tribals from exploitation. Further, the TRIFED and the co-operative farming were not seen functioning in the tribal area.

Analysis of the tribal economy of the Kalrayan hill presented in Chapter VI depicts their actual socio-economic conditions during the post-land reform period. In the hill no difference in the size of the family was found between the lower as well as upper hill villages. The distribution of population portray that more percentage of tribals (50.55 per cent) were found in 15-59 age-group of the total population. The main occupation of the hill tribal was farm occupation (87.18 per cent). As indicated in the chapter majority of the tribals were illiterate.

The economic analysis shows that the major wealth was the value of land. The major proportion of wealth was 58.93 per cent when compared to the value of livestock 12.52 per cent, value of house 11.81 per cent, value of consumer durables 9.8 per cent and value of agricultural implements 6.94 per cent.

Land allotted by the Government was 51.25 per cent of the total land. The land under dispute between the Government and the tribals was 40.99 per cent of the total land. According to the records of the State, there is no disputed land, but the firsthand information as depicted in Table 6.6 provides support for the existence of disputed land. The views of the tribals presented in Chapter VI, explain only incomplete implementation of land reforms in the Kalrayan Hills.

The principal crops cultivated by the tribals were Varagu and Samai 50.69 per cent of land and Paddy in 31.11 per cent of land. The other crops were Ragi (7.43 per cent), Tapioca (7.41 per cent), Groundnut (1.62 per cent) and Plantain (1.33 per cent). The tribals sow the paddy seed called "punal kattu nellu", which was suitable to the hill area. The high-yielding varieties of seed and technology provided through Tribal Sub-Plan were inappropriate.

In the employment, only one tribe was working in a Bank and others engaged in their own traditional work under the new environment. They also work in other's farm for wage or on exchange of labour or reciprocal labour and employed in other works like building construction, non-farm works etc., sometime, they also move out of their habitation to seek employment elsewhere in the low country. The male tribes work on an average 277 days in a year, of which 179 days in farm and 98 days in other works. Whereas, female labour work for 148 days in a year, of which 105 days in farm and 43 days in other works. Further, both male and female on an average work for 425 days in farm and other work.

The per capita income of the sample tribals was Rs. 2712. The per capita income of the sample villages was Rs. 3008 in Kendikkal, Rs. 2233 in Vellimalai, Rs. 2340 in Karialur, Rs. 1955 in Mavadipattu, Rs. 1951 in Nochimedu, Rs. 1497 in Kundiyanatham, Rs. 3509 in Vazhapady, Rs. 3225 in Pottiyam and Rs. 3517 in Malliampady.

The per capita household expenditure was Rs. 12048 per annum, whereas, their per capita annual household income was Rs. 13834. The loans borrowed from moneylenders constitute the major proportion (71.59 per cent). The village wise data also shows that the loans outstanding were more to the moneylenders than to the Government agencies. The loan outstanding to moneylenders was 90.86 per cent in Vellimali. It was because the village exposed to the non-tribals due to its locational advantage.

The inputs used and output from crops like paddy, varagu, samai ragi and tapioca analysed with multiple regression, simple regression, Karl Pearson's correlation coefficient shows that given the soil condition, technology, irrigation and the cost of cultivation, the hill area was more suitable for raising millets like varagu, samai and ragi rather than the other crops.

In the study, a significant variation was observed between the land under dispute and the total land of the tribals. Further, the study found a significant change in the land use pattern during the post-land reform period. In the analysis, a significant change in the crop pattern was observed in the hill area from 1986 to 1996. The fact presented in the thesis proves the vicious pray of prejudices of good towards the tribals in the land reform measures. Even though, land reform measures are capable of advancing economic growth of the tribals, it is not implemented in its right spirit and method.

Similarly the accompanied package measures are brought from conventional frame meant for the non-tribals.

Hence, the resulting condition is traumatic and failed to affect the desired results in the Kalrayan hill. On the other hand, the transition from non-ryotwari to ryotwari system had changed many tribals' farmers as landless labourers and also brought a new category of land called disputed land in the Kalrayan hill. As found in other tribal areas of the country, forest officials are problems to the tribals in the Kalrayan hill. Altogether, the Kalrayan hill requires a need based administrative reform for an effective tribal development programmes as suggested below.

Suggestions

1. As per the guidelines given by the Government, the census authorities cannot enumerate the Malayali tribes if they move out of their villages during the census enumeration work. However, Kadar and Irular tribes of Tamil Nadu are exempted from such "area restriction" in the census enumeration. It is suggested that the Malayali tribals are the major tribals of the State they should not be subject to the "area restriction" during the census enumeration.

2. The growth rate of non-tribal population is alarming compared to the growth rate of tribal population in the tribal areas. Such a condition would result in non-tribals usurping the benefits meant for the tribals. Therefore, Government should prohibit the settlement of non-tribals in the tribal areas.

3. Educational attainment of tribals is low compared to the others. The performance of the Government Tribal Residential Schools are not upto the standards. Further, tribal villages in the inaccessible areas do not have schools. Moreover, the schools run by the Non-Governmental Organisation are performing well. Therefore, they must be encouraged for a better educational system for the tribal areas.

4. Government should encourage tribals to start business or trade in their areas. Similarly, adequate number of fair price shops for selling of essential items should be opened and they should be run by tribals themselves. Such a move would reduce the non-tribals entry into tribal areas as businessmen and traders.

5. The non-farm occupation is the lowest in the tribal areas. Therefore, job opportunities should be created in the off-season period. Perhaps, this step would control migration of tribals into non-tribal areas and also increases their employment opportunity and income.

6. Statutory minimum wages must be fixed exclusively for the tribals.

7. Indebtedness is rampant among the tribals. Since indebtedness result in land alienation law must be enacted to protect the tribals from the dispossession and alienation of tribal lands.

8. In Tamil Nadu, there is no law to prohibit land alienation in the tribal areas. The 'Revenue Standing Order' that controls the land alienation in the tribal areas does not have any constitutional authority. Therefore, special law must be enacted in this regard.

9. Disputed land between Government and the tribals were reported by the tribals. Therefore, fresh look is needed to solve their land problems by allotting some more lands to the tribals or fresh survey should be conducted in the areas.

10. Government should allow the tribals to use the forest land and to collect the minor forest produce. This will be possible only if it amends the Forest Conservation Act. In order to safeguard the

valuable forest wealth, responsibilities should be fixed on the tribals in the preservation of forest and forest land.

11. A close coordination between forest officials and tribals and officials and officials of other department is all the more needed to assert their purposeful role in the tribal areas.

12. LAMPS should not club credit and non-credit function. To perform the non-credit function more effectively, a separate agency should be formed.

13. The Tribal Sub-Plan should come out evolving and implementing the routine development programmes. The sub-plan should be need-based and it should involve the native tribals in its functioning.

14. To review the working of programmes in the tribal areas a committee should be formed with due representation of tribals and officials in different capacities.

15. The scheduled castes and Scheduled Tribes have subtle differences in terms of social and economic features. However, presently the Director of Adi-Dravida and Tribal Welfare is the authority for implementing various schemes and policies for both the groups. Here, it will be perfect if the department is separated for an effective administration and development.

16. The administrative machinery in the tribal areas should be totally revamped. To begin with the offices of the Government departments must be located only in the tribal areas and not in non-tribal areas. To this effect the taluk office must be shifted from Sankarapuram to the Kalrayan hill area.

Appendix 1

Average Cost of Cultivation of Varagu and Samai Crops in the Selected Villages (in Rs.)

(Per acre)

Sl. No.	*Name of the Village*	*Seed Cost*	*Ploughing Cost*	*Manure and Fertilizer Cost*	*Labour Cost*	*Total*
1.	Kendikkal	33 (7.16)	76 (16.49)	57 (12.36)	295 (63.99)	461 (100.00)
2.	Vellimalai	29 (8.31)	77 (22.06)	55 (15.75)	188 (53.86)	349 (100.00)
3.	Karialur	41 (9.62)	107 (25.12)	70 (16.43)	208 (48.83)	426 (100.00)
4.	Mavadipattu	31 (6.46)	95 (16.94)	77 (16.04)	277 (57.71)	480 (100.00)
5.	Nochimedu	35 (7.13)	147 (29.94)	91 (18.53)	218 (44.4)	491 (100.00)
6.	Kundiyanatham	38 (7.82)	128 (26.34)	63 (12.96)	257 (52.88)	486 (100.00)
7.	Vazhapady	37 (9.84)	84 (22.34)	58 (15.43)	197 (52.39)	376 (100.00)
8.	Pottiyam	32 (6.27)	130 (25.49)	71 (13.92)	277 (54.31)	510 (100.00)
9.	Malliampady	39 (8.90)	110 (25.11)	75 (17.12)	214 (48.86)	438 (100.00)
	Total	315 (7.84)	954 (23.75)	617 (15.36)	2131 (53.15)	4017 (100.00)

Source: Computed, (values in parentheses are percentages to the total).

Appendix 2

Total Population and Percentage of Scheduled Tribe under TSP-1991

Sl. No.	*India/State or Union Territory*	*Total Population ('000)*	*Scheduled Tribe Population ('000)*	*Scheduled Tribe Percentage of Total Population*
	INDIA	8,38,584	67,758	8.08
1.	Andhra Pradesh	66,508	4,200	6.31
2.	Assam	22,414	2,874	12.82
3.	Bihar	86,374	6,617	7.66
4.	Gujarat	41,310	6,162	14.92
5.	Himachal Pradesh	5,171	218	4.22
6.	Karnataka	44,977	1,916	4.26
7.	Kerala	29,099	321	1.10
8.	Madhya Pradesh	66,181	15,399	23.27
9.	Maharashtra	78,937	7,318	9.27
10.	Manipur	1,837	632	34.41
11.	Orissa	31,660	7,032	22.21
12.	Rajasthan	44,006	5,475	12.44
13.	Sikkim	406	91	22.36
14.	Tamil Nadu	55,859	574	1.03
15.	Tripura	2,757	853	30.95
16.	Uttar Pradesh	139,112	288	0.21
17.	West Bengal	68,078	3,809	5.59
	UNION TERRITORIES			
1.	Andaman & Nicobar Islands	281	27	9.54
2.	Daman and Diu	102	12	11.54

Source: Union Primary Census Abstract for Scheduled Castes and Scheduled Tribes, Series-I, 1991.

Bibliography

Books

Basu, Ashok, R., *Tribal Development Programmes and Administration in India.* (National Book Organisation, New Delhi, 1985).

Bezy, Fernand. (Ed.,) "Belgian Congo" in Adamantious Papelasis, *et.al., Economic Development : Analysis and Case Studies.* (Universal Book Stall, Delhi, 1967).

Boserup, Ester. *The Conditions of Agricultural Growth: The Economics of Agrarian Change.* (George Allen and Unwin Ltd., London, 1965).

Burman, B.K. Roy. *Towards Poverty Alleviation Programmes in Nagaland and Manipur* (Mittal Publications, Delhi, 1984).

Chand, Mahesh and Puri, V.K., *Regional Planning in India,* (Allied Publications Pvt. Ltd., New Delhi, 1983).

Dorner, Peter. *Land Reform and Economic Development.* (Penguin Modern Economics Texts, C. Nicholls and Company Ltd., Middlesek, England, 1972).

Dubey, S.N. and Murdia, Ratna (Ed.,) *Land Alienation and Restoration in Tribal Communities in India,* (Himalaya Publishing House, Bombay, 1977).

Edminster, Robert. (Ed.,) "Mexico", in Adamantious Papelasis *et al., Economic Development : Analysis and Case Studies.* (Universal Book Stall, Delhi, 1967).

George, Jose and Sreekumar, S.S. *Tribal Development Legislation and Enforcement.* (Commonwealth Publications, New Delhi, 1994).

Gilder, George. *Wealth and Poverty.* (Kalyani Publishers, New Delhi, 1981).

Griffin, Keith. *Land Concentration and Rural Poverty.* (The Macmillan Press Ltd., Madras, 1976).

Gispert, P. *Tribal India: A Synthetic View of Primitive Man* (Rawat Publications, Jaipur, 1983).

Gupta, Dipankar. "Integrated Tribal Development Programme : An Evaluation of ITDP in Birbhum District, West Bengal" in M.L.Dantwala *et.al.,* (Ed.,), *Asian Seminar on Rural Development : The Indian Experience.* (Oxford and IBH Publishing Co. Pvt. Ltd., New Delhi, 1986).

Gupta, Ranjit (Ed.) *Planning for Tribal Development.* (Ankur Publishing House, New Delhi, 1976).

Herring, Renold J. *Land to the Tiller: The Political Economy of Agrarian Reform in South Asia.* (Oxford University Press, Delhi, 1983).

Khusro, A.M. *Economics and Social Effects of Jagirdari Abolition and Land Reform in Hyderabad.* (Osmania University Press, Hyderabad, 1958).

Kottakayam, Jacob John. *Social Structure and Change among the Tribals.* (D.K. Publication, New Delhi, 1983).

Kulkarni, M.G. *Problems of Tribal Development: A Case Study*. (Parimal Prakashan, Aurangabad, 1974).

Kuppuswamy, B. *Social Change in India*. (Vikas Publications, New Delhi, 1972).

Kurien, C.T. and James, Josef. *Economic Change in Tamil Nadu: A Regionally and Functionally Disaggregated Study*. (Allied Publishers Private Limited, Bombay, 1979).

______ *Poverty, Planning and Social Transformation* (Allied Publishers Private Limited, Bombay, 1978).

Kuznets, Simon. *Modern Economic Growth: Rate, Structure and Spread,* (Vakils, Feffer and Simons Private Ltd., Bombay, 1966).

______ *Economic Growth and Structure: Selected Essays,* (Oxford and IBM Publishing Co., New Delhi, 1965).

Jacoby, E.H. and Jacoby, C.F. *Man and Land: The Fundamental Issues in Development,* (Andre Deutsch, London, 1971).

Jain T.L. *Poverty in India: An Economic Analysis*. (Ess Ess Publicatons, New Delhi, 1987).

Jones, Steve *et al.,* (Ed.) *Rural Poverty and Agrarian Reform* (Allied Publishers, Bombay, 1982).

Joshi, P.C. *Institutional Aspects of Agricultural Development: India from Asian Perspective*. (Allied Publishers Pvt. Ltd., New Delhi, 1987).

______ "Problems of Land Reforms in the Second Stage" in V.S. Mahajan (Ed.) *Studies in Indian Economy* (Deep and Deep Publications, New Delhi, 1983).

Majumdar, D.N. *Races and Cultures of India.* (Asia Publishing House, Bombay, 1961).

Mencher, Joan P. *Agriculture and Social Structure in Tamil Nadu : Past Origins, Present Transformations and Future Prospects* (Allied Publishers Private Limited, Madras, 1978).

MIDS. *Tamil Nadu Economy: Performance and Issues,* (Oxford and IBH Publishing Co. Pvt. Ltd., Bombay, 1988).

Mukherjee, Ramakrishna. *Social Indicators.* (The Macmillan Company of India Limited, Bombay, 1975).

Mukhopadhyay, Sundhi K. *Sources of Variations in Agricultural Productivity: A Cross Section Time-Series Study in India.* (The Macmillan Company of India Limited, Bombay, 1976).

Myrdal, Gunnar. *Economic Theory and Underdeveloped Regions.* (Methuen and Co. Ltd., London, 1969).

Nair, M.K. Sukumaran. *Tribal Economy in Transition.* (Inter-India Publishers, Tribal Studies of India Series T122, New Delhi, 1987).

Rangachari, A.V. and Elango, R. (Ed.) *Basic Needs Planning.* (Department of Economics, Annamalai Univesity, Annamalai Nagar, 1990).

Ramaiah, P. *Tribal Economy of India* (Light and Life Publishers, New Delhi, 1981).

Saradamoni, K. *Divided Poor: Study of a Kerala Village.* (Ajanta Publications, New Delhi, 1981).

Sen, Amartya. *Employment Technology and Development.* (Oxford University Press, Delhi, 1975).

Sidhu, B.S. *Land Reform, Welfare and Economic Growth.* (Vora and Co. Publishers Pvt. Ltd., Bombay, 1976).

Schultz, Theodre W. *Economic Growth and Agriculture.* (McGraw Hill Book Company, New Hork, 1968).

______ *The Economic Organisation of Agriculture.* (Tata McGraw Hill Publishing Company, Bombay, 1953).

Singh, Baldev. "Planning for Rural Development: Economics of Land Redistribution (A Study Based on a Regional Programming Model) in D.M. Nanjundappa and R.K. Sinha (Ed.,) *Backward Area Development, Problems and Prospects* (Sterling Publishers Pvt. Ltd., New Delhi, 1982).

Singh, Karan. *Population, Poverty and the Future of India,* (National Institute of Family Planning, New Delhi, 1975).

Singh, Tarlok *et.al.,* (Ed.) *Impact of Land Reforms on Agriculture and Rural Development.* (National Institute of Rural Development and Indian Association of Social Science Institutions, New Delhi, 1992).

Sonachalam, K.S. *Land Reforms in Tamil Nadu: Evaluation of Implementation* (Oxford and IBH Publishing Company, New Delhi, 1970).

Srivastava, S.K. *et.al.,* (Ed.,) *Agricultural Economics and Co-operation. (A Study in Agricultural Economy and Co-operative Development with Special Reference to India),* (S.Chand and Co., Delhi, 1970).

Srinivasan, T.N. *"Income Distribution: A Survey of Policy Aspects"* in Charan D. Wadhva, *Some Problems of India's Economic Policy.* (Tata McGraw Hill Publishing Company, Bombay, 1977).

Venkataramani, G. *Land Reform in Tamil Nadu.* (Sangam Publishers, Madras, 1973).

Vidyarthi, L.P. and Rai B.K. *The Tribal Culture of India.* (Concept Publishing Co., New Delhi, 1976).

Vyas N.N. *Land and Tribals* (Ed.) (Published by M.L.V. Tribal Research and Training Institute, Rajasthan, 1983).

______ *Bondage and Exploitation in Tribal India.* (Rawat Publications, Delhi, 1980).

______ and Mann, R.S. *Indian Tribes in Transition.* (Rawat Publications, Jaipur, 1980).

Warriner, Dorren. *Land Reform in Principle and Practice.* (Clarendon Press, Oxford, 1969).

Journals

Balakrishnan, V. *et.al.,* "Changing Tribal Economy of the Nilgiris-An Appraisal", *Indian Journal of Agricultural Economics,* Vol. 47, No. 3, July-September 1992.

Bandyopadhyay, Rekha. "Global Review of Land Reform: A Critical Perspectives", *Economic and Political Weekly,* March 16, 1996.

Bardhan, P. K. "On the Minimum Level of Living and the Rural Poor", *Indian Economic Review,* Vol. V, No. 1, April, 1970.

Bhaduri, A. "Class Relations and the Pattern of Accumulation in an Agrarian Economy". *Cambridge Journal of Ecnomics,* 1981.

Barthakur, I.K. "Tribal Economy" *Yojana,* Vol. 33, No. 2, December 1-15, 1989.

Bhattacharjee, P. R. "New Horizons of Tribal Development in Tripura", *Journal of North East Indian Council of Social Science Research,* Vol. 11, No. 1, April, 1987.

Burman, B.K. Roy. "Issues in Tribal Development", *Mainstream,* Vol. XXIII, No. 20, January 12, 1985.

Choudhari, Kalyan. "Bonded Labour", *Economic and Political Weekly,* Vol. XI, No. 11, March 13, 1976.

Conference Number, *Indian Journal of Agricultural Economics,* Vol. 47, No. 3, July-Sep. 1992.

______ *Indian Journal of Agricultural Economics,* Vol. XXXIII, October-December 1978.

Dandekar, V.M. "From Agrarian Reorganisation to Land Reform", *Artha Vignana,* Vol. VI, No. 1, 1964.

______ and Rath, N. "Poverty in India", *Economic and Political Weekly,* Vol. VI, January, 1971.

Dantwala, M.L. and Shah, C.H. "Pre-Reform and Post-Reform Agrarian Structure", *Indian Journal of Agricultural Economics,* Vol. XXVI, No. 3, July-September, 1971.

Flores, E. "Issues of Land Reform", *Journal of Political Economy,* Vol. 78, No. 4, July-Aug. 1970.

George, P. T. "The Evolution of Land Tenure in India", *Artha Vignana,* Vol. 12, 1970.

______ "Land System and Land Legislation in Madras", *Artha Vignana,* Vol. 12, 1970.

Ghosh, Ratan. "Land Reforms and the Draft Five Year Plan 1978-83", *Economic and Political Weekly,* Vol. XIV, No. 45, Nov. 10, 1979.

______ and Nagraj, K. "Land Reforms in West Bengal", *Social Scientist*, January-February, 1978.

Goswami, Atul. "Tribal Development with Special Reference to North-East India", *Social Scientist*, Vol. 12, No. 8, August, 1984.

Gupta, Tirath and SAMBRANI, Sreekant. "Control of Shifting Cultivation: The Need for an Integrated Approach and Systematic Appraisal", *Indian Journal of Agricultural Economics*. Vol. 33, October-December, 1978.

Hanumantharao C.H. "Structural Adjustment: Lessons from East Asian Experience", *The Times of India*. February 10, 1995.

______ "Farm Mechanisation in a Labour Abundent Economy", *Economic and Political Weekly*, Vol. 7, (Annual Number, February, 1972).

______ "Ceilings on Agricultural Land-Holdings: Its Economic Rationale", *Economic and Political Weekly*, Vol. 7, No. 26, June 24, 1972.

Jahangir, B.K. "Tribal Peasant in Transition : Chittagong Hill Tracts", *Economic and Political Weekly*, Vol. 14, No. 11, March 17, 1979.

Khan, Sayeed Ahmed, "Dry Lands Development", *Yojana*, Vol. 33, No. 22, December 1-15, 1989.

Khaund, J.P. "A New Strategy for Tribal Development", *Yojana*, Vol. XXVI, No. 14 & 15, 1982.

Kulkarni, S.D., "Alienation of Adivasi Lands: Government Not Serious", *Economic and Political Weekly*, Vol. IX, No. 35, August 31, 1974.

_____ "Adivasi Sub-Plan : A Mid-Term Appraisal", Economical and Political Weekly, Vol. XII, No. 3, Janunary, 15, 1977.

Kunhaman, M. "The Tribal Economy of Kerala: An Intra-Regional Analysis", *Economic and Political Weekly*, Vol. XX, No. 11, March 16, 1985.

Ladejinsky, Wolf. "Land Ceilings and Land Reforms". *Economic and Political Weekly*, Vol. 7, (Annual Number, February, 1972).

Lakshman, T.K. *et.al.*, "Controversies over Ceilings on Land Holdings in India", *Southern Economist*, Vol. XII, No. 10, September 15, 1973.

Lakshmaiah, T. "Socio-Economic Development of Tribals", *Mainstream*, Vol. 18, December 19, 1984.

Lavania, G.S. and Dixit, R.S. "Economics of High-Yielding Varieties Programme in Package District, Aligarh", *Indian Journal of Agricultural Economics* (Research Co-Reprinters, New Delhi, Vol. XXVIII, 1968).

Mahalingam, S. "Role of Co-operatives in Tribal Economy", *Yojana*, Vol. 33, No. 22, December 1-15, 1989.

Malhotra, R. "Tribals : Which Way Justice", *Mainstream*, Vol. XXIII, No. 36, May 4, 1985.

Minhas, B.S. "Rural Poverty, Land Distribution and Development Strategy", *Indian Economic Review*, Vol. V, No. 1, April 1970.

Murdia, Ratna. "Land Allotment and Land Alienation: Policies and Programmes for Scheduled Castes and Tribes", *Economic and Political Weekly*, Vol. IX, No. 32, August 9, 1975.

Narayanan, Sachindra. "Plan and Planned Development: A Case Study of Primitive Tribe", *Mainstream*, Vol. XXII, No. 49, August 4, 1984.

Oommen, T.K. "Agrarian Legislations and Movements as sources of Change: The case of Kerala", *Economic and Political Weekly*, Vol. X, No. 40, October 4, 1975.

Parmer, Mary. "Tribal Planning in Himachal Pradesh", *Yojana*, Vol. 33, No. 22, December 1-15, 1989.

Patnaik, Utsa, "Capitalist Development in Agriculture", *Economic and Political Weekly*, Vol. 6, No. 39, September 25, 1971.

Prasad, Lal Mani. "Tribal Development Administration in India", *Social Change*, Vol. 18, No. 1, March 1988.

Prasad, R.R. "Tribal Development in India, Strategies, Programmes", *Journal of Rural Development*, Vol. 7, No. 1, January 1988.

Raj, K.N. "Ownership and Distribution of Land", *Indian Economic Review*, Vol. V, No. 1, April 1970.

Rajagopalan, V. and Varadarajan, S. "Impact of Risk and Uncertainty on Farm Production and Income in the Hills of the Nilgiris, Tamil Nadu", *Indian Journal of Agricultural Economics*, Conference Number Vol. XXXIII, October-December 1978.

Raj, Krishna. "Agrarian Reform in India: The Debate on Ceilings", *Economic Development and Cultural Change*, Vol. 7, No. 3, 1958-59.

Rammunny, Murkot. "Great Concern: Little Action". *The Hindu*, August 26, 1987.

Rao, N.V.N. and Reddy, P. Ram. "Minor Irrigation and Tribal Development: An Empirical Study", *Kurukshetra*, Vol. 34, No. 2, November, 1985.

Rath, N. "Garibi Hatao : Can IRDP do it", *Economic and Political Weekly*, Vol. XX, No. 6, February, 1985.

Sain, K. "Economic Analysis of Shifting Cultivation", *Indian Journal of Agricultural Economics*, Conference Number, Vol. XXXIII, October-December 1978.

Sen, Biswajit. "Impact of Tribal Welfare Programmes", *Yojana*, Vol. 33, No. 22, December 1-15, 1989.

Shrivastava, K.B. "Land Distribution in U.P: A Case Study", *Kurukshetra*, Vol. XXIV, No. 20, July 16, 1976.

Singh, Bhupinder. "Tribal Development in Retrospect and Prospects: Sixth Plan Mid-Term Appraisal", *Indian Journal of Public Administration*, Vol. XXX, No. 4, October-December 1984.

Singh, Sakendra Prasad. "Development Programmes for the Tribals: Need for New Approach", *Indian Journal of Public Administration*, Vol. XXIX, No. 4, 1983.

Singh, Hoshiar. "Oh, to have a piece of own land", *Kurukshetra*, Vol. XXXI, No. 18, June 16-30, 1983.

Thirunavukkarasu, S. "Strategy for Integrated Rural Development: A Study in a South Arcot Village", *Social Science Digest*, Vol. IV, July, 1986.

Reports

Reserve Bank of India. *Report of the Committee on Agricultural Productivity in Eastern India.* (Publication Division, Bombay, Vol. 1, 1984).

Government of India, *Report of the Commissioner for Scheduled Caste and Scheduled Tribes.* (Ministry of Welfare, New Delhi, 28th Report, 1986-87).

______ *Report of the Study Team on Tribal Development Programmes* (Planning Commission, New Delhi, 1966).

______ *Report of the Working Group on Tribal Development during the Sixth Plan*, 1980-85, (Planning Commission, New Delhi, 1981).

______ *Report of the Committee on Forest and Tribals in India* (Ministry of Home Affairs, Tribal Development Division, New Delhi, 1982).

______ *Report of the Committee on Scheduled Tribes* (Ministry of Home Affairs, Tribal Development Division, New Delhi, February 1976).

______ *Reports of First Five Year Plan to Eighth Five Year Plan* (Planning Commission, New Delhi, Published in 1952, 1956, 1961, 1969, 1976, 1981, 1986, 1991).

______ *Report of the Commissioner for Scheduled Castes and Scheduled Tribes, 1960-61* (Manager of Publications, Part-I, Delhi, 1961).

______ *Study Team on Social Welfare and Welfare of Backward Classes*, (Committee on Plan Projects, Planning Commission, New Delhi, 1958).

______ *Reports of the Scheduled Areas and Scheduled Tribes Commission.* (Chairman U.N.Dhebar) 1960, (Ministry of Home Affairs, New Delhi, 1961).

______ *Report on Indian Food Crisis and Steps to meet it*, (Ford Foundation Agricultural Production Team, New Delhi, 1959).

______ *Indian Agriculture in Brief* (Directorate of Economics and Statistics, Delhi, 1971).

______ *Reports of the Committees of the Panel of Land Reforms* (Planning Commission, New Delhi, 1959).

______ *Report of the Working Group on Development of Scheduled Tribes duirng Seventh Five Year Plan (1985-90)*, (Planning Commission, New Delhi).

Government of Tamil Nadu, *Annual Tribal Sub-Plan*, (Issued by Director of Adidravidar and Tribal Welfare, Ezhilagam, Chennai, 1976 to 1996).

______ *A Sub-Plan for Tribal Development : For Implementation in the Fifth Five Year Plan*, (State Planning Commission, Ezhilagam, Chennai, August 1974).

______ *An Economic Appraisal*-Various Issues (Government Press, Chennai).

______ *Various Five-Year Plan Reports from the First Five-Year Plan to Tenth Five-Year Plan*, (State Planning Commission, Ezhilagam, Chennai).

______ The Tamil Nadu Land Reforms (Fixation of Ceiling of Land), Act, 1961 (Modified upto 1980), (Law Department, Chennai, 1980).

______ The Madras Inams (Supplementary) Act, 1963 (Modified upto 1966) (Law Department, Chennai, 1980).

______ The Tamil Nadu Lease-Holders (Abolition and Conversion into Ryotwari) Act, 1963 (Modified up 31.12.1979), (Law Department, Chennai, 1980).

______ The Scheduled Castes and the Scheduled Tribes (Prevention of Atrocities) Act, 1989, (Law Department, Chennai, 1994).

______ The Bonded Labour System (Abolition) Act, 1976 (Central Act 19 of 1976).

Government of Maharashtra. The Maharashtra Tribals Economic Condition (Improvement) Act, 1976.

Index

A

Abolition of Big Landed Estate and Land Reforms Act, 47
Acts and Regulations in Orissa, 49
Adi-Dravida and Tribal Welfare, 10, 242
Adi-Dravid—Department, (TN), 35
Administration, 26, 28, 54-55, 113, 161, 188, 231
• and Development, 242
Administrative Reforms, 23
Agrarian
• Reform, 59
• Revolution, 60
• Structure, 23-24, 70, 79, 88
• System, 79, 88
Agricultural
• Colonies, 77
• Economy, 79
• Implements, 41-42
• Labourers, 126, 128
— and Horticulture, 26
— and Industry, 24, 39
— Debt Bondage Abolition Regulation, 52
— Policy, 60
Andhra Pradesh, 42, 49
• Scheduled Areas Moneylanders, Regulation, 1963, 52
Andhra Pradesh, Kerala, and Tamil Nadu, 90
Andhra Pradesh—West Bengal, 85
Apatanis of Apatani Valley, 43
Aravalli Hills, 72
Ariya, Goundan, 111, 116, 230
Arts and Crafts, 73
Arts and Culture, 79
Arunachal Pradesh, 43
Assam, 72, 80, 85
Assam Moneylanders' Regulation, 1968, 52
Assam—Bihar, 41
Assam—Rajasthan, 82
Assam—Tripura, 73
Attur Taluk, 109
Australian Aborigins, 40

B

Badaga of Nilgiri Hills (TN), 43

Baigas of Madhya Pradesh and Orissa, 41

Banswara (Raj), 45

Bihar and Maharashtra, 40, 54

Bihar Moneylanders' Act, 52

Bihar—West Bengal, 85

Binami Transfer of Land, 48-49

Bombay Agricultural Debtors' Relief Act, 52

Bombay Land Revenue Code, 48

Bombay Tenancy and Agriculture Land Act, 48

Bombay—Assam, 72

Bonded

- Labour, 51
- Labour System (Abolition) Act, 1976, 169, 230
- Labour System, 99, 234
- Labourers, 113

British Colonial Rule, 235

C

CAEC, 58

CAPCS, 58

Ceiling

- Acts, 86
- Laws, 76
- on Land Holdings, 79, 82, 84, 86

Central

- Advisory Board for Tribal Welfare, 78
- Land Reform Committee, 89

Chinese Movement, 61

Civil War, 60

Commercial

- Banks, 51
- Cooperatives, 195
- Crops, 236

Community Development, 73, 77, 83

Community Development and Extension Programme, 77

Consolidation, 71, 80, 84, 86, 89, 91

Conventional Land Revenue Measures, 26-27

Cooperative

- Banks, 51
- Credit Societies, 173, 237
- Farming Society, 175
- Farming, 71-72, 84, 175-76, 213
- Societies, 48, 175

Cottage Industries, 83

Cottage/Village Industries, 69

Criminal

- Tribal Acts, 74
- Tribals, 79
- Tribes, 74

Crop (Cropping Pattern), 43-44, 109, 128, 156, 166, 190, 193, 195, 220, 236, 239

Crop Rotation, 72

Cuban Revolution, 60

Cuddalore District, 110

Cultural and Economic System, 188

Customary Laws, 33

D

Declaration of American President, 59

Delhi, Dadra and Nagar Haveli, 85

DERGUE, 59

Development Bridges, 57

Development Programme for Agriculture, 170

Dharmapuri, 109

Dheber, UN, 78

Distribution of Land, 156, 164

DTDP (Dispersed Tribal Development Programme), 99

Dungarpur (Raj), 45

E

Ecological Security, 53

Economic

- Development, 40, 54, 61, 69, 181, 188, 229, 232,
- Farming, 70
- Growth, 239
- Reforms, 27
- Schemes, 174
- Structure, 27
- System, 201

Economy (ies), 39-40, 54, 56, 72, 74

- Tribal, 76, 188

Education, 73, 79, 83, 97, 99, 169, 188, 234-35

- Elementary, 184

Educational Status of Tribals, 188

Eighth Plan, 103, 234

Extension Education, 42

F

Fair Price Shops, 241

Farm Forestry, 53

Female Labour, 238

Fifth Plan, 94, 103, 233-34

Financial Institutions, 51

Five Year Plan (1st), 70

Five Year Plan (2nd), 74-77

Five Year Plan (3rd), 78-79

Five Year Plan (4th), 84

Five Year Plan (5th), 27, 29, 87, 231

Five Year Plan (6th), 27, 95

Five Year Plan (7th), 97

Five Year Plan (8th), 98-100

Five Year Plan (9th), 101

Five Year Plan (10th), 101-02

Five Year Plans, 72

Food Crops, 135

Food Gathering and Hunting, 39-40

Forest

- and Tribal, Report of Committee on-, 53
- Areas, 118
- Gitteri Hills, 118
- Jawadhi Hills, 118
- Kalrayan Hills, 118
- Kolli Hills, 118
- Pachamalai Hills, 118
- Palni Hills, 118
- Shervarry Hills, 118
    - — Conservation Act, 128, 156, 230, 241
    - — Department, 9
    - — Economic, 73
    - — Labour Cooperatives, 73, 77, 83
    - — Labour Cooperative and Tribal Development Blocks, 233
    - — Land, 9-10
    - — Policy and Forest System, 53
    - — Policy in India, 53-54
    - — Resources, 30, 109

Forest/Land Policies, 74

Forestry Oriented Programme, 234

Forestry, 54

Fourth Plan, 80, 84, 87-88, 93, 103, 233

Freedom of Hunting, 40

G

Garo Hills, 44

German Minority, 60

Gingee, 111

Glossary of Terms, 15-16

Goa, 85

Gomugi Dam, 110, 155, 168, 195, 207

Gond, Bhills and Bhilala (MP), 43

Government Tribal Residence Schools, 124, 240

Gram Panchayats, 49

Gujarat, 45, 48, 54, 80, 85

H

Haryana, 89

Haryana and Punjab, 234

Hills Administration, 230

Himachal Pradesh Consolidation of Holdings Act, 47

Himachal Pradesh Land Regulation Act, 47

HO of Bihar and Bengal, 43

Holdings and Tenancy Reforms, 28

Horticulture, 42, 97, 234

HP Transfer of Land (Regulation) Act, 1968, 50

I

Illiteracy, 9, 48

Illegal Land Transfers in UP, 49-50

Inam Estate

- Abolition Act, 113
- Abolition and Conversion into Ryotwari, Act, 29, 230
- Estate, 113
- Estate Administration, 160

Indebtedness and Tribal Rights, 235

Indian Agriculture, 70

Indian Tribals, 9

Indian Tribes, 26

Indian Tribes,

- Classification, 26
- Cultural Contacts, 26
- Linguistic Affiliation, 26
- Occupational Economy, 26
- Physical and Racial Charac., 26
- Religious Beliefs, 26
- Social Customs, 26
- Territorial Distribution, 26
- Traditions & Beliefs, 26

India—South America, 42

Industrial Development, 229

Industries, 53, 186

Infrastructural Facilities, 101

International Monetary Fund, (IMF), 23-24

Irrigation, 42, 44, 73, 83, 97, 110, 169, 175, 234

ITDP (Integrated Tribal Development Projects), 95, 102, 173, 175, 234

J

Jadaya Goundan, 111, 115-16

Jagirdars, 11, 29, 113, 115-16, 160-61, 166, 168-69, 230-31, 233, 235

- Administration, 29, 111

Jagirs, 29, 42, 112-13, 124, 126, 161, 166, 184, 188, 192

- Regime 235

Jhumming, 42-43

K

Kalamath Food Gatherers of North America, 40

Kalrayan Block, 236

Kalrayan Halls Tribes, 235

Kalrayan Hills (TN), 9, 10, 28-31, 33, 35, 40, 43, 45, 88, 95, 109-11, 113, 115, 117-18, 122, 124, 128, 135, 155-56, 159-63, 166-67, 169-70, 172-73, 175-76, 181-82, 184, 186-87, 192, 194, 201, 203, 208-09, 211, 219, 230-31, 234-38, 240, 242

- Administration, 116

• Distribution of Land in-, 164
• Population, 118
• Tribal Economy, 36
• Tribes, 30, 36, 110, 112, 118, 166, 217, 231

Kancheepuram, 102, 110
Kanyakumari District, 160
Karialar, 122, 126, 153, 167-69, 183, 190, 194, 199, 206, 208, 212, 214-15, 222
Karialar Community, 110
Kerala, 80, 85
Kerala Moneylanding act, 1968, 52
Kerala—Andaman, 40
Koraput (Orissa), 45
Krishna Devaraya's Regime, 29 see under Raja also
Krishna Devaraya of Vijayanagar Kingdom, 111
Kurumba Goundan, 111, 116

L

Land
• Alienation, 25, 39, 45-50, 52, 77, 87, 162, 166, 232, 235-36, 241
• Ceiling
— Acts, 71

Laws, 90
Legislation, 86
• Development Measures, 233
• Disputes, 31
• Redistribution, 57-58, 60
• Reform Act, 49
• Reform Act in Tamil Nadu, 236
• Reform and Peasant Association, 59
• Reform Centre Poona, 87
• Reform Implementation Committee, 84
• Reform in Tamil Nadu, 160
• Reform Measures, 28-31, 33, 35, 70, 76, 84, 93, 160, 192, 229, 235
• Reform Movements, 58
• Reform Policies, 232
• Reform Programme, 87
• Reform Tribunals, 234
— In Sample Villages, 165-67
• Reforms in-, 55
— Africa, 55
— Algeria, 57
— Argentina—Peru, 58
— Cameroon, 55
— China, 60-61
— Cuba, 59
— Ethopia, 59
— Nigeria, 55
— Tanzania, 55
— Tunisia, 56

— Uganda, 55

— Yugoslavia, 60

- Reforms Laws in Himachal Pradesh, 47
- Reforms Measures (LRM), 9, 24, 54
- Reforms, 10, 23-24, 27-28, 31, 33, 35, 39, 43, 69-70, 73, 75-76, 79, 83, 85-90, 92-93, 95, 100, 103, 159, 163, 165, 167, 169, 176, 184, 190, 192, 229-32, 234
- Tenure Policy, 56
- To Tiller Act, 48
- Use Pattern, 166

Landless Agricultural Labourers, 23, 39, 57

Landless Labourers, 240

Landless Tribals, 234

Large Scale Multi-purpose Societies (LAMPS), 10, 31, 51, 117, 168, 172-76, 237, 242

- Cooperative Societies, 102
- Schemes, 175

Latin America, 58-59

Law Reforms, 54, 58

Legal System, 9

Legislation, 82, 84-85, 90-91, 233

Literacy, 33, 124, 182, 184, 187-88

Literacy Index, 44

M

MADA, 94-95, 234

Madhya Pradesh, 42, 45

Madhya Pradesh Cooperative Societies, 233

Madras, 82

Maharashtra, 54, 80, 85

Maharashtra—Rajasthan, 85

Maidu of California, 40

Malayalis or Sholagars, 28, 163

Malliampady, 122, 167-68, 183, 188, 194, 199, 203, 205-06, 210-11, 239

Manipur, 40, 45, 54, 72

Marginal Farmers, 23

Market Reforms, 23-24

Meghalaya, 42, 44-45

Migration, 51, 122

Military Training, 57

Ministry of

- Land Reform, 92
- Welfare, 174

Minor Forest Produce, 9, 25, 77 174, 230, 241

Mizos and Mizoram, 43

Mottampatti Taluk, 32

MP Anusuchit Jan Jati Rin Sahayata Act, 52

Multipurpose Cooperative Societies, 73, 77, 83

Mysore, 82

N

Naga Tribals of Assams, 41
National Development Council, 84
Negritos of Malay, 40
Nehru, Pandit Jawahar Lal, 28
New Economic Policy (NEP), 23, 229
NGO, 240
Nilgiri District (TN), 43
Ninth Plan, 235
North East Region, 41
North Eastern States, 42

O

Orissa, 49, 80
Orissa Cooperative Society Act, 49

P

P. Shilu Ao, 84
Panchayat Samities, 49, 83
Panchayats, 83
Planners, 75
Planning, 23, 72, 99, 175, 201
Planning Commission, 27, 71, 84
Plantation Schemes, 53
Pottiyam, 167-68, 183, 190, 192, 195, 199, 203, 205-06, 215, 239
Poverty Alleviation Policies, 229
Presidents' Rule, 1976, 115
Primitive Tribal Group Projects, 234
Punjab Tenancy (HP Amendment) Act, 1952, 47
Punjab Tenancy Act, 47
Punjab Tenants Security of Tenure Act, 1950, 47
Punjab, Haryana and Uttar Pradesh, 86
Punjab—Andhra Pradesh, 89

R

Raja Krishna Devaraya of Vijayanagar Kingdom, 230, 235
Rajasthan, 80
Religious and Charitable Institutions, 80
Reservation of Forest, 25
Revenue
- Administration, 112, 116
- Department, 9, 10
- Standing Order, 173, 194, 241
Revenues, 29
Rivers, 110
- Gomugi, 110
- Kottaputhur, 110
- Mainmukha, 110
- Mayura, 110
- Melmalai, 110
- Pulavapady Ponnanganmi, 110
- Sundapady, 110

Rubber and Coffee Plantations, 42
Rubber Plantation, 76
Rural
- Development, 23-24, 181, 229-30
- Development Programme, 58
- Population, 79

Ryotwari Sagri System Abolition Act, 1961, 52
Ryotwari System, 32, 70, 233, 240

S

Sago Industries, 109, 195
Salem District, 50, 109, 115, 120, 215
Salem Kalrayan Hills, 120
Samai Cultivation, 211
Sample Village, 122, 124, 182, 236
- of Kalrayan Hills, 183
- Tab., 33

Saora of Orissa, 43
SC/ST (Prevention of Atrocities), Act, 1989, 235
Scheduled Areas or Dispersed Tribals, 26
Scheduled Castes and Scheduled Tribes, 27, 46, 48, 50, 54, 92, 118, 235, 242
Scheduled Tribe, 49, 122
- Population, 94, 234
- under TSP, 244

Scientific Management, 25
Second World War, 60
Seerapattu Taluk, 32
Sericulture and Horticulture, 186
Seventh Plan, 98, 234
Shifting Cultivation, 39-33, 73, 77, 83, 97, 112, 194, 203, 230-32, 234-36
Sixth Plan, 234, 238
Slavery, 169
Small Industries, 169
Social and Economic Injustice, 159
Social Forestry, 53
Social Justice, 69, 88, 232
Social Structures, 181
Societies Act, 174
Society (ies), 74, 77, 90-91, 94, 159, 237
Socio-Cultural and Economic Systems, 33
Socio-Economic
- Development, 23, 188
- Structures, 184

Special Central Assistance, 169
Special Central Assistance Programme, 27
Special Economic Development Programme, 101
Special Multi-Purpose Tribal Blocks, 78
State of Madras, 160
State Planning Commission, 10

State Tribal Cooperative Fed of Forest Cooperative, 174

Sugar Industries, 76

T

Talent Search Training Programme, 102

Tamil Nadu, 29-30, 50, 69, 71-72, 81-82, 85, 87, 89, 96, 98-100, 102, 113, 115-16, 118, 124, 160, 162, 166-67, 169, 173, 175, 188, 230, 232, 234-35, 240-41

- Agri Land Records of Tenancy Rights Act, 235
- Cultivation Tenants (Payments of Fair Rents) Act, 235
- Cultivation Tenants Protection Act, 235
- Land Reform Act, 160, 235
- Land Revenue Act, 29
- Public Trusts Act, 1961, 235
- Survey and Boundary Act, 1923, 162

Taxes, 112

Telangana, (AP), 85

Tenancy Act, 48

Tenancy Reform, 70-71, 75, 84, 85, 89, 90

Tenancy Reform Acts, 89

Tenants, 81-82, 85, 233

Tenants Acts–Tamil Nadu, 100

Tenth Plan, 235

Terrace Cultivation, 39, 73

Tharu and Korwa of UP, 43

Tharu Tribal Community, 51

Third Plan, 82-84, 87

Tirunelveli District, 160

Traditional Rights, 25

Transfer of

- Land, 46

Tribal Land, 78

Tribal Areas, 9, 24-28, 35, 44-45, 47, 51-52, 73, 77-79, 87, 91, 96-97, 103, 126, 153, 160, 162, 166, 172-75, 181, 190, 201, 229-30, 232-34, 236-37, 240-42

- Administration, 79
- Bharmour and Pangi, 47
- of Orissa, Bihar and MP, 77

Tribal Community, 46, 69, 72, 74, 94, 96, 118

Tribal Cooperative Market Development Federation of India, (TRIFED), 174-75, 237

Tribal Development, 28, 35, 69, 74, 83-84, 95, 231-32, 234

- Bharmour and Pangi, 47
- Blocks, 83-84, 88
- Development Reforms, 27
- Measures, 31, 69, 87, 103, 231

- Programme, 73, 87-88, 94, 96, 235
- Projects, 172
- Schemes, 181

Tribal
- Economy, 24, 28, 35, 43, 55, 237
- of Kalrayan Hills, 181
- Groups, 25, 28, 79, 230
- Land, 25, 48-49, 241
- Population, 32, 73, 78, 95, 98-99, 102, 118, 122, 169, 234-35, 240
- Population Major Distribution, 120
- Sub-Plan (TSP), 27, 30, 87, 93-99, 101-02, 169, 195, 233-35, 237-38, 241
- Women, 97, 103

Tribals, 26, 44

Tribals of Madhya Pradesh, 41
- Korku, 41
- Korwa, 4
- Maria, 41
  - — Baiga, 41

Tribals Rights over Land, 29

Tribals, Chotanagpur (South Bihar), 44

Tribals' Fundamental Rights, 43

Tribes in Tamil Nadu, 102
- Irular, 26, 102
- Kadar, 26, 102
- Kanikar, 102
- Kattunayakan, 102
- Kurumba, 102
- Malayali, 26, 102, 110-11
- Palaiyan, 102
- Paniya, 102
- Sholagar, 102
- Toda, 102
- Veddar, 102

Tribes, 26, 33, 40, 72, 74, 113, 185, 197

Tribes,
- Apatanis of Arunachal Pradesh, 26
- Garo and Khasi Hills-Meghalaya, 26
- Irular, 240
- Jhumia, 42
- Kadar, 240
- Malayali, 109, 118, 185, 240
- Primitive, 95

Tzarist Russia, 60

U

Union Territories, 80

USA, 58

Uttar Pradesh, Maharashtra and Himachal Pradesh, 90

Uttar Pradesh—Delhi, 81

V

Valsad Dist., 51

Vedar of Ceylon, 40

Vellimalai, 115-17, 122, 153, 168-69, 173, 183, 192, 199, 201, 205, 207, 211-12, 214-16, 221-23, 232, 239

Vellimalai Taluk, 32-33, 231

Vellore District, 110

Vellupuram District, 109

Vindhyas/Satpura Mountains, 72

W

Welfare Measures, 169

Welfare Programmes, 76, 78, 87

West Bengal, 42, 48-49

West Bengal Land Reforms (Amendment), Act, 1965, 48

World Bank (WB), 23

Z

Zamindari System, 70